EVERYDAY DIRTY WORK

GLOBAL LATIN/O AMERICAS
Frederick Luis Aldama and Lourdes Torres, Series Editors

EVERYDAY DIRTY WORK

INVISIBILITY, COMMUNICATION, AND IMMIGRANT LABOR

Wilfredo Alvarez

THE OHIO STATE UNIVERSITY PRESS

COLUMBUS

Library of Congress Cataloging-in-Publication Data

Names: Alvarez, Wilfredo, 1978– author.

Title: Everyday dirty work : invisibility, communication, and immigrant labor / Wilfredo Alvarez.

Other titles: Global Latin/o Americas.

Description: Columbus : The Ohio State University Press, [2022] | Series: Global Latin/o Americas | Includes bibliographical references and index. | Summary: "Recognizing the need to further understand co-cultural communication practices in the workplace, Everyday Dirty Work explores how Latin American immigrant janitors communicate from their marginalized standpoints in a predominantly White academic organization and how everyday interpersonal encounters create discursive spaces that welcome and disqualify people based on symbolic and social capital"—Provided by publisher.

Identifiers: LCCN 2021046629 | ISBN 9780814214671 (cloth) | ISBN 0814214673 (cloth) | ISBN 9780814282007 (ebook) | ISBN 0814282008 (ebook)

Subjects: LCSH: Intercultural communication—United States. | Foreign workers, Latin American—United States—Case studies. | Janitors—United States—Case studies. | Immigrants—United States—Social conditions—Case studies. | Organizational sociology. | Communication in organizations—United States.

Classification: LCC HM1211 .A48 2022 | DDC 303.48/2—dc23/eng/20211223

LC record available at https://lccn.loc.gov/2021046629

Cover design by Alexa Love
Text composition by Stuart Rodriguez
Type set in Minion Pro

To Maria, my beloved and incomparable life partner

Mira, no solamente somos Latinos, eh . . . somos la gente que también
limpiamos su basura. Esas dos cosas ya son problematicas de por si,
entonces añade el hecho que casi todos somos mulatos y morenitos,
que la mayoria de nosotros no hablamos su idioma y te metes en
una situación bien interesante con mucha de esta gente . . .

Look, not only are we Latinos, we are also the people who
clean their waste. Those two things are already bad enough,
then you add the fact that most of us are brown and black, that
many of us don't speak their language and you get into a really
interesting situation with many of these people [Whites] . . .

—Ricardo (janitor in Housing Services)

CONTENTS

ACKNOWLEDGMENTS

COMPLETING THIS JOURNEY was possible thanks to the kindness, perseverance, love, and support of many people. First, Kristen Elias Rowley, editor in chief at The Ohio State University Press. Thank you so much for your guidance and excellence during the manuscript development process. Your steady leadership made this manuscript possible. I am also grateful to the series editors, Drs. Frederick Luis Aldama and Lourdes Torres, for believing in this project and offering a platform for its publication. I am deeply grateful to the readers who reviewed this manuscript. Your candid feedback made it possible for this book to reach its full potential. Lastly, I want to acknowledge Bailey Kirby's copyediting prowess to ensure that my words communicate my ideas clearly and elegantly. This book's publication would not have been possible without your writing skills, intellectual sophistication, humor, and persistence during the manuscript development process.

As I reflect on the journey thus far, I offer gratitude to the mentors who have guided my path like beacons in the night. Two very special women who believed in me when I did not believe in myself during a critical time in my life: Aida Dadian and Helen Baldwin at Theodore Roosevelt High School in the Bronx, New York. Your love and kindness served as the catapult that elevated me to unimaginable heights. To Dr. Keith Jenkins, at the Rochester Institute of Technology, you changed my life when you introduced me to the communication discipline. But most importantly, you poured in me lessons filled with selfless love which were the catalysts in my evolution. Your beautiful soul and care for humanity is admirable. Keith, you represent a major turning point in my life because you embody everything that I ever aspired to be. I am eternally grateful to you. To Dr. Brenda J. Allen, you are the best mentor anyone could have. You are superlative! Thank you for your continuous guidance, kindness, fabulous style, and grace. You have a special place in my heart for eternity. Muchas gracias por todo!

This book would not have been completed without the generosity of the 25 beautiful souls that accompanied me in this research journey. Thank you for trusting me with your life stories. It was an honor getting to know your complex humanity beyond the uniforms and stereotypes' superficialities. With this book, your life stories will reach the eyes and hearts of many people who will hopefully be touched and changed by you, just as I have been changed. I am eternally indebted to you for all you have given me and many others.

To my parents, Natividad Lajara and Wilfredo Alvarez, for sacrificing so much to make me the person who I am today. Your love is something that I cherish every single day. Thank you for planting the seed so that I could reach this milestone. I also want to express my gratitude to my uncle José Alvarez for insisting I enroll in high school during a time when I had no interest in returning to school. Your encouragement represents the genesis of the journey that led to me writing and completing this manuscript. To Zulma M. Homs, thank you for your unconditional love and support. You have been, and continue to be, a steady force in my life; always cheering for me as well as offering wisdom when needed. To all of you, los amo mucho!

Finally, the following people planted a seed of confidence in me during challenging junctures in my professional journey. Without your care, compassion, and willingness to take a chance on me, I would not be here and this book would not have materialized: Bruce Austin, Starky Bibb, Timothy Maisonave, Felecia Jordan-Jackson, Mark Zeigler, Julie Yun, Arturo Aldama, Lisa Flores, Patrick De Walt, Mark Orbe, Katrina Bell-Jordan, Tony Adams, and Jeff Miller. You have one thing in common: You believe in humanity's potential to be and do better. I will continue to do my best to carry on with your legacy going forward.

Communication in Everyday Life

Arriving in *Nuebayol*[1]

UNCLE JONATHAN: Bueno tu sabes que este es un pais donde hay muchas oportunidades, pero tu tienes que trabajar duro para conseguir esas oportunidades.

[Well, you know, this is a country where there are a lot of opportunities, but you have to work hard to reach those opportunities.]

ME: Bueno, ayudeme a conseguir un trabajo. Yo trabajo donde sea; donde puedo comenzar a buscar?

[Well, help me find work; I'll work wherever. Where can I start looking?]

UNCLE J.: No te apures, yo voy a preguntar en el golf club. Pero pregunta en otros lados a ver si hay trabajos en las factorias.

[Don't worry, I'm gonna ask at the golf club, but ask in other places such as factories.]

ME: OK, si no hay problema. Yo le empiezo a preguntar a otras personas.

[OK, no problem. I'll start asking other people.]

UNCLE J.: Una cosa si te digo, si tu te vas a quedar viviendo aqui en los Estados Unidos tu tienes que aprender Inglés.

[I'll tell you one thing, though: If you are staying here in the United States, you have to learn English.]

---

1. Slang term that Dominican Republic nationals use to refer to the city of New York.

This conversation occurred between my uncle and me, at 16 years old, on my third day as a newly arrived immigrant to the United States from the Dominican Republic. It was a hot summer evening and my father, my two uncles, and I were chatting in the living room of our shared dwelling in the Bronx borough of New York City—a rundown co-op apartment owned by my father's younger brother in a drug-infested area. At the time, the exchange seemed mundane, but I remember it vividly because it has become more meaningful to me over the years.

These multilayered concerns—work, education, and language—are the reality of many Latin American[2] immigrants,[3] as well as other non-English-speaking immigrants, who join the workforce in the United States unable to speak the dominant English language. Traditionally, in the United States, people who do not speak English are socially marginalized and discriminated against: Latin American immigrants in particular are hypermarginalized when we consider the low symbolic value this country ascribes to non-native English speakers, racial-ethnic minorities, and recent immigrants. As a result, many Latin American immigrants have to take service jobs, regardless of their education, work experience, or socioeconomic status. This low value has become a more accentuated reality since Donald Trump entered the political scene in 2015. This social organization means that Latin American immigrants who work in service occupations, for example as janitors, are a meaningful starting point for exploring issues related to workplace communication and its intersection with individuals' race, social class, occupation, and immigrant status (B. J. Allen, 1995, in press; Alvarez, 2016; Crenshaw, 2017; hooks, 1989).

The opening exchange with my uncle highlights important themes that I address in this book. Unbeknownst to my uncle and me, we were talking about my sociocultural and economic integration into my new host society, the United States (Y. Y. Kim, 2017). Additionally, we were discussing an immigrant's need to learn the host society's dominant language, which has direct implications for the person's ability to acquire cultural, social, and economic capital and thus improve their overall quality of life and social mobility (Bourdieu, 1987, 1991). Lastly, one of the main subtexts of our conversation

2. This term refers to Spanish-speaking immigrants from countries in the geographic region known as "Latin America." For this reason, I use the term "Latin American" throughout the book. With this language choice, I by no means attempt to refute the emergent use of the term "Latinx." On the contrary, I embrace and support this linguistic choice as a mode of gender inclusiveness. I use "Latin American" because it is the term with which the janitors in this study and I identify the most outside of our respective countries of origin.

3. For this study, I consider immigrants to be people who were born outside of the United States and made it their permanent place of residence, regardless of the legality of that residence.

was the vital relationship among work, social and cultural integration, and language acquisition.

At the time of our brief exchange, my uncle and I were not aware of its larger importance beyond securing my place in my new home; today, that conversation becomes a significant point of departure for the story that unfolds in the following pages, as I journey into the nuances of how everyday communicative encounters embody the struggles and hopes of people working in the margins of both organizations and society.

Language, Communication, and the Immigrant Experience

"If he doesn't learn English now . . ."

A conversation with a counselor when I was enrolling in high school in the Bronx, New York:

COUNSELOR: How many credits does he have?

UNCLE RAMIRO: Cuantos creditos tienes?
    [How many credits do you have?]

ME: No se; mire el record de notas.
    [I don't know; take a look at my transcript.]

COUNSELOR: OK, he should do two years here.

UNCLE RAMIRO: El dice que tu deberias hacer dos años mas por lo menos.
    [He says that you should do two more years [of schooling] at least.]

ME: Por que? Yo termine el bachillerato en Santo Domingo. Puedo hacer un año más y ya?
    [Why? I finished high school in Santo Domingo. Can I do one more year and that's it?]

COUNSELOR: Here's the thing, I think he should spend the time here in high school and learn English. If he doesn't learn English now, professors are not going to wait for him to learn in college.

"English, English, English! You must learn English! It is very, very important!"

A conversation with my English as a second language (ESL) teacher a few months later:

MRS. DUNBARN: I like your progress in the class so far; you are doing very, very well. I am so proud of you!

ME: OK, thank you. I see so many other students who do not look very interested in learning.

MRS. DUNBARN: I know, I know, they don't know how much harm they are doing to themselves. If they don't learn English, they are going to hurt their future. But you are not, because you are learning a lot.

ME: Thank you. I just feel that I want to have a voice. I don't want to live in a place where I can't express my voice.

MRS. DUNBARN: That is why learning English is so important. That's why I tell the students all the time: "English, English, English! You must learn English! It is very, very important!"

My experiences learning English and communicatively navigating my host society during the early days of my arrival to the United States serve as part of the impetus for writing this book. Reflecting on these experiences led me to ask questions about what living and working in the United States is like for Latin American immigrants with low cultural, social, and economic capital (Bourdieu, 1987). I wanted to explore some of the ways people communicatively navigate U.S. society, as well as what the perceived outcomes of those experiences are for them.

Therefore, in this book, I explore co-cultural communication practices in the workplace, specifically how Latin American immigrant janitors communicate from their marginalized standpoints in a predominantly White organization. From the non-White immigrant janitors' standpoints, White people's perceptions of their race, ethnicity, social class, and occupation complicate co-cultural communication and cross-cultural language use in the workplace (Orbe, 2017). Principally, I examine how the janitors perceive, interpret, and thematize routine messages related to race, ethnicity, social class, immigrant status, and occupation and how those messages and overall communicative experiences constitute their work and personal lives in the United States (Alvarez, 2016; Delgado, 2009; Dyer & Keller-Cohen, 2000).

In the following pages, I will share some of my personal and professional journey, but largely, I will use the platform of this book to amplify the voices of the participants. In particular, I will provide opportunities for communication scholars and practitioners and organizational leaders (particularly in higher education) to understand how communication shapes intercultural interaction and immigrants' lived experiences in work and personal contexts. This text thus develops readers' understanding of intercultural communication processes between nondominant society members (e.g., Latin American immigrants) and dominant society members (e.g., middle-class Whites).

As immigrants from Latin America, the janitors who participated in this study occupy a traditionally nondominant position in the U.S. social hierarchy, and, as history shows, this social position has material consequences (Ore, 2018). This study sought to affirm the janitors by creating a communication space where they have an opportunity to enact their voices in this platform (Bernal, 2002). As a result, this book seeks to advance knowledge about intercultural communication processes for social sciences and humanities scholars in general, communication scholars and advanced students in particular, and organizational leaders and practitioners.

The Significance of Culture for Communicating (Identity)

Latin American immigrants are *not* a small part of the economic landscape of the United States. Contemporary shifts in internal demographics and immigration patterns have contributed to the increase of people of Latin American descent in the U.S. labor force (e.g., as service workers; U.S. Bureau of Labor Statistics, 2020). Per the U.S. Bureau of Labor Statistics (2020), approximately 24% of people who hold service positions in the United States are Latin American immigrants or U.S.-born people of Latin American descent—a higher percentage than any other racial or ethnic group. In 2020, the percentage of Latin American women employed in service occupations (e.g., housekeepers, food service workers, janitors) is at least four percentage points higher than Black/African American women, 31% to 27%, and at least 10 percentage points higher than other racial groups, 19% for Whites and 20% for Asians. The difference for men was eight percentage points higher, 19% to 11% compared to Asians and seven percentage points compared to Whites, 19% to 12%, with only Blacks/African Americans having a higher percentage of people working in service occupations than men of Latin American descent, with 19.6% (U.S. Bureau of Labor Statistics, 2020). Given the number of Latin American immigrants who have entered the United States in the last decade, these percentages could easily rise, not only in low-status occupations but also across organizational hierarchies.

In spite of the previous statistics, the United States continues to struggle with creating welcoming environments for new immigrants. Public discourse plays a key role in creating and maintaining negative images of immigrants—especially Latin American immigrants (Alvarez, 2016, 2018; Cisneros, 2008; Flores, 2003; Jiménez Román & Flores, 2010; Ono & Sloop, 2002; Santa Ana, 1999). These negative images tend to reside in this country's collective imagination through popular culture, causing them to become embedded in the national psyche (K. R. Chávez, 2009; L. R. Chávez, 2008, 2017) and lead to the kinds of negative reactions many immigrants receive when they speak their native language in public or the kinds of ridicule they are met with when they speak limited or accented English. The fact that the United States shares a direct border with Mexico—and the rest of Latin America is not far beyond—lends further negativity to an already fraught immigrant image (Flynn, 2018).

Several meanings that the term "immigrant" has been historically assigned in U.S. society are "outsider," "illegal," "dangerous," and "polluted" (Cisneros, 2008). Even the 45th president of the United States, Donald Trump, has referred to deported immigrants as "animals" (Hirschfeld Davis, 2018). These labels, or embedded metaphors, are translated from general discourses, through interpersonal and media interactions, to a deep-seated feeling of negativity (K. R. Chávez, 2009). This Latino threat narrative (LTN) infuses Latin American immigrants with negative meanings that affect how they are perceived and treated in the public spheres of social life (Delgado, 2009). According to L. R. Chávez (2008),

> The Latino Threat Narrative (LTN) works so well and is so pervasive precisely because its basic premises are taken for granted as true. In this narrative, Latinos, whether immigrant or U. S. born, are a homogeneous population that somehow stands apart from normal processes of historical change. They are immutable and impervious to the influences of the larger society and thus are not characterized as experiencing social and cultural change. (p. 41)

This LTN is a particular brand of social imaginary—not a set of harmless ideas but a discourse that shapes and enables a society's dominant practices (A. J. Aldama, 2001; DeChaine, 2009; Taylor, 2002). Because metaphors, including labels, are critical to how people think and make meaning in their lives (G. Lakoff & Johnson, 1980; R. T. Lakoff, 2017), they are fundamental to shaping and sustaining the national social imagination. Additionally, this work helps to inform connections between janitors' narratives and the concept of a "social imaginary," as these ideas are influential for individuals and groups because they inform how people send and receive messages at the interpersonal level (Butler, 1995; Collier, 1991; Drzwiecka, 2000).

Today, in the United States, the (Latin American) immigrant as a social imaginary is filled with tension and disapproval (Villegas, 2019). And, worse, that imaginary maps from the abstract concept of an immigrant to actual immigrant *bodies,* contributing to the hypermarginalization of Latin American immigrants (Bogel-Burroughs, 2019). Accordingly, public discourse is not just conceptual: It can have serious implications for immigrants in many social contexts, beginning with the link between societal discourses and interpersonal interactions (K. R. Chávez, 2009). Immigrants are "read" as unwanted and potentially dangerous by individuals who draw from negative societal discourses to make sense of and to interact with immigrants (Alvarez, 2018). In other words, the target group of the discourse becomes the embodied representation of those discourses; consequently, this group is the target of those who follow the fundamental ideas that those discourses advance. As a whole, these observations suggest that when a group is demonized consistently in popular culture, it typically is the case that we hear about aggression toward those group members (Alvarez, 2016, 2018).

Media and societal images are deeply ingrained in interpersonal interactions between dominant group members and immigrants, especially in the case of a power differential (e.g., police and immigrant, supervisor and worker). A prime example of this transfer from negative discourse to negative interactions (especially aggression) is the Chandler Roundup, a July 1997 immigration raid in Chandler, Arizona. In her study of how law enforcement agents and presumed migrants interact, K. R. Chávez (2009) discusses the role of history in shaping those interactions, especially in historically conflict-ridden contexts such as the state of Arizona (i.e., conflicts due to Mexican immigration). Law enforcement officers' perception of brown-skinned people as outsiders who deserved to be removed from the country was, in part, driven by the corresponding societal narrative.

Another, more recent example of this dynamic is one of the many mass shootings in the United States in 2019 (a total of over 300 at the time of writing). A young White male drove nine hours to El Paso, Texas, and opened fire on a group of Walmart shoppers (mostly Mexicans and Mexican Americans). In this instance, the killer was a self-avowed White supremacist who sought to kill Mexicans because he perceived that they were "invading" the country (Bogel-Burroughs, 2019). This rhetorical framing is increasingly common in mass media and encourages some consumers of that media to act accordingly. This shooting has accelerated a national conversation about the relationship between the promotion of hateful discourse in the mass media (social media in particular) and physical violence—specifically, race-based hate against primarily Black and brown people (Alvarez, 2021, 2022; Ott, 2017; Ott & Dickinson, 2019).

Understanding the influence of broad societal messages on interpersonal interactions also requires analyzing common social contexts such as the workplace (Zlolniski, 2003). The struggle for legitimacy and inclusion is especially amplified at work, where communication is central. Still, the communicative experiences of working-class Latin American immigrants in service occupations have not been well documented (for an exception, see Amason et al., 1999). For instance, a search in multiple major academic online databases yields only a few relevant articles from the keywords "Latina/o/x" or "Latin American," "Organizational" or "Workplace," "Service Work(ers)" and "Communication." This outcome suggests that researchers have not seized the opportunity to conduct investigations that illuminate the communication-related service work experiences of Latin American immigrants in the United States. My work is motivated by this opportunity. In the following sections, I will identify the key communication processes that are at the center of understanding this book's subject in depth.

Key Communication Processes at Work

The communication processes this book highlights pertain to how organizational members engage in verbal and nonverbal interactions in specific relationship types, such as superior–subordinate and among coworkers, in addition to communication between people from different cultures and social identity positionalities (Bridgewater & Buzzanell, 2010). *Superior–subordinate communication* involves message exchanges between two employees, one of whom has formal authority over the other (Campbell et al., 2001; Steele & Plenty, 2015; Tanner & Otto, 2016). *Coworker communication* is defined as message exchanges between employees equal in hierarchy (Kram & Isabella, 1985; Madsen, 2016; Sollitto & Myers, 2015). Lastly, *co-cultural communication* is communication between cultural group members with more or less power, prestige, and privilege based on the social contexts in which they interact, including the workplace (Orbe, 1998b, 2017; Zirulnik & Orbe, 2019).

Vertical and Horizontal Communication Processes

Workplace relational processes are crucial for the effective functioning of both employees and organizations (Bartoo & Sias, 2004; Fix & Sias, 2006; Jablin, 1979; Mills, 1997; Teven, 2007; H. Wang et al., 2014). One of the most significant relationships that people have in the workplace is the relationship with their superior(s) (Krone, 1992; Sias & Jablin, 1995), and most formal organizational structures have superior–subordinate role attachments. Understanding this type of relationship is significant to this study because when Latin American immigrant janitors describe their everyday interactions at work, they often emphasize their exchanges with their supervisors. This type of workplace dynamic is critical to understanding communication at work with a co-cultural dimension, as the interactants are more often people who embody unequal positions in the hierarchy of U.S. society. This vertical, dyadic relationship is contrasted by peer-to-peer interactions, a horizontal, transactional set of processes critical to communication at work.

Workplace peer relationships, also called "equivalent-status" relationships (Sias et al., 2002), are relationships between coworkers with no formal authority over one another. Because most organizations traditionally have had hierarchical structures, these relationships represent the majority of organizational relationships (i.e., most people have *one* supervisor and *many* coworkers). These relationships serve many functions in organizations because "peer coworkers are the most likely, and most important, sources of emotional and instrumental support for employees, primarily because coworkers possess knowledge and understanding about the workplace experience that external sources do not" (Sias, 2005, p. 379). Consequently, constructive coworker relationships are significant for all employees, but especially for peer coworkers (T. D. Allen et al., 1999). Still, research on coworkers' communication has received less attention than has superior–subordinate communication (Sias & Cahill, 1998).

Examining this type of relationship is also significant to this book because peer coworker research generally presumes that most employees go through similar career stages. However, similar to the trend in superior–subordinate research studies, investigators have focused almost exclusively on white-collar employees. Peer coworker research also assumes that certain message types—such as workplace information sharing, advice, and social support—are exchanged in each career stage. As a result, much of this research emphasizes the functions of peers in specific career stages, in a specific order (Spillan et al., 2002). These assumptions and traditional models of peer communication have excluded the experiences of persons in low-status occupations/nondominant group members, so the insights of this case study contribute to that line of research.

Co-Cultural Communication Processes

Scholars like B. J. Allen have claimed that studying traditionally marginalized groups is critical to enhancing our knowledge of communication practices and systems. As B. J. Allen (1996) advanced:

> Knowledge available from the study of women's [and minority groups'] lives
> might enable women and other oppressed groups to improve the conditions

of their lives because, as "strangers" or "outsiders," they can identify patterns that are not easily identifiable by "natives" or "insiders." (p. 259)

Such observations indicate that a need still exists today to highlight issues related to communication between marginalized and dominant social groups, as Orbe et al. (2006) signaled over a decade ago. Engaging in such efforts would push those who study organizations to understand a wider range of experiences across organizational and social hierarchies. Co-cultural communication theory is one theoretical framework that has been useful to help organizational researchers understand the lived experiences of marginalized group members.

Within traditional social hierarchies, people of Latin American descent have especially been marginalized or perceived as a "nondominant social group." Working-class, lower-status employees also have been considered nondominant in formal organizational structures and communication systems. These combined factors suggest that an investigation of Latin American immigrant janitors' communication could be better approached using Orbe's (1998a) model of nondominant group members' communication practices and orientations. As Orbe and Spellers (2005) explain, "Co-cultural theory offers a framework to understand the process by which individuals come to select how they are going to interact with others in any given specific context" (p. 174). The following statement captures the essence of co-cultural communication theory:

> Situated with a particular *field of experience* that governs their perception of the *costs and rewards* associated, as well as their *capability* to engage in various communicative practices, co-cultural group members will adopt certain *communication orientations*—based on their *preferred outcomes* and *communication approaches*—to the circumstances of a specific *situation*. (Orbe, 1998a, p. 19)

Co-cultural communication theory was founded on the central tenets and ideas of standpoint theory and muted group theory (Kramarae, 1981, 2005; D. E. Smith, 1987). Muted group theory advances that societies have social hierarchies where some groups are privileged over others, with the groups at the top of the hierarchies establishing the communication system of that society (E. Ardener, 1978; S. Ardener, 1975). Over time, these communication structures become (re)produced by both dominant and nondominant members' discourse and, thus, the dominant communication systems remain in place (Giddens, 1984). As Orbe (1998a) describes, "This process [of social reproduction] renders marginalized groups as largely muted because their lived experiences are not represented in these dominant structures" (p. 4). Co-cultural communication theory explains that because unequal power relations exist in all societies, there always is a muted group framework in place (Meares et al., 2004). Additionally, people who have been "muted" often engage in communication practices to resist the system's attempt to keep them muted.

Overall, this examination follows research that promotes a deeper under-standing of communication processes in organizations from historically mar-ginalized perspectives (Alvarez, 2016; Buzzanell, 1994; Pertúz, 2017; Ray, 1996; Razzante & Tracy, 2019; Zirulnik & Orbe, 2019). This line of research also contributes to understanding human communication because "the oppressed can see with the greatest clarity, not only their own position but . . . indeed the shape of social systems as a whole" (Frankenberg, 1993, p. 8).

> Look, not only are we Latinos, we are also the people who clean their waste. Those two things are already bad enough, then you add the fact that most of us are mulatos y morenitos [brown and black], that many of us don't speak their language and you get into a really interesting situation with many of these people [Whites]. (Ricardo, a janitor in the residence halls)

Communicating Social Identity

Kimberlé Crenshaw (1991) introduced the concept of "intersectionality" in the late 1980s/early 1990s to highlight how multiple overlapping systems of oppression "intersect" to affect individuals' lived experiences in material ways. Crenshaw (1991) argued that we can only understand discrimination through a deeper understanding of how interlocking systems of oppression function to reinforce each other (in the original example, an organization hiring the usual Black man and White woman as tokens—but not hiring a Black woman) (P. H. Collins, 1986, 2000). According to Crenshaw, Ricardo's experience (as represented by his quote above) is symbolic of how his ethnicity, occupation, and language use "intersect" to create a complex structure of societal oppres-sion that is more insidious than considering each of those identity categories in isolation. This point highlights Crenshaw's idea that in U.S. society overlap-ping or intersecting systems of oppression are evident in a person's or group's lived experience when they face the negative consequences of occupying two or more marginalized identities (e.g., Black and woman). Therefore, in this book, I also follow Crenshaw's call to consider intersecting identities as a factor that Latin American immigrant janitors experience material disadvantages through everyday discourse in their occupation as service workers.

Overall, I seek to understand how overlapping systems of oppression are constituted through everyday discourse. The narratives that unfold in the following pages stem from the janitors' points of view, which is this book's primary goal. More specifically, I was interested in listening to and learning more about the janitors' interpretations and experiences of communicating with culturally (dis)similar others in the workplace context—in other words, how they communicated their social identities to others and their perceived responses from others. The results depict discursive features of their experiences as marginalized members of society. For instance, several janitors interviewed for this project explicitly expressed that their multiple marginalized identities are the main reason for their experiences of exclusion and subordination in the workplace.

It is evident from the janitors' narratives that who they are is significant to culturally different others and that these others communicate in ways that demonstrate that degree of significance. What I mean by this is that from phenotypic traits (hair color and texture, skin complexion, and facial features) to dress and speech, the janitors noted that, in their experiences, all these symbolic aspects of a person were "read" in harmful ways and those "readings" led to some type of verbal or nonverbal social rejection. I argue that these communicative encounters contribute to, and are illustrative of, what Crenshaw noted when she claimed that a person is not only disadvantaged because of any one aspect of their social identities but because of multiple aspects operating in tandem. The janitors' narratives shown in this book illustrate a discursive layer that people give life to in their everyday interactions with each other. It is my goal in this book to illustrate the implications of intersectionality in and through micro-level interactions in the ever-significant work sphere of social life.

Research Framework: Converging/ Diverging Immigrant Realities

"I'm sorry, but I don't speak English"

ME: Que yo le digo entonces si me preguntan algo?
[What do I tell them if they ask me something?]

UNCLE RAMIRO: Si te preguntan algo tu le dices "I'm sorry, but I don't speak English."
[If they ask you something you tell them, "I'm sorry, but I don't speak English."]

"Stop talking that shit!!!"

Having a conversation with a classmate at my high school, in Spanish, when a student walks by:

ME: O si tu sabes que eso es lo que tu tienes que hacer.
[Oh yeah, you know that's what you have to do.]
RAUL: No, yo se; eso fue lo que el maestro dijo en la clase.
[No, I know; that's what the teacher said in class.]
STUDENT: Stop talking that shit!!!

These scenes depict some of my early experiences as a Latin American immigrant in the United States. The first scene shows my uncle coaching me as I was preparing to begin high school only a few weeks after I had arrived from Santo Domingo. The conversation was about language use in everyday interactions. The second scene shows one of my early experiences with social rejection based on my language use—also in my daily interactions with people. As a Latin American immigrant, I still find myself constantly rehearsing my lines before I deliver them in social situations in general and in organizational settings in particular. These might be common communicative struggles that many immigrants face as they transition from a native to a foreign culture. Further, because of my struggles with language use, I have experienced a great deal of interpersonal rejection in various social contexts, including educational settings like the one in which this case study takes place.

My personal and professional experiences provide the backdrop that informs the choices that I made as a researcher. I believe my background as a Latin American immigrant endows me with unique perspectives that I bring to the research framework that I use to write this book. Those perspectives rely on my direct lived experiences, as I have "walked the walk" that many immigrants walk before they enter the United States and during their time here. For instance, I had to learn a new language as an adult, wait for long hours at the Office of Immigration and Naturalization Services (INS) to take various types of written and oral tests, and endure continuous questions ("What are you?" and "Why do you sound like that?") from "curious" native-born English speakers. For many years, I have had to communicatively navigate a European-dominated host society that is more concerned with sustaining its ethnolinguistic vitality (Ehala, 2015) and strengthening its dominant group identity than accepting and welcoming culturally different others. As a result, my positionality helps me to view and understand the phenomenon about which I write in ways that native-born persons may not.

In addition to my lived experiences as a Latin American immigrant, I have extensive experiences in diverse roles (i.e., student, staff, faculty) at organizations geographically dispersed across the United States. These experiences inform the perspectives and knowledge that I bring to this book. In sum, I bring the "real-world" experiences of a Latin American immigrant who has navigated various types of institutions in the United States for over 20 years. At the outset, I acknowledge that my personal experiences and related assumptions may direct attention to certain issues and not to others. However, these same experiences equip me with perspectives that enrich the insights that I bring to writing this manuscript. The choices that I made as a researcher are a direct reflection of both my personal and professional experiences and also why I was drawn to this topic to begin with. I foreground this point because my goal is not to claim I am a "detached" observer but to honestly depict my experiences as someone who is invested in understanding myself in relation to others. I believe that this process of seeking to understand requires me not only to be introspective but also to externalize my thoughts and feelings about that process. For this reason, I sought to understand the work experiences of people with whom I perceived some degree of kinship given our immigrant status—as well as because I perceived that we had shared struggles related to cultural transition and adaptation, language use, and navigating often-hostile workplaces and society at large.

This book further highlights how a focus on language use and social identity can stretch research and theory's assumptions about dominant and nondominant individuals' communication practices. For example, established communication theories, like co-cultural communication theory (Orbe, 2017), assume that social actors have the ability to select a particular communication orientation in a given situational context. In the United States, then, the assumption would be that all actors are able to freely select from the dominant verbal repertoire, English. The implication of these assumptions is that people like the Latin American immigrant janitors who participated in this case study have additional layers of social disadvantage, exclusion, and subordination, particularly in terms of discursive/linguistic/communicative layers. The argument I make in this book is that the communicative layer is a critical layer that directly contributes to individuals' and groups' marginalization and oppression in everyday life (e.g., the communicative layer directly affects people's cultural, economic, and social capital—their power and prestige). I believe that extending scholarly and practical understanding of low-status employees' communication experiences can advance organizational research, theory, and practice related to how organizational members in all types of organizations orient toward those who work in stigmatized occupations. My hope is that this book can function as a source of information to improve organizational practices that consider multiple levels of stakeholders, not just people on the middle and higher rungs of organizational hierarchies. It could, most importantly, be used to improve working conditions of historically marginalized workers (e.g., service workers, immigrants, racial and ethnic minorities).

Target Audiences, Objectives, and Organization of the Book

This book highlights the work experiences of one group of people (Latin American immigrant janitors) to illustrate how everyday communication processes constitute broader social systems of exclusion and subordination. Throughout the book, I interleave the janitors' narratives of their work experiences to highlight key themes and issues. For instance, a typical day in one of the participants' work life would include symbolic gestures such as people walking over them or direct insults. As Angelina, a veteran janitor, pointed out in her narrative, "We are the dirtiest of the dirtiest to them [Whites] so of course they treat us like filth." Through this exploration of micro-level interactions from the janitors' standpoints, this book attempts to extend organizational communication, labor relations, and Latin American/Latinx/a/o studies research. In addition, this book seeks to inform organizational leaders and scholars about intercultural communication complexities and practices in diverse contemporary organizations.

This book is intended for, but not limited to, audacious and innovative mid-level and senior-level nonprofit organizational leaders, particularly in higher education, who are interested in understanding and maximizing relational processes across institutional hierarchies—especially leaders seeking to develop their understanding of the significance of relationships to improve their organization's performance. In addition, this book is for social sciences and humanities scholars interested in relational processes in complex systems such as organizations. Lastly, this book is of particular interest to organizational communication and intercultural communication teachers, scholars, and students. Overall, this book aims to broaden the readers' imagination pertaining to what organizational leadership is and *who* can lead and *how*.

Therefore, this book's central objectives are to develop organizational leaders' appreciation for the significance of human relationships across institutional hierarchies. This deeper degree of understanding advances leaders' capacity to lead more innovative, compassionate, empathetic, and equitable organizations. Second, this book offers insights into the organizational lived experiences of critical, but often undervalued and invisible, organizational members (e.g., janitorial staff and other service workers). Seeking to connect with and tap into so-called lower-status employees' potential can unlock the entire organization's greater potential. Lastly, this book provides practical recommendations to organizational leaders, based on theoretical insights and research data, to improve the ways in which they relate to and support *all* stakeholders, and thus develop their overall organizational functioning.

To achieve these objectives, this book is organized as follows. In chapter 1, I discuss the research methods used to study the janitors' communication experiences. Specifically, this chapter highlights the case study's antecedents, approaching key stakeholders at the research site, the qualitative methods used for data collection and analysis, and the assumptions with which I had to contend as I conducted the research.

Chapters 2, 3, and 4 present selections from my participant interviews, divided into three areas: organizational communication, co-cultural communication, and the impact of social identity categories on communication. Chapter 2 underscores relevant research related to organizational communication themes, issues, and practices. Specifically, the chapter focuses on central processes of organizational hierarchies and roles. Some of these themes are typologies of coworker communication and superior–subordinate communication practices in traditional organizational bureaucracies. Chapter 3 explains co-cultural communication practices and approaches. This chapter delves into the ways co-cultural communication processes play out in organizational settings in general and the setting of this case study in particular. Co-cultural communication theory functions as a conceptual framework that helps the reader understand and structure the central problematic presented in this book—that is, the communication experiences of Latin American immigrant janitors within a higher education organization. In chapter 4, I discuss key issues and concepts related to organizational communication, language, and social identity. Particularly, this chapter focuses on the role that language plays to structure communicative encounters in organizational life. In this chapter, I also make connections between language, communication, and social identity categories.

Chapter 5 draws together narratives from the janitors that touch on their experience with learning English, how they perceive the overlap of language with social integration, and their outlook on their immigrant experience as a whole. The final chapter, chapter 6, provides theoretical and practical implications for mid-level and senior-level organizational leaders, social sciences and humanities teachers, scholars, and students interested in communication processes in complex systems, and others interested in the scope of this work.

You will find that I weave discussions of social identity throughout all of the following chapters, even though chapter 4 is the one specifically designated as "about" social identity. This integration is purposeful: A truly intersectional view of workplace and co-cultural communication cannot separate people's identities from their communicative experiences. My hope is to demonstrate, both to organizational leaders and scholars, that employees' demographics and individual experiences matter—and that, more importantly, negative workplace communication experiences that result from intercultural conflict are embedded in overarching organizational structures. I aim to amplify the study participants' voices while keeping my long-term orientation toward more inclusive communication research in perspective.

CHAPTER 1

Research Methods

TO EXAMINE how social identities' meanings emerge through interlocutors' exchanges, it is important to overview how I captured those communicative nuances through the research methods and practices I employ in this research study. My approach to this research is just as important as my motivations for undertaking it.

This chapter explains the design of the research study. First, I discuss the rationale for using an interpretive conceptual framework. Next, I overview the research site's usefulness for this case study and explain the data collection and analysis procedures. Then I situate myself within the research site, explaining my relationship with the research site, how I see my role as a researcher and participant, and how my identity and my assumptions shape my research in this site. Finally, I offer some ethical considerations and the study's limitations.

The Research Site: A Public Ivy in the Southwest

Rocky Mountain University[1] (RMU) is located in the southwestern region of the United States. The university was established, along with the state where it

---

1. This is a pseudonym used to preserve the research site's anonymity.

is located, in 1876 (University Website[2]). Nestled in the foothills of the Rocky Mountains in a city of roughly 100,000, RMU is the flagship institution of the state's four-campus public university system. RMU hosts approximately 35,000 students, out of which approximately 30,000 are undergraduates and 5,000 are graduate or professional students. The student body is composed of 55% men and 45% women; 60% in-state residents and 40% out-of-state; 66% White/ Caucasian American, 11% Hispanic/Latino, 5% Asian, 5% multiracial, 1.6% Black/African American, 0.2% American Indian or Alaskan Native, 0.06% Native Hawaiian or Pacific Islanders, and 9% international students (University Website).

RMU offers more than 90 academic programs within nine colleges and schools. It employs approximately 1,500 full-time faculty members, of which 15% are racial minorities and 47% are women. Additionally, the university is known as a Public Ivy—the unofficial term for institutions that offer the rigor of an Ivy League school without the attendant price tag. Over 90% of the full-time instructional faculty members hold doctorates or other advanced terminal degrees, and several faculty members are Nobel Prize winners. As noted on the university website (2020), RMU "ranks in the top five U. S. universities, excluding military academies, in the number of astronaut alums and is the top NASA-funded university in the world."

Because of its history as an academic center of the state, RMU's campus has driven the growth of the surrounding community. In the early part of the 20th century, this growth began to accelerate. To prepare for infrastructural improvements that could accommodate increased enrollment, the university administration debated their approach to the architecture of the campus. The eventual agreement was that buildings should have a consistent style, a unique feature among universities that persists to this day. The university presents an environmental façade of homogeneity that has, in part, served to conceal underlying racial tension.

Race Relations at RMU

The foundation of this prestigious university and its unique architecture includes the work experiences of those who help keep RMU running through their everyday silent efforts: janitorial workers. Janitors—also called custodians, housekeepers, frontline workers, or environmental services staff—are in charge of maintaining RMU's picturesque facilities, keeping them inhabitable

---

2. The website is not provided to maintain the organization's anonymity.

and in good condition for people to carry out their intellectual endeavors. Of the more than 400 custodians on the RMU campus, 150 (37.5%) are considered Hispanic or Latina/o, according to the University Office of Planning, Budget and Analysis; this is a slightly lower rate for Hispanic or Latina/o custodians than that of the United States (50%) but a significantly higher proportion than that of the city's Hispanic or Latina/o population as a whole (9.8%; U.S. Census Bureau, 2020).

According to several veteran janitors I interviewed for this study, the relationship between Latin American immigrant janitors and RMU has gone through a lot of variation in the last 40 years, but it seems to be directly affected by the larger social climate of the time. Latin American immigrant custodians at RMU have lived through U.S. President Ronald Reagan's controversial amnesty program in the 1980s, drastic shifts in this racial-ethnic group's presence within the custodial staff across departments, and persistent racism on campus, just to name a few significant events.

Several of the janitors I interviewed have been working at RMU since the early 1980s. That decade brought interesting experiences to them. For example, according to one of the janitors, "Esos eran tiempos mejores; eran mas tranquilos" [Those were better days; calmer days]. She said, "La mayoria eramos Latinos entonces nos llevavamos bien todos" [There were mostly Latinos on campus so we all got along well]. This person also said that people wanted to work and worked harder than today's workers. In an event that reflected the circumstances of the time, she shared with me that she had moved to the United States illegally and someone reported her at work, which led to her losing her job at RMU. A few years later, President Reagan pushed for an amnesty program that would legalize people living illegally in the United States. When the amnesty program came into effect, this janitor became legal and asked for her job back, which she got. She told me that despite her one bad experience, Latin Americans around her usually took care of each other and worked hard to preserve their jobs. She said that those days were much different than today. She also said she has witnessed a big shift in the number of Latin American janitors on campus.

Several janitors expressed that the 2010s brought a shift in racial-ethnic demographics within the custodial staff across departments on campus. Several participants shared that Latin American people used to be the majority of janitors on campus, and they feel that the reduced percentage has been calculated and premeditated. For example, 40 years ago, two-thirds of the janitors on campus were Latin Americans; today those numbers have decreased dramatically. It is apparent that other racial-ethnic groups have gained a stronger presence on campus: The current main racial-ethnic group originates from Southeast Asia. According to several participants, this shift in janitors' demographics is mainly due to administrators having blatant prejudices and biases, against Mexicans specifically. Some janitors disclosed that they perceive that administrators' prejudicial feelings align with modern-day larger societal views about Mexican immigrants. Other events that have transpired in the last two decades support janitors' perceptions of the campus negative racial climate.

Mitigating Racism on Campus

During my time conducting this research study, I listened to many people's stories about bigotry and acts of racial hatred on campus. It was thus not surprising to hear the janitors' stories about overt communicative acts of disrespect and prejudice in places like residence halls. This negative climate seemed to reach its peak in the past 10 to 15 years, when students would do things like spit in janitors' faces and utter racially charged statements. In one well-known incident on campus, a White student yelled "Clean my shit, you fucking Mexican!" to a middle-aged Mexican woman cleaning a bathroom in one of the residence halls on campus. Other incidents included students knocking down trash bins and saying that "the Mexicans would clean them."

Acts of prejudice against janitors paralleled incessant racially motivated acts against Black, Latin American, and Asian faculty members and staff on campus. Students' hateful comments escalated to such a degree that some residence hall staff members decided to organize what became known as the Dialogues on Immigrant Integration, which mirrored a local community program with similar goals. When asked about the campus program's goals years ago, one of the initial organizers stated that the dialogues "got people with very different points of view to sit and talk with each other . . . the whole idea was this respectful exchange of viewpoints on the issue of immigration" (Talbott, 2009). The second organizer added, "There isn't a position or an agenda. It is really about opening a discussion about immigrant integration" (Talbott, 2009). In particular, residence hall staff wanted to address students' treatment of Latin American immigrant custodial workers. Several janitors mentioned during our interviews that the dialogues have helped alleviate the racist climate that once existed on campus. Campus dialogues started years ago, and they continue to take place today. According to both the janitors with whom I talked and residence life staff, the campus dialogues have yielded positive results for many RMU organizational stakeholders.

Access to the Site and Interest in the Study

It was that tense racial climate that led me to this study. Because I had been a student there, I knew RMU had the potential to be rich with symbolic currency, especially with regard to exploring the everyday communication experiences of Latin American immigrant janitors. Specifically, I became interested in issues of communication and social identity while doing research in organizational communication and difference/diversity. After immersing myself in scholarly literature related to organizational communication and difference/diversity (e.g., notions of identity such as race, ethnicity, gender, and social class), I became interested in understanding the communication experiences of occupationally marginalized organizational actors—those working on the lower levels of U.S. organizational hierarchies. The idea for the present project came to me one evening, and a year later, I was working as a part-time janitor in the department of Facilities Management.

To gain entry to employment with Facilities Management, one of my mentors referred me to two staff members in the department of Human Resources (HR), both in the area of organizational development and training. At our meeting, they offered to connect me with the staff coordinator in Facilities Management. I explained to the staff coordinator my goal of understanding Latin American janitors' communication experiences and how, to achieve that goal, I wanted to work as a janitor. I offered to periodically meet with her to check on the status of my request and to revisit the goal of my study. She communicated with her superiors about the possibility of hiring me as an employee within this department. About five months after our first meeting, I got an email from the staff coordinator to inform me that I had been approved to start working as a part-time janitor. This arrangement was ideal for a number of reasons, which I outline below.

Size and Location

RMU's size and geographic location made it a practical site to study Latin American immigrant janitors' communication. First, RMU is a large public university that serves the public higher education needs of the state and the country. RMU has a mildly diverse faculty, staff, and student population (in terms of race, ethnicity, social class, gender, occupation, and education level). Although the majority of RMU's faculty, staff, and students are White, its demographics reveal a certain variety of organizational actors—with, for instance, roughly 50% of the RMU full-time faculty being women and 15% of the student population belonging to a racial minority group. These demographics make RMU a strong candidate for an organizational setting to study workplace communication. Janitorial workers did have opportunities to come into contact with diverse individuals, which is practical for a study about communication and social identity.

At the macro level, RMU is located in the southwestern region of the United States; due to its geographic location, the university offers an institutional context that exists in the middle of continuous contentious debates and discourses about "Mexican illegal immigration." This context is relevant because most of the janitors at the time of my study were self-identified *Mexicanos*.[3] Moreover, RMU was an appropriate site considering the tense past and bloody history of race relations in this region of the United States, specifically between Mexicans and Anglo-Saxons (A. J. Aldama, 2001; Gomez, 2018; Rodriguez, 2007). In sum, both the organization's size and location within the United States contributed to informing janitors' communication.

Organizational Actors

Although RMU, on the surface, appeared at the time to be an organization that lacked what is commonly understood to be diversity, a careful inspection revealed that this organization is diverse with respect to other aspects of social difference besides race-ethnicity (e.g., gender, sexual orientation, social class, occupation, and education level). As the statistics outlined above suggest, RMU displays some diversity specifically in terms of gender and organizational role. RMU is a relatively diverse institution if one considers various social identities and not just race-ethnicity.

The participants of this research project (Latin American immigrant janitorial workers) also represented a diverse group of people (see Table 1). For instance, participants exhibited differences in terms of regional origin, age, and socioeconomic, educational, and occupational backgrounds. They originated from different parts of Mexico and other Latin American countries, such as Perú, Honduras, and El Salvador. The majority of Mexican participants originated from the Mexican states of Michoacán, Zacatecas, Durango, and Chihuahua. Five participants originated from El Salvador, two participants originated from Honduras, and one from Perú. Participants' ages ranged from 37 to 62 years old, with a mean age of 47 years old. Most

---

3. Spanish word for "Mexicans."

TABLE 1. Research Participants' Demographic Data

*PARTICIPANT	AGE	SEX	COUNTRY OF ORIGIN	DEPARTMENT
Rodolfo Pérez	58	Male	Perú	Student Union
Raul Matos	59	Male	Mexico	Student Union
Manuel Lopez	47	Male	Mexico	Recreation Services
Manuela Ortiz	50	Female	Mexico	Recreation Services
Ofelia Martinez	46	Female	Mexico	Student Union
Juan Pulido	47	Male	El Salvador	Facilities Management
Daniela Cruz	43	Female	Mexico	Facilities Management
Margarita Dominguez	37	Female	El Salvador	Student Union
Ruben Rodriguez	40	Male	Honduras	Facilities Management
Rodrigo Rocha	48	Male	Honduras	Facilities Management
Maria Guerrero	59	Female	Mexico	Facilities Management
Morelia Perdómo	46	Female	Mexico	Facilities Management
Roberto Aquino	41	Male	Mexico	Facilities Management
Ramona Genao	44	Female	Mexico	Housing Services
Antonia Garcia	50	Female	Mexico	Housing Services
Isaura Ramirez	45	Female	Mexico	Housing Services
Carlota Gomez	52	Female	Mexico	Facilities Management
Johan Quezada	48	Male	Mexico	Facilities Management
Aurelia Rojas	49	Female	Mexico	Facilities Management
Ricardo Acosta	41	Male	El Salvador	Housing Services
Mirella Robles	39	Female	El Salvador	Housing Services
Lucia Peralta	38	Female	Mexico	Housing Services
Juana Castellano	55	Female	Mexico	Housing Services
Pedro Alcantara	48	Male	El Salvador	Facilities Management
Artemia Tavarez	62	Female	Mexico	Housing Services

*Names are pseudonyms used in the manuscript to protect the participants' identities.

participants migrated to the United States as young adults (in their mid- to late teens) or when slightly older. Many participants were married and had children. Most participants had lived in the United States for at least 10 years. These differences, even alongside their similarities, made for rich perspectives and lived experiences.

The participants came to their current janitorial jobs from occupations as diverse as hotel housekeeper, factory worker (including turkey, tire, and canned vegetable factories), dishwasher, nongovernmental organization administrator, kitchen helper, landscaper, secretary, and accounting assistant.

This job diversity also reflected participants' educational diversity. Whereas some participants had achieved some college education, others never went past the fifth grade, and some could not read or write. The large majority of participants' formal education was in their native countries. Several participants were highly articulate and used sophisticated words to communicate with me, whereas others relied on basic diction.

RMU's various departments and services also contributed to the organization being a practical site for this study. The janitorial staff worked in departments or units that were very distinct, and thus, the staff members had different structural and cultural experiences. These departments made the Latin American immigrant janitors' communication experiences qualitatively different. In this project, I included the four major departments that provide janitorial services to the university: Facilities Management, Housing Services, Recreation Services, and the Student Union[4] (SU). Each of these departments has its own culture, goals, and customer needs. Hence, RMU's structural diversity was an asset for this study.

Organizational Structure

By interviewing participants across departments, this study indirectly explored whether there were any salient similarities and differences across janitors' departments and their communication experiences. RMU's mixture of organizational substructures also contributed to making RMU a constructive research site. Facilities Management serves the cleaning needs of various buildings on campus—primarily classrooms, offices, hallways, and conference rooms; Housing Services is in charge of student dormitories and other housing units for graduate students and faculty and staff; Recreation Services serves the student recreation centers on campus (i.e., gymnasiums and recreational facilities); and the Student Union is the university's "living room," where the university community comes for activities, speakers, meetings, and food. Janitors working in these departments can have very different communication experiences because the facilities and the people they serve vary. For example, Housing Services janitors (who are officially called housekeepers) rarely interact with faculty members because they work in the student dormitories. In contrast, Recreation Services and SU janitors have opportunities to interface with the campus community at large, as do Facilities Management janitors.

---

4. Pseudonym.

Positioning Myself as a Researcher

My structural position in the university similarly affected my interactions with the participants in my study. Even though I spent several months in the research site working as a janitor, I had spent several years as an active participant within the organization in different capacities, including student and instructor. This circumstance gave me additional knowledge about the organization and its history, culture, and people. Hence, I had a developed relationship with this organization and the people I dealt with that is much longer than the time that I spent officially "studying" it. This relationship gives me a vantage point that was useful in researching the phenomenon under investigation. For instance, my role as a researcher and as a participant is not that of the traditional researcher who comes into an organization because they are interested in studying symbolic processes in that organization. I already had been immersed in the organization and, therefore, was more sensitized to its day-to-day happenings. This circumstance, of course, presented me with both advantages and disadvantages.

My organizational role may have shaped how the janitors perceived me in the organization. Although I am Latino and an immigrant, I also have acquired much cultural capital (i.e., learning the dominant language and about U.S. culture) during my time in the United States, and this capital has allowed me to climb various "social ladders" (e.g., educational and socioeconomic). In this society, I am part of an elite group of people—the educated elite. This reality might have shaped whether the janitors viewed me as an in-group or out-group member. Additionally, age difference might have been an issue for some janitors, as I was in my 30s, whereas most participants were middle-aged (45 years old or older). These circumstances might have shaped how the workers oriented toward me and what information they chose to disclose.

In contrast, participants also could have perceived me as a positive role model or as someone who is motivational for other people of Latin American descent, regardless of age and occupation. In fact, several participants explicitly communicated to me that they were proud of me and "all my accomplishments." Several janitors even encouraged me to "continue representing Latinos well." Such perceptions might have motivated them to open up to me, to help me meet the study's goals. In sum, who I am within the research site may have had both positive and negative consequences due to my relationship with the organization and its members. My role as researcher may have been affected by my other roles within the organization.

My relationship with the university partially shaped my assumptions as I prepared to interact with the research participants. From my perspective, I had the idea that the janitors were unhappy and that they were likely suffering and living a despondent life because of the jobs that they held. I came into the study ridden with assumptions about who the janitors were and what their feelings were about work and life, ready to discover all the wrongs that were being committed against them. Those views, however, were partially shaped by me "watching" them from my privileged standpoint within the organizational setting. Throughout the research process, I had to reposition myself and my views about who the janitors were and their life experiences. Additionally, I learned that it is critical to enter a research site and approach people with an awareness of the assumptions and standpoints that cloud our perceptions, working hard as a researcher to suspend preconceived assumptions. Through building relationships with the janitors before and during the data collection process, I heightened my awareness and better understood my role as a researcher at this organization.

Because I recognized my positionality early on, I was able to design my study in a way that allowed more opportunities for me to set aside my assumptions and foreground the participants' stories. It was and is my goal to use my privileged social positionality to give voice to people who might otherwise never be heard by the audiences of a scholarly book like this one.

Situating Work Experiences Within an Interpretive Framework

Methodology

The core of my study is interpretive research. An interpretive framework is useful for conducting this research because "for interpretivists, it is axiomatic that we need to see social action from the actors' point of view to understand what is happening" (Lindlof & Taylor, 2017, p. 31). The philosophical principle that undergirds my research for this book is what Wilhelm Dilthey called *Verstehen*. I centralize the notion of "seeking to understand" as I attempt to broaden and deepen my understanding of the experiences of Latin American immigrant janitorial workers within a higher education organizational setting.

The interpretive paradigm is useful for developing research agendas on issues related to social identity and qualitative scholarship (Denzin & Lincoln, 2017). Social scientists have advocated the need to conduct qualitative research studies, in general, due to their emphasis on localized, situated meaning-making among social actors and between social actors and researchers (Denzin & Lincoln, 2017; Tracy, 2020). As Denzin and Lincoln (2017) explained, qualitative research "locates the observer in the world," "involves an interpretive, naturalistic approach to the world," and "involves researchers making sense of phenomena in terms of meaning people bring to them" (p. 3).

Therefore, this research seeks to interpret the meanings that janitors cocreate with others through their everyday interactions. I embrace an interpretive framework because, according to Hecht et al. (1990), interpretive research methods have "a unique ability to capture the actor's point of view and allow the cultural perspective to emerge from the participant's own words" (p. 35). Interpretive approaches have strategically equipped scholars to take on certain historically neglected topics in the academy (e.g., race and ethnicity issues; Clair, 2003). An example of this paradigm shift (from positivistic to interpretive approaches) in communication studies is the trend to use interpretive frameworks to study communication and social identity issues (Alvarez, 2016; Ciszek, 2017; Hogg, 2018).

Concerning relationships between interpretive research and studies of race and ethnicity, Orbe (2000) explains that there is "a clear need to extend beyond social scientific research methodologies. To advance current conceptualizations of racial–ethnic minority groups in intercultural scholarship, research must begin to focus on the 'experiential' as much as the 'experimental'" (p. 604). This book represents an effort to answer such calls to action for more experiential research about communication and social identity by investigating relationships between communication processes and social identities such as race, ethnicity, occupation, and social class (Alvarez, 2017).

An interpretive framework was further suitable for this project because the framework's philosophical tenets advance that social actors' realities are constantly created, sustained, and modified through their interactions as they create and exchange—and make sense of—localized meanings and communicative performances (Denzin & Lincoln, 2017). The strength of this paradigm is that it produces knowledge "inductively through the iterative testing of tentative explanations against the experience of ongoing interaction with group members" (Lindlof & Taylor, 2017, p. 11). The implications of such a conceptual stance are that the knower can seek to understand social actors' communicative practices and meanings through a deep textual reading of their symbolic performances, as they simultaneously participate in co-constructing meaning throughout the research process.

Such a research approach implies that the researcher does not have to be a passive observer, as required in some positivistic paradigms, but can be an active participant in social actors' situated, localized, and emergent realities. As Lindlof and Taylor (2017) explained, "True knowledge is gained through prolonged immersion and extensive dialogue practiced [by researchers] in actual social settings," and "intimate familiarity with the performance and significance of social practices . . . is a requirement for [their] adequate explanation." Therefore, within an interpretive paradigm, "the researcher *is* the instrument" (Lindlof & Taylor, 2017, p. 11). Because I wanted to be an active participant in the participants' lived experiences, using qualitative methods provided the opportunity to proactively and symbolically engage participants in their own world.

Several additional characteristics of the interpretive paradigm further highlight its usefulness for the present study. First, the position, background, and researchers' choices tend to inform interpretations, such that researchers' values are unavoidably instilled in the research. Second, researchers' knowledge of their position and values allows for an understanding of issues that lead to certain choices being made and to achieve intersubjective understanding with those they study. This strategy allows for reliable findings and constructive interpretations of research claims (Goodall, 2019). Third, researchers' reflexivity is important during the research process and when reporting findings. By reflecting on the choices, positions, and values that are at play during data collection and analysis, researchers can offer specific and useful accounts of actual relationships between them and the persons they study (Tracy & Geist-Martin, 2013). These methodological characteristics are important because they contribute to "thick description" (Clark & Chevrette, 2017). When researchers are carefully tuned in to cultural context cues, they can provide nuanced interpretations and descriptions in ethnographic research; in relation to this study, thick description relies on meaningful symbolic manifestations such as words, actions, and nonverbal behaviors. Accordingly, I employed in-depth interviews to collect much of the discourse from the research participants.

Methods

In this study, I employ qualitative methods to collect, analyze, and interpret data to answer the research questions. Qualitative research has no specific defining method but, instead, uses a variety of methods to capture social action from multiple angles (Glaser & Strauss, 2017; Lindlof & Taylor, 2017). For instance, whereas naturalistic inquiry almost always relies on researchers' immersion in the world of the social actors' being studied, and ethnographers almost always use participant observation as a methodological strategy, qualitative research is a broad umbrella term that can employ strategies such as participant observation, interviewing, and document and artifact analysis. In this research, I employed in-depth interviewing as a primary strategy to collect and examine Latin American immigrant janitors' discourse (Tracy, 2020).

Interviewing is the primary method of data collection because it creates a space where participants narrate their behaviors, thoughts, and feelings. Interviews allow participants to recreate their lived experiences in ways that other forms of data collection such as surveys or experiments may not achieve. Such situated narratives are rich in description and, thus, ideal for an interpretive study (Tracy, 2020). One key feature of contemporary forms of interviewing is that they have become a more interactive—but still not neutral—process than traditional positivistic ways of interviewing (Hawkins, 2018; Nathan et al., 2019).

I used three types of interviews in this study, with the goal of capturing participants' experiences in multiple contexts at multiple times. The first interview type, the *informant interview*, "inform[s] the research about key features and processes of the scene—what the significant customs and rituals are and how they are done" (Lindlof & Taylor, 2017, p. 176). This type of interview provided an opportunity for me to gain knowledge about happenings and situations in the scenes. Next, during *respondent interviews*, I encouraged interviewees to "express themselves on an issue or situation, or to explain what they think or how they feel about their social world" (Lindlof & Taylor, 2017, p. 178). The last type of interview I conducted, in addition to formal in-depth interviews, was *ethnographic interviews*, which were informal and impromptu interviews conducted during my time working as a janitor. In concert, these types of interviews helped to gain a deep understanding of the social actors' lived experiences, as well as the departments' cultures and everyday activities.

In each interview, I employed a semi-structured, conversational approach with the janitors (Agarwal, 2020). Approaching interviewing as an interactive process where knowledge is co-created with participants can yield powerful narratives about their lived experiences. Janitors were able to ask questions, take their own route to answering *my* questions, and guide the discussion in a way that demonstrated their intercultural perspective and resulted in "a shared responsibility for the discovery of knowledge" (Orbe, 2000, p. 612). I created interview guides to align with general criteria recommended by interpretive scholars (e.g., Lindlof & Taylor, 2017; see Appendix A). Some of these criteria were that (a) the topics and questions should stay broad so the interviewer can ask the questions differently to different participants, (b) the interview guide should not rigidly dictate the order of how questions are asked, (c) the guide should provide the interviewer the freedom to ask optional questions, and (d) the interview guide should allow the researcher to reframe questions and adapt to interviewees' verbal style as the interview unfolds (Lindlof & Taylor,

2017). Some of the questions included in the interview guide were the following: During a regular work day/night, who do you talk to regularly? Do you feel that language affects your day-to-day communication with others? Has anyone ever asked for your suggestions about tasks, problems, or particular situations at work? Please describe some of the relationships that you have formed and developed at work and with whom.

The janitors with whom I conducted formal, sit-down, in-depth interviews were recruited through a snowball sampling strategy ($N = 25$). The snowball sampling strategy allowed recruitment of individuals who worked in four organizational units and with whom I did not have the opportunity to interact. To reach potential participants across departments, I asked janitors with whom I had built relationships to connect me with friends and colleagues. I then contacted those referrals via email and telephone to set up dates and times to meet for a sit-down interview. I interviewed eight janitors from Housing Services, five janitors from the SU, four from Recreation Services, and eight from Facilities Management.

Regarding sample size, the guideline that I followed was to conduct interviews until no new information was gained in relation to answering the research questions—that is, until the point of "theoretical saturation" was apparent (Glaser & Strauss, 2017). I reached saturation at 25 interviews, as themes of our discussions were clearly repeating themselves. I conducted the interviews in classrooms, in break rooms, in lobbies, and at janitors' homes. The interviews lasted 90 to 105 minutes on average. All interviews (including informant, respondent, and ethnographic) were, at the interviewees' request, conducted in the janitors' native language, Spanish. With the interviewees' permission, in-depth interviews were audio-recorded and then transcribed verbatim in Spanish. I transcribed half of the interviews and a professional transcriber transcribed the other half. I use pseudonyms for all participants in all data texts. In total, the interviews yielded 234 pages of transcribed text. I translated all portions of the interviews used in the manuscript from Spanish to English. My background as a native Spanish speaker and my formal education in both English and Spanish allowed me to translate transcripts and to record interview notes in English and Spanish as I conducted the interviews.

Conducting interviews in participants' native language was important for the study's purpose and outcomes, as I wanted to acquire participants' voices in their raw form. Namely, I wanted to effectively communicate participants' experiences to both English- and Spanish-speaking audiences. Interviewing participants in their native language and then translating the text to English best accomplished that goal (Mandal, 2018; Regmi et al., 2010). For ethical considerations, I employed plain diction that was free of regional colloquial-isms and idiomatic phrases during the interviews (see the interview protocol in Appendix A). Furthermore, although using two languages added time and labor, doing so meant that this project would contribute to translinguistic qualitative communication research (J. Choi et al., 2012; Ho et al., 2019). My research responds, in particular, to a call by Lopez et al. (2008):

> Cross-cultural qualitative studies conducted in languages other than the investigator's primary language are rare and especially challenging because of the belief that meaning—which is at the heart of qualitative analysis—cannot be sufficiently ascribed by an investigator whose primary language differs from the study's participants. (p. 1729)

Because the participants' native language is also my first language, I believe I straddled the bilingual fence effectively to manage how the data were obtained and interpreted.

Interviews were conducted in participants' native language for two addi-tional reasons. First, research that is inclusive of English language learners (ELLs) is virtually nonexistent in the communication discipline. Second, this research study highlights potential challenges that might be encountered when conducting research with ELL populations. I admit at the outset that conduct-ing interviews in a language other than English and translating the text can pose some methodological challenges, but in this study, I had confidence in my bilingual abilities to translate text from Spanish to English and vice versa. Furthermore, I was well aware that even though standards of rigor exist for qualitative research, there are not necessarily similar standards for translating text. In this vein, this study also serves as a "conversation starter" regarding what standards of rigor scholars should have in place when conducting quali-tative research with ELL persons.

Existing studies with ELL populations largely exist in health communica-tion contexts (e.g., Al-Amer et al., 2015, 2016; Lopez et al., 2008; Marshall & While, 1994; Twinn, 1997). These disciplines have highlighted several pre- and during-interview issues that also were apparent in the present study. Specifi-cally, ELL participants tend to be apprehensive about participating in research studies in which researchers do not speak their language (Marshall & While, 1994). This was the case during the present study, as a large number of poten-tial participants declined to participate in this study. I am not sure why this happened, but one potential reason might be that some people perceived me as an out-group member although I too originated from Latin America and spoke Spanish. Additionally, if I had conducted the interviews in English, I probably would not have been able to probe as deeply as I was able to do using participants' native language.

Participant Observation

Participant observations allowed me to witness social actors' communicative performances in their environment as they happened. The value of participant observation lies in "researchers' *having been there*" (Lindlof & Taylor, 2017, p. 135). Accordingly, I used participant observation to immerse myself in janitors' work lives. I also wanted to intimately get to know what it is like to interact with others from a janitor's perspective.

When employing participant-observational methods, researchers can accomplish their goals by embodying one of four roles: *complete participant, participant-observer, observer-participant,* and *complete observer* (Lindlof & Taylor, 2017). As a participant-observer, I entered the field with the clear expectation that I was in an investigator role. I studied the scene from my vantage point of working as a part-time janitor who was in the building learning about janitorial culture and individual and group symbolic performances. In this role, "participation is part of a 'deal' negotiated with gatekeepers (or sponsors) and usually involves a special status—usually a part-time, temporary, voluntary, and/or 'play' role" (Lindlof & Taylor, 2017, p. 147). In this role, I worked as a part-time janitor and was not expected to master all the cleaning duties that veteran janitors mastered. I was in this role for about four months, working four-hour shifts three times a week for a combined total of approximately 12 hours a week.

I worked in various buildings on campus, including the School of Business and the Administrative Center. My work duties consisted primarily of dusting and wiping down top surfaces in offices, classrooms, and meeting rooms. I also swept and mopped floors. During that time, I was fully engaged in performing the duties of a janitor but without having all the expectations and responsibilities that affect full-time janitors. I did not have to finish a certain number of offices by a certain time. I could also take, although briefly, some time off to write field notes and to ask the supervisor and my coworkers questions about their work activities and specific happenings in the scene. In total, I spent approximately 110 hours in the field, which yielded roughly 30 pages of handwritten field notes. Halfway through the data collection, I came back into the field and spent several hours with the janitors, this time in an observer-participant role.

In the observer-participant role, observing was my primary goal, but I still interacted with participants as they worked (Lindlof & Taylor, 2017). I came back to the field a year later because I wanted to reengage in janitorial work life after spending months reconceptualizing the study. As the project unfolded, and as I continued to engage research topic–related texts and data, I wanted to observe firsthand how scholarly literature and completed interviews related to janitors' lived experiences. Another important reason for returning to the field was that, as an iterative process, qualitative research allows researchers to leave and come back to the field to better capture and understand the social actors' *lebenswelt* (lifeworld) and symbolic performances (Lindlof & Taylor, 2017). In total, I spent an additional 25 hours in the field.

Participant-observation data were collected from three scenes in the research site: staff meetings, breaks, and during work hours—or on the "front-lines," as being on the clock is formally known across campus units. These three scenes displayed janitors' routine interactions with supervisors, coworkers, and customers.

First, I observed staff meetings led by the supervisor. I participated in seven meetings, in which, typically, the supervisor discussed upcoming events and miscellaneous work-related activities with janitors. Staff meetings were regularly scheduled, every other week or so, and mandatory. These meetings usually took place before the beginning of janitors' work shifts. The meetings typically lasted no more than half an hour and took place in a classroom in the School of Business building (I spent most of my working hours in this facility). As a scene in the research site, these staff meetings provided a discursive space where I could observe superior–subordinate interaction and decision-making and collaboration processes. I saw how the supervisor verbally addressed the workers and how workers responded to the supervisor and to their colleagues (Jian & Dalisay, 2017, 2018). Staff meetings also allowed me a glance into the department's culture, as I could observe behaviors related to leadership style and organizational discourse. In sum, staff meetings offered a discursive space where I could examine department-specific attitudes, knowledge, and behaviors within the work group I observed (Herdman et al., 2017; B. B. Jones, 2020).

In the second scene, I observed janitors interacting with others during their break hours. I had various opportunities to sit down and "break bread" with the janitors. I observed janitors when their "veils" were down, as they were typically relaxed, joking around, and sharing food and stories with each other. In that scene, I was able to see a more laid-back side of the workers. We also talked about their dreams, fears, personal lives, and their feelings about their work. It was during breaks that I conducted some informant interviews and ethnographic interviews. It also was during break hours that I learned about janitorial work in general, as well as the department's culture and janitors' perspectives about their supervisors and the department's leadership. These casual moments led to conversations that deeply enriched my knowledge about janitorial work (Holmes, 2005; Mahalingam et al., 2019).

The third scene I observed was "the frontlines," the official name that departments gave the work of cleaning the physical facilities. I spent most of my time in the field doing janitorial work, but I also observed janitors doing their jobs and interacting with other people. Janitors, including myself, spent most of the time on the frontlines isolated, with some rare, brief, and casual encounters with coworkers and customers (i.e., faculty, students, and noncustodial staff). In the time I spent working as a janitor, I experienced the boredom and monotony of janitorial work. I recall thinking to myself, "I could not do this for very long." I constantly thought about the communicative isolation in which I was immersed for those hours that I spent cleaning facilities. However, I gained valuable insights into janitors' day-to-day communication during those hours, as I experienced firsthand who they talked with and what they talked about, as well as the frequency, breadth, and depth of their conversations.

Ethical Considerations

It is important to note that I deeply considered ethical issues related to janitors' privacy and protection, as they were people who some may consider to be vulnerable subjects. Although this study had minimal risk for the participants and their well-being, I used several precautions to protect the participants.

First, I used informed consent throughout the study. Participants were informed well in advance of the study's purpose and of their participation. Each participant had the opportunity to read and sign informed consent forms written in participants' native language of Spanish. For those participants who could not read the form, I read the form to them verbatim. Second, all pertinent documents (e.g., interview guide) were translated into Spanish to provide participants with access to all information pertaining to their participation in the study. Third, all information regarding participants was kept confidential throughout the final manuscript, with all names being pseudonyms. Fourth, to the extent possible, I translated all interview text in participants' exact words. I strategically employed plain diction such that all questions and answers were free of regional colloquialisms and idiomatic phrases that might not be understood by a larger audience. I knew that translating information from one language to another could represent ethical issues, and for that reason, I was sensitive to what participants said and to how I represented their words in the manuscript. Lastly, all information related to the research study that does not appear in the manuscript is in my possession.

Data Analysis

To analyze the texts (interviews and observations) I gathered, I employed an inductive conceptual framework based on a process that examines and produces concepts and themes that emerge from the data—grounded theory (Glaser & Strauss, 2017). The data analysis and collection occur almost simultaneously "by identifying some important issues that guide the collection of data" (Ezzy, 2002, p. 12). Preexisting theories, concepts, and issues sensitize researchers to specific questions in an iterative process of observation and analysis during the research project; therefore, "theory is built up from observation. . . . Theory is 'grounded' in data" (Ezzy, 2002, p. 12). Grounded theory, in practice, involves creating codes and categories to sort the data while still collecting said data. Those codes and categories are constantly changing, as new field experiences alter the researcher's perspective (Lindlof & Taylor, 2017). This mutability might suggest that the coding process could last for an indefinite period of time, but research endeavors, in general, reach a point of "theoretical saturation" (Glaser & Strauss, 2017):

> What keeps the process under some control is the fact that the analyst is comparing each incident to other incidents in order to decide in which categories they belong. Thus when considering any new incident, the analyst compares it with incidents that have already been coded into categories. (Lindlof & Taylor, 2017, p. 219)

It was within this iterative analytical process that I analyzed raw data from interview texts for this study.

Throughout my coding process, I constantly discussed initial and subsequent findings with my mentors and colleagues, and I reflected on scenes and interviews and on my positioning as a researcher. Having the data-analytic process always in the back of my mind allowed me to home in on salient coding categories that shed light on the issues under investigation, even as I was in the field. Throughout the coding process, I paid attention to data that informed the everyday communication experiences of the janitors and how they perceived themselves, others, and their interactions. Keeping these sensitizing concepts in mind helped to identify larger themes when they emerged from the data. For example, some of those themes are (a) Social effects of language use, (b) Feelings and attitudes toward language use, (c) Language use and everyday communication challenges, (d) Intercultural communication accommodation, (e) Interpersonal conflict avoidance, (f) Gossip; supervisor and coworker issues, (g) Coworker relationships, and (h) Interpersonal networks. Such a process also was useful in helping to understand my position as a researcher studying the research site and the people in this study.

Researcher's Assumptions: My Story, Their Story, Our Story?

Following my dedication to the interpretive framework, I remained self-reflexive during the research process. I kept my positionality in mind and talked with the research participants, friends, peers, mentors, colleagues, and strangers to consider my work from multiple angles. Throughout the writing process, I asked others for feedback on my interpretations of the findings. I engaged in these practices in part to keep my assumptions "in check" and to be intentional about remaining cognizant that my immigrant experiences are both similar and dissimilar to the Latin American immigrant janitors with whom I worked on this project.

Based on my experiences and background as a Latin American immigrant and stakeholder in different types of organizations during my time living in the United States, I clearly hold assumptions that frame how I approached conducting this investigation and writing this manuscript. I was dedicated to unpacking those assumptions at the outset because they embody taken-for-granted knowledge that initially informed my perception of the people whose voices and life experiences I attempt to represent in my written discourse.

Assumption 1

Non-Native English Speakers, Specifically Spanish-Speaking Latin American Immigrants, Struggle to Communicate Effectively at Work

This assumption is partially based on my experiences as a Latin American immigrant, someone who is aware of the communication struggles Latin American immigrants who do not speak English experience in the United States. I have regularly witnessed friends and family members struggle to find work and communicate with others in the most mundane of circumstances due to their limited English language skills. During my time living in the United States, there have been numerous occasions when I could not communicate my thoughts and ideas in English to another person, which led to exceptionally uncomfortable situations. Even though I have acquired a considerable amount of language skills over the years, I still struggle to communicate in some social contexts. These experiences led me to ground my study in the assumption that struggling to communicate at an English-only workplace is a common occurrence for all Spanish-speaking Latin American immigrants.

Assumption 2

Non-Native English Speakers Rely on Same-Race and Same-Language Peers for Comfort, Affirmation, and Coping When Faced With Communicative Adversity

Throughout my experience as an immigrant, I have consistently found solace during difficult times in my interactions and relationships with my same-race and same-language peers. I believe that there was a commonality of experiences that pushed us to support and affirm each other during stressful circumstances as out-group members in U.S. society. Furthermore, those same-culture/same-language peers often were the only people with whom I felt safe disclosing certain thoughts and feelings related to institutional challenges I encountered. I felt that some people viewed me as an outsider, or even someone who could not be trusted, because of my social differences. In these circumstances, same-race peers tended to understand my perspectives because they could relate to my lived experiences. Even now, they are the people who most consistently affirm me in times of identity crisis and in relational conflicts with cross-cultural others. These experiences led me to consider my participants' interpersonal relationships rather than just organizational ones—but it also caused me to be careful not to assume my participants do not interact outside their same-race, same-language groups.

Assumption 3

Within the Social Parameters of Their Intersections of Social Identity, Non-Native English Speakers Are Discontent With Their Circumstances Because They Tend to View Themselves Negatively

Even within my privileged social position as a college professor, I struggle tremendously due to my perceptions of how other people view me. I fight to view myself as someone who is worthy of others' acceptance and affirmation. Although I have acquired cultural and social capital, other people's constant verbal and nonverbal messages—straddling the fence between hostility and fear—constantly push me to reflect on the sources of their communication orientations. My assumption was that immigrants have negative views of themselves that are shaped by dominant discourses as being socially undesirable or stigmatized and that, because of negative self-perceptions, immigrants actively desire better socioeconomic circumstances for themselves. Their social locations shape how others perceive and communicate with them, which, in turn, shapes how they perceive themselves. Rather than forming the basis of my study, this assumption colored my perceptions: I had to actively keep from projecting my insecurities onto the participants.

Assumption 4

Workplaces Can Be Unwelcoming and Difficult Spaces to Navigate Communicatively, Especially for Non-Native English Speakers

The last assumption is based on the premise that, historically, in the United States, people who identify with certain social identities have experienced great hardship in different social settings (Alvarez, 2016, 2018). Specifically, because of their race, ethnicity, social class, and immigrant status, as well as their occupation, Latin American immigrant janitors may experience regular verbal and nonverbal rejection and offensive behaviors from other employees. People's communicative behaviors toward different others are shaped by dominant discourses about individual differences in the United States. As a Latin American immigrant, I can relate to people who have experienced verbal and nonverbal violence due to their marginalized racial–ethnic social positions. For this study, I had to ensure that this assumption did not bleed into my interactions with participants and cause them to think differently about their own experiences at RMU.

I believe that frontloading my assumptions gives the reader a sense of who I am as a person and researcher and helps contextualize why I decided to study the research setting and participants while employing the methods used in this study. My hope is that this book will open a window into the lived experiences of people who inhabit the margins to illuminate their experiences in ways that foment consciousness and, ultimately, more just and humane workplaces and society at large. I aim to elevate their stories by adding my story, with the hope of facilitating more positive narratives and stories for us and others who come behind us.

CHAPTER 2

Communicating at Work

Si, es que una cosa es ser lider administrativo y otra es ser lider en medio de la gente. Sabes por qué? Si tu eres lider administrativo desde aqui giras las ordenes y no mas dices: dile a la gente esto y esto yo giro, pero creeme que yo me atrevo a decirte y sin temor a equivocarme que creo que yo seria mejor lider que tu, sabes por que? Porque yo se manejar los caracteres, las actitudes, la manera de comportarse de la gente yo estoy trabajando de una manera directa con ellos el administrativo no lamentablemente, no consiste el trabajo en que todo este limpio; hay personas que tienen que limpiarlo y ahi es que esta el asunto.

[Yes, it is one thing to be an administrative leader and it's another thing to be a leader among people. You know why? If you are an administrative leader from over there you give your orders and you only tell people to do this and that. If I were to give orders, believe me and I would dare to say unequivocally that I am a better leader than you, you know why? Because I know how to deal with people's characters, attitudes, their behaviors, I would be working directly with them, the administrative leader is not. Lamentably, the work is not just about everything being clean; it is people who have to do the cleaning and therein lies the point.]

—Raul

Pues hablamos muy bien; hacemos el trabajo y todo bien aqui. Es un ambiente muy unido con todos nosotros. Conversamos de la familia; ya tenemos tiempo trabajando y nos conocemos de años. Compartimos la comida como si fueramos familia todos.

[We talk and all is well; we do the work and everything is fine here. It is a very united environment with all of us here. We talk about the family; we have a long time working here and we know each other for years. We share our food like we are all family.]

—Manuela

THESE NARRATIVES, excerpted from transcripts of my interviews, exemplify Latin American immigrant janitors' routine communication experiences with their supervisors and coworkers. The janitors' workplace experiences are rich with both heartbreaking and joyful moments, and their relations of those experiences display the complexity inherent in human communication in general and workplace communication with culturally different others in particular. This chapter's goal is to carefully situate these narratives in the existing scholarship on organizations' interpersonal hierarchical roles—like superior–subordinate and coworkers—and communication practices in traditional organizational bureaucracies. My hope, in part, is to highlight how the stories and experiences of Latin American, immigrant, low-status-occupation individuals can complicate what researchers and organizational leaders understand about both workplace and intercultural communication.

Workplace Communication

Workplace communication, a central concept in this analysis, is any engagement in verbal and nonverbal interactions in specific organizational relationship types, such as superior–subordinate and coworkers, in addition to communication between co-cultural group members in those and other roles (Hall, 2016; Mikkola & Valo, 2020; Orbe, 2017). These interpersonal relationships are crucial for the effective functioning of both employees and organizations (Caillier, 2017; Colbert et al., 2016; Sias, 2013; Sias & Shin, 2020).

Perhaps the most influential relationship that people have in the workplace is their relationship with their superior(s) (Kramer, 2017; Myers, 2017; Steele & Plenty, 2015), as superior–subordinate arrangements are found in most organizational structures. In this book, *superior–subordinate interaction* is defined as "exchanges of information and influence between organizational members, one of whom has formal authority to direct and assess the actions of the other organizational member (as defined by official organizational sources)" (Jablin, 1979, p. 1202)—in short, message exchanges between two organizational members, one of whom is positioned hierarchically above the other (Bakar et al., 2020; Campbell et al., 2001).

Research largely suggests that positive superior–subordinate interactions are linked to employees' satisfaction, organizational commitment, and relational satisfaction with coworkers (Babalola, 2016; Kram & Isabella, 1985; Liao et al., 2017). *Coworker communication* exists with or without a superior-subordinate relationship and consists of dyadic message exchanges between organizational members who occupy equal hierarchical positions (Ploeger-

Lyons & Kelley, 2017). Coworker relationships help employees to cope with work-related stress and job burnout (Teven, 2007; Wright, 2011).

In either kind of relationship, research shows that asymmetrical co-cultural interactions result from communicative conflicts between in-group and out-group members in organizations (Cranmer & Myers, 2015; Morton et al., 2012). These conflicts typically stem from stereotypical meanings ascribed to individuals' social identities (B. J. Allen, 2017; Orbe, 2017). This finding is crucial to my motivation to immerse myself in Latin American immigrant janitors' workplace communication, and I found strong evidence of the importance of superior–subordinate communication and coworker communication in this context.

Superior–Subordinate Communication

The body of literature on superior–subordinate communication stretches back almost 60 years. Katz and Kahn's (1966) classic model of superior–subordinate communication identified five basic types of downward communication from superior to subordinate: job instructions, job rationale, organizational procedures and practices, feedback about subordinate performance, and indoctrination of goals (pp. 239–241). In contrast, upward communication from subordinate to superior involves information about the subordinate, information about coworkers and their problems, information about organizational practices and policies, and information about what needs to be done and how it can be done (p. 245). This model and others (e.g., Eilon, 1968; Melcher & Beller, 1967; Yoder, 1970)—in addition to Graen et al.'s (1972) and Dansereau et al.'s (1975) research on leader–member exchanges—serve as much of the impetus for scholarly study of superior–subordinate organizational interactions.

From its genesis in organizational behavior research in the early 1970s, the study of superior–subordinate interactions has focused on supervisors' communicative behaviors and the outcomes associated with those behaviors (Bisel et al., 2012; Dansereau et al., 1975; Graen et al., 1972; Kramer, 2017; Lloyd et al., 2015). This line of work has been influenced by leader–member exchange theory (LMX; Jian, 2015). According to LMX theory and research, supervisors have distinctive relationships with their subordinates and, therefore, subordinates receive different amounts and qualities of resources (primarily material) from their supervisors (Dansereau et al., 1975). These origins might explain why subsequent research on superior–subordinate interaction has had underlying assumptions of linearity or cause and effect. For instance, much of this research has focused on the effects of supervisors' behaviors on subordinates' job satisfaction and organizational commitment (B. J. Collins et al., 2014; Loi et al., 2014; Valaei & Rezaei, 2016), as well as the amount, quality, and consequences of downward information-giving (Cho, 2014; Sias, 2005). Other works have focused on superior–subordinate relational quality (Falcione et al., 1977; Gates, 2008; Infante & Gordon, 1985; Redmond et al., 2016) and dyad–organization relationships (Muterera et al., 2018).

Leadership Studies

Early LMX research focused on the so-called average style of leaders and not on dyadic leader–member interaction processes (Graen et al., 1972; Graen & Cashman, 1975). This "average style" assumed that leaders had relationships with groups and not with individuals. LMX research later shifted to show relational differences that existed between leaders and each of their followers. For instance, Graen and colleagues' research brought attention to the vertical dyad linkage (VDL; e.g., Dansereau et al., 1975). VDL suggested that a leader's relationship to their group was made up of groups of vertical dyads (Graen & Scandura, 1987). Instead of viewing two entities as the unit of analysis (leader and group of followers), researchers began to view the leader as one entity in a relationship with various groups, which were called in-groups and out-groups. In-groups were made up of individuals who had better relationships with their leaders, whereas out-group members had poorer relationships with their leaders.

From the previous research emerged specific distinctions between the notions of "leadership" and "supervision" (Jacobs, 1971). *Leadership* came to mean that the "basis of influence is anchored in the interpersonal exchange relationship between a superior and a member," whereas *supervision* focuses on "the nature of the vertical exchange . . . such that a superior relies almost exclusively upon the formal employment contract in his exchanges with a member" (Dansereau et al., 1975, p. 49). Positioning supervision as role-taking and leadership as role-making facilitated the notion that superior–subordinate relational outcomes are *not* universal and need to be negotiated in everyday interactions (Graen & Cashman, 1975).

Dansereau et al.'s (1975) study of 60 managers at the housing division of a large public university found that in-group members (those individuals who were closer to their leaders) expressed higher satisfaction with their jobs than did out-group members (employees who were not part of the supervisors' inner circle). Moreover, in-group members reported better personal relations with their supervisor and higher value of their job performance rewards. These findings suggest that more and higher-quality information exchanges between superiors and subordinates can not only engender better job outcomes for subordinates but also better relational quality, something the janitors in my study noted on multiple occasions.

Communication Studies

It was not until Fairhurst et al.'s (1987), Fairhurst and Chandler's (1989), and Fairhurst's (1993) studies of LMX in the late 1980s and early 1990s that superior–subordinate research took a turn toward more communication-oriented investigations. These studies found that high-quality, superior–subordinate relationships (in-groups) were characterized by greater information breadth and depth than were low-quality relationships (out-groups). Further studies followed that focused on employees' information experiences, relationship quality, and superiors' and subordinates' individual differences (e.g., Abu Bakar et al., 2007; Abu Bakar & Mustaffa, 2008; Kniffin et al., 2014; Yang & Cho, 2015). These factors still form the central understanding of communication between superiors and subordinates. Sias (2005) found that superior–subordinate interaction dynamics were strongly associated with both the amount and quality of information that employees reported receiving from their supervisors. This study also showed that employees in a supervisor's in-group have an information advantage compared to out-group members. These results raise questions about whether individual variables, such as race or gender, affect who becomes part of supervisors' in-groups, not least because people tend to be drawn to others they perceive as being similar in terms of race, ethnicity, class, gender, education level, religion, and so on (Acker, 1990; Adkins & Lury, 1999; S. Gordon et al., 2019; Paustian-Underdahl et al., 2017).

Furthermore, Teven (2007) showed that supervisors, regardless of sex, produce more positive subordinate perceptions of credibility by being more nonverbally immediate (welcoming in attitude, posture, manner of engagement, etc.). One implication is that certain communication orientations with subordinates might be perceived as more effective to enhance superior–subordinate rapport in the workplace (Lybarger et al., 2017). These results also indicate that subordinates find nonverbally immediate supervisors to be more trustworthy, caring, and competent than supervisors who are less nonverbally immediate and who are antisocial. These relational outcomes can, thus, have a positive effect on the organization's functioning as a whole.

Fix and Sias (2006) research found that the extent to which employees anticipated that their supervisors would use person-centered communication was positively associated with their perceptions of the quality of their superior–subordinate interactions. These results, in addition to Fairhurst's (1993) findings, suggest that communication processes are central to the study of superior–subordinate workplace interactions.

Limitations of Existing Communication Research

Existing communication-oriented studies of superior–subordinate interactions have a few underexplored avenues of research that I hope to grow with my case study. First, demographically diverse population samples have been largely absent—especially diverse racial-ethnic ones (Abu Bakar & Mustaffa, 2008). This research has also focused on white-collar occupations and middle-class college students and has fully neglected blue-collar occupations. Second, much of this work has relied primarily on experimental and survey-based research designs (Lybarger et al., 2017). For a long time, the empirical emphasis overlooked qualitative, interpretive methodological frameworks (for exceptions, see Fairhurst, 1993; Gates, 2008; Maji & Dixit, 2020); instead, the focus was on testing hypotheses regarding population samples. Interpretive frameworks can help nuance results and offer insight that goes deeper than the basic mechanics of relationships.

Third, this line of research has a strong emphasis on individual difference such as sex, communicator style and ability, and organizational outcomes (Abu Bakar et al., 2007), factors often addressed in isolation from one another. This focus on individual differences and abilities has overlooked complex processes of dyadic communication such as identity negotiation and conflict management. Theoretical frameworks such as social exchange theory (SET) and equity theory (ET) have attempted to bridge this research gap: Since the 1980s, SET and ET have centrally informed superior–subordinate workplace communication scholarship (Sias & Jablin, 1995). For instance, through these theoretical lenses, researchers have claimed that superior–subordinate relationships evolve over time based on interactants' perceived costs and rewards.

Still, I see space for work that accounts for a broader sample of workplace communication experiences *and* complicates the inevitable individual differences by situating them in the organizational and social structures that make them significant sources of interpersonal negotiation.

Summary

Superior–subordinate interaction research has a rich history that has evolved into the study of more communication-oriented foci. Early research focused on positive superior–subordinate relationships and the tangible outcomes that those relationships produced. Later, research focused on the processes that lead to organizational outcomes, and, as a result, an emphasis emerged on information exchanges, relational quality, and sex/gender differences. Although significant, an exclusive emphasis on individual differences, such as sex or gender, does not give a full picture of organizational processes. Most studies of superior–subordinate communication overwhelmingly have used White participants (for exceptions, see Gates, 2005, 2006, 2008; Kamal Kumar & Kumar Mishra, 2017), with the implicit assumption that findings from such research are applicable to racially homogeneous populations. Relying primarily on White participants in fact excludes other experiences that would contribute to a more comprehensive understanding of organizational members' routine interactions. By considering historically overlooked organizational members and occupations, this book seeks to contribute to the body of knowledge about vertical dyadic communication.

These omissions suggest that studying particular groups of people and individual and situational variables (e.g., language use ability, people working with culturally different others, and the university setting) might not be as relevant in organizational research—an implication I reject and challenge. To expand the paucity of research on superior–subordinate communication that is inclusive of lower-status workers, this project investigates the nature and processes of organizational interactions focusing on traditionally subjugated organizational members. In tandem it investigates strong links between positive superior–subordinate relationships and positive peer coworker relationships.

Peer Coworker Communication

Workplace peer relationships, also called "equivalent-status" relationships (Fay & Kline, 2011; Ploeger-Lyons & Kelley, 2017; Sollitto & Myers, 2015), are relationships between coworkers with no formal authority over one another. Because most organizations traditionally have had hierarchical structures, these relationships represent the majority of organizational relationships (i.e., most employees have one direct supervisor and many coworkers). These relationships serve multiple functions because peer coworkers are the most common source of "emotional and instrumental support for employees," largely because of their tacit insider knowledge of the organization (Sias, 2005, p. 379). Hence, constructive coworker relationships are especially significant among peers (T. D. Allen et al., 1999; Love & Dustin, 2014). Most people's everyday workplace interactions are with their coworkers; however, peer communication has received less attention from researchers than has superior–subordinate communication (Methot et al., 2016).

Coworker communication research has primarily focused on (a) creating typologies of peers and their functions in organizations according to career stages (Kram & Isabella, 1985), (b) identifying relationships between superior–subordinate and coworker communication (Sias & Jablin, 1995), and (c) studying interaction processes according to peer types (J. Gordon & Hartman, 2009). Kram and Isabella's (1985) groundbreaking research on the role of peer relationships in career development inspired scholars from several disciplines to study coworkers' relationship formation, development, and outcomes in organizational contexts (see, e.g., Fritz, 1997; Odden & Sias, 1997; Spillan & Mino, 2001). Though this research, like that in superior–subordinate communication, originated in organizational behavior studies, communication scholars have contributed in their own right (e.g., Fay & Kline, 2011; Fix & Sias, 2006; Sollitto & Myers, 2015).

Level and Purpose of Peer Communication

The peer coworker research literature generally presumes that employees go through similar career stages of increasing responsibility and thus have similar workplace experiences. However, investigators have focused almost exclusively on white-collar organizational members, which contributes to assumptions that certain message types are universally exchanged, such as workplace information sharing, advice, and social support. As a result, much of the research on peer relationships emphasizes common career stage (Spillan et al., 2002).

Kram and Isabella (1985), for example, "suggest that peer relationships offer an important alternative to conventional mentoring relationships by providing a range of developmental support for personal and professional growth at each career stage" (p. 116). These findings narrowed peer relationships to mentoring but ultimately provided the foundation for one of the most widely used typologies of peer relationships in the workplace: *Information peers* are those individuals whose primary function is workplace information sharing; *collegial peers* are those with whom people not only exchange job-related information but with whom they also have a friendship; and *special peers* are those with whom organizational members are emotionally the closest and to whom they provide emotional support, friendship, personal feedback, and validation. Different peers can serve different functions across their careers: establishment, advancement, middle, and late career stage.

One's information peers in the establishment stage, for example, aid others in "learning the ropes and getting the job done" (p. 125). In contrast, one's special peers during this career stage help create a "sense of competence, commitment" and discuss "work-family conflicts" (Kram & Isabella, 1985, p. 125). What this and subsequent studies on peer relationships seemed to assume was that most if not all organizational members across bureaucratic levels "climb the ladder" in more or less similar ways. Importantly, it is unclear how research has accounted for blue-collar employees—such as janitors, housekeepers, and domestic servants—who historically have remained on a linear career path and experience minimal differences in their hierarchical position and typical communicative encounters.

Differential Treatment

Peer coworker research that focused on communication processes did not surface until the early to mid-1990s (Sias, 1996; Sias & Jablin, 1995). At that time, much of that research had a strong LMX essence and thus was conducted by organizational behavior and management scholars. Sias and Jablin led the way in studying peer coworker communication, seeking to understand, among other issues, how organizational members talk about differential treatment and how their communication is related to workplace relational outcomes. Much of this research advanced that workplace relationships do not happen in a vacuum and that what happens in organizational dyads has the potential to affect other parts of the organizational system (Sias & Jablin, 1995). Similarly, Ambrose et al. (1991) argued that information regarding the outcomes of other individuals' interactions and relationships is a central attribute of any social context that, by extension, can affect all people in that context.

Once again, researchers have not paid comparable attention to relationships between social groups' variables such as race, ethnicity, and social class, or to vertical and horizontal communication in organizations. The main line of research, like that on superior–subordinate communication, has continued to show a bias toward the experiences of white-collar organizational members. Central scholars such as Jablin and Sias continued the research legacy that placed LMX theory at the center of their investigations, even further embracing the theory's (often exclusionary) underlying assumptions and tenets.

In a striking example, Sias and Jablin (1995) examined differential treatment in superior–subordinate and peer coworker communication. They found that employees who were perceived to receive preferential treatment from their superiors tended to be isolated from coworker groups, whereas employees who were perceived to be fairly rewarded became part of the in-group. Moreover, employees who others perceived to be punished fairly tended to be isolated from coworkers, whereas those who were unfairly punished were drawn into the peer group communication network. Many participants reported that negative differential treatment from a supervisor often instilled feelings of vulnerability in the rest of the coworker groups. In a similar study, Sias (1996, 2005) found that organizational members' perceptions of differential treatment are often socially constructed by coworkers through communication. Also, Kramer (1995), in a longitudinal study of job transferees, found that organizational members who perceive that they are in a high-quality relationship with their superior (e.g., high in trust, support, and openness) also developed collegial and special relationships with their peers that were characterized by trust, self-disclosure, and open communication (Myers et al., 1999).

Taken together, perceptions of superiors' differential treatment and communication about differential treatment may be related to coworkers' attitudes about the quality of their superior–subordinate relationship (Kramer, 2017; Mueller & Lee, 2002; Myers, 2017). Simultaneously, perceptions regarding the quality of subordinates' relationships with superiors may relate to how subordinates perceive the fairness of their superiors' behaviors and how they communicate with their coworkers about such behaviors. Organizational members often perceive that they can highly trust coworkers, providing opportunities for them to voice their problems when they cannot do it with their supervisor. In sum, these studies offer some evidence that superior–subordinate interactions affect others outside of the dyad—in particular, superior–subordinate relationships affect interactions with coworkers.

Much of the research on peer coworker communication has investigated differences and similarities of information, collegial and special peers' communication, and outcomes associated with these interaction processes (Myers, 2017; Myers & Johnson, 2004). For example, Sias and Cahill's (1998) classic study of peer coworker relationship development showed key factors (e.g., context, type of communication network) related to the transition from coworker to becoming good friends. Myers and Johnson (2004) found that coworkers' perceived similarity and trust were lower with information peers than with collegial or special peers.

Together, these studies offer evidence that there are qualitative differences among the types of peer coworkers. However, this line of research primarily has relied on students and white-collar workers of European descent, with little mention of social identity categories other than sex/gender and, sometimes, individuals' occupations and age (Fritz, 1997; Odden & Sias, 1997). Moreover, there seems to be a methodological bias toward postpositivism (J. Gordon & Hartman, 2009; Ji & Jan, 2020; Zhuang et al., 2019) in that cause–effect frameworks appear as the norm.

What this work fails to account for is the effect of individual difference on the individual experience and outsider perception, *as well as* its effect on the organization itself. Is the composition of in-groups affected by supervisors' race, gender, ethnicity, and so on? Is peer response to employee punishment and reward similarly affected? Are blue-collar workers especially susceptible to differential treatment from culturally different others, either supervisors or peers? These questions and others add further weight to the tendency for studies of superior–subordinate and peer coworker to focus on White, white-collar participants.

This book moves away from these trends—and toward a foundation for more inclusive, intersectional research—by examining Latin American immigrant janitors' communication with their coworkers through an interpretive lens to offer further insights into their communication processes. One contribution of this expansion is a likely new understanding of how in-groups and out-groups form in culturally heterogeneous organizations. Superior treatment is not the only factor, as individuals tend to gather and bond with people who are similar to them in visible, significant ways. This bonding is often facilitated by affinity-seeking strategies, that is, strategies that increase the "degree of liking" among peers (R. A. Bell et al., 1987).

Affinity-Seeking Behaviors

To illustrate how coworkers enact affinity-seeking strategies, J. Gordon and Hartman (2009) examined peer coworker communication in relation to open communication and the use of affinity-seeking strategies (e.g., providing feedback and job-related support). The findings supported two out of four hypotheses. First, special peers were more likely to use affinity-seeking strategies than were informal peers, but special peers did not use affinity-seeking strategies more often than did collegial peers. Second, communication openness is used more by special peers than by informational peers. Because the main purpose of communication with informational peers is to exchange work-related information, communication focusing on building more intimate relationships would not be expected.

Unclear in this line of research is how communication openness differs in level and depth based on peer type, although communication openness can lead to more cohesive work environments, job satisfaction, and organizational commitment, and can lead to better communication among coworkers (Givens & McNamee, 2016; Hall, 2016). One of my hypotheses for the Latin American janitors' communication context is that, as peer coworkers of similar cultures, they are more open with one another and more likely to cohere as peers. Additionally, I hypothesize that their relationships with their superiors are not as cohesive and in fact suffer from a serious imbalance in in- and out-group communication due to intercultural differences.

Case Study Findings and Research Implications

Following the need for empirical, interpretive studies that recognize the unique workplace communication experiences of non-White, immigrant, lower-status individuals, I provide an analysis and interpretation of the major findings, themes, issues, and practices related to workplace communication processes—particularly, communicating with supervisors and coworkers.

Overview

Most of the janitors who participated in this book's case study perceived that workplace interactions vary significantly depending on the person with whom they interact. First, they said that communication with supervisors is often harmful. Most janitors expressed that their supervisor was almost like a dictator in their leadership approach, who relied on an aggressive communication style during routine interactions. In contrast, interactions with coworkers were mostly positive. Most janitors expressed that relationships with coworkers were somewhat superficial but mostly positive, as these were the people with whom they talked the most. Overall, janitors described most vertical communication (with supervisors) as toxic and horizontal communication (with coworkers) as supportive.

Communicating With Supervisors

The janitors in this case study expressed that their supervisors were people who behaved like authoritarians whose authority was not to be challenged in any way. The janitors interpreted supervisors as people whose role gave them all the power necessary to mistreat their subordinates. Particularly, the janitors shared that many supervisors engaged in constant verbal mistreatment, displayed preferential treatment of certain people, and seemed to display blatant racial prejudices.

Treatment by Supervisors

The majority of the janitors interviewed for this investigation report that they perceive varying degrees of favoritism from their supervisors. For example, Manuel's comment illustrates perceptions of employee preference: "Todos sabíamos que el [supervisor] tenía preferencia por ese empleado. El le decía a otros; _____ es el empleado como todos deben ser. Y sus acciónes lo demonstraban consistentemente" [We all knew that he preferred that employee. He'd [the supervisor would] tell others _____ is the employee that everyone should be like, and his actions showed it consistently]. Blatant showings of preferential treatment from supervisors pushed some janitors to embrace a nonassertive separation communication orientation toward their supervisors (Orbe, 2017). According to most janitors, they often chose, unless necessary, to avoid any type of interaction with their supervisor.

The majority of janitors also indicated that their superiors addressed them in condescending and disrespectful ways. Janitors expressed, almost across the board, that supervisors simply did not know how to treat the people who worked for them. They agreed with each other when they said that supervisors' interpersonal skills were not up to par with the demands of their organizational role. Similar supervisor communication patterns existed across departments. Most janitors interviewed stated that their supervisor had been verbally aggressive toward them. This comment illustrates how most janitors described their work experiences with their supervisors:

> Right now . . . this is something recent . . . with our supervisor we are having problems . . . serious . . . the whole group . . . of mistreatment . . . yes, verbal abuse. Some of us complained already; if I'm not mistaken four or five coworkers complained with administration and they don't do anything. The people are afraid, they are stressed out, frustrated, they don't want to talk. . . . [W]e are steeped in a very serious problem and we can't say anything . . . [because] if you say anything . . . you know what happens . . . (Rodolfo)

This pattern suggests that supervisors' leadership approaches demonstrate some similarities across departments. Comparable cross-department patterns in leadership and communication styles suggest that supervisors may not be properly trained to communicate effectively with their subordinates. Additionally, these similarities in leadership style suggest that supervisors might be indoctrinated somewhat equally into their departments' culture, as different departments display some overlap in leadership approaches and what leadership means for people in supervisory roles.

Superior–subordinate communication practices in this research setting exemplify the differences in both the execution and the effect of role-taking (leadership) and role-making (supervision) efforts. Latin American immigrant janitors perceived that several people became supervisors due to their seniority status and by "knowing the right person." These observations point to issues related to who gets to become supervisor in the organization and what qualifies them to hold such position, in addition to likely implications for the treatment and potential for advancement of the janitors themselves. Communication experiences with supervisors reflect that most janitors are not satisfied with their immediate supervisor. They expressed that they were happy to have a job but that they were very unhappy with the leadership. This is how Ofelia talked about the climate that supervisors' communication style creates:

> She was exasperating, one would do their work and for her it was never enough. She was always aggressive . . . when we have meetings sometimes they ask if we have questions and I don't feel comfortable giving my opinion. Many times it's better to avoid speaking up (laughter). But there isn't a climate to give suggestions because I do not trust it.

Similarly problematic, Juan described how some supervisors manage communication in meetings:

> Um, there are meetings and people do not talk, but I notice that they are afraid, because if you accuse a supervisor then the supervisor goes after you and reprimands you or gives you more work. Recently, there was a meeting and he told me, no more; I was talking because people don't want to talk; what we need is for people to talk, that's what meetings are for; there is something wrong happening here.

This finding shows the significance of understanding organizational experiences beyond middle- and upper-management levels (i.e., white-collar employees). Supervisors in this organization may not perceive any tangible rewards for having respectful equal exchanges and relationships with their subordinates. In this research setting, supervisors' distributive (win–lose) treatment toward their subordinates creates a defensive communication climate that is harmful to their workplace relationships.

Relational Challenges Due to Race

Superior–subordinate relationships in the organization are also influenced by factors such as everyday relational challenges associated with intercultural communication ineffectiveness. Janitors indicated that the majority of their supervisors are European American (White) men. Supervisor–subordinate relationships are cross-race in that most janitors were either of Latin American or Asian descent and their supervisors were White, which is significant considering that this organization is a predominantly White university that is located in a largely White city and state. Supervisors' communicative patterns with their subordinates potentially exemplify the embodiment of negative attitudes based on prevailing discursive constructions of race, ethnicity, social class, and occupation in U.S. society. Though this study did not investigate supervisors' perspectives and motivations, the data suggest that supervisors, being White and of a higher social class status, may perceive themselves as occupying a higher level not just in the organizational hierarchy but also in the macrolevel racial-ethnic and socioeconomic hierarchies in the United States' social imaginary (Barreto & Lozano, 2017; Carter & Pérez, 2016).

Such perceptions of social location can give individuals a sense of entitlement that becomes enacted in various contexts of social life. Therefore, it might not be a coincidence that the majority of janitors indicated that their supervisor had verbally attacked them on more than one occasion. Within prevailing U.S. social hierarchies, and coupled with current public discourses about Latin American immigration, it is plausible that supervisors act out feelings of rejection and racially prejudicial attitudes toward Latin American immigrant janitors. This exposes some of the communication complexities of low-status organizational actors with cross-race supervisors (Deitch et al., 2003; K. P. Jones et al., 2016; Van Laer & Janssens, 2011).

Most supervisors in the organization are White European Americans, which has direct implications for language use and intercultural communication. Janitors indicated that they perceived some supervisors as being unwilling to attempt to negotiate some degree of politeness during their interactions. Such unwillingness to accommodate their subordinates, in addition to employing aggressive communication styles, suggests that supervisors might be enacting prejudicial biases against the janitors. Such communicative behaviors can also be related to dominant societal discourses and how these discourses shape supervisors' perceptions of people of Latin American descent (K. R. Chávez, 2009; L. R. Chavez, 2017). Given the organizational and broader societal context, it is possible that many supervisors view their interactions with their Latin American subordinates through a prejudicial lens. Some supervisors might believe that they are there to impart orders to their subordinates and bristle at the thought of having to teach them English, despite the janitors' expectations of superiors simply reducing their communication speed and complexity. Chapters 3, 4, and 5 explore the themes of these experiences—co-cultural communication, social identity categories, and language use, respectively.

Communicating Within an Organizational Hierarchy

These results about janitorial staff supervisors' communication behaviors reinforce previous organizational research (Ashcraft, 2007, 2017; Mikkelson et al., 2019; Mumby, 2010). This scholarship posits that dominant societal discourses shape how people perceive and communicate with the people who are the target of negative discourses. The information that people receive from dominant societal discourses functions as the antecedent of interpersonal contact. For example, according to several janitors, an administrator in one of the organization's departments was once heard saying that she "preferred 20 Laotians to one Mexican." Several participants also indicated that this administrator's interactions with them matched her alleged comment, in that she was consistently impolite and hostile toward Latin American janitors. Additionally, when asked how often they interacted with administrators, most janitors said almost never. Janitors' negative perception of the leadership suggests that they work within a defensive communication climate where they do not give feedback because their supervisors would not welcome their input. Second, in this environment, janitors often do not go to their superiors for resources, opinions, or advice. It is not surprising, therefore, that most janitors mainly sought out support from their coworkers, which reinforces research on the importance of strong, positive peer coworker communication (Omilion-Hodges & Ackerman, 2018).

Janitors' relational processes with key organizational leaders made them feel powerless and voiceless, working in a toxic communication climate. These feelings were evident in janitors' narratives, some of which displayed feelings of deep mistrust. Though most janitors said that they felt established in their job, they also said that they live in constant fear of losing their job. Consequently, janitors constantly negotiated the tension between permanence and impermanence. They perceived that they could not communicate openly with their superiors. Janitors also perceived that language barriers created a communication chasm where some of them retreated or remained distanced from their supervisors. Overall, the organization's culture forced janitors to engage in self-subordinating behaviors (Doyle, 2000; Foucault, 1977). Supervisors' communicative behaviors created an atmosphere where supervision, not leadership, was dominant (Jacobs, 1971).

The participants have little to no voice in this communication environment, with dissent getting suppressed and feedback discouraged. This type of workplace atmosphere reflects what Deetz (1992) called *"discursive closure"* (p. 187). Once the culture is established and set in motion through everyday communication practices, janitors learn through socialization, storytelling, and lived experiences that enacting voice is an unwelcomed practice, which fundamentally disciplines their actions. In this context, Latin American immigrant janitors exist in this organization's interstice, which functions as a microcosm of the larger society (Aparicio & Chávez-Silverman, 1997). Janitors in this organization are stuck in limbo, a socially liminal space that is disciplined by the discursive mechanisms operating around and on them. Janitors are powerless, lack opportunities to enact their voices, and exist in a tension of permanence–impermanence (L. R. Chávez, 2017; Foucault, 1977). Janitors' proactive communication and conflict avoidance behaviors embody their powerlessness and voicelessness in this setting.

Several janitors indicated that they avoid communicating with their superiors and engaging in any conflict, in general. They viewed conflict as destructive, rather than productive, and constantly feared that conflict would ultimately lead to their termination. For many janitors, lacking a formal education and the ability to speak English, such an outcome would be catastrophic. Within this context, less interaction with others means a lesser likelihood of getting into a conflict either with a superior, coworker, or customer. The costs heavily outweigh the rewards of having a serious conflict with anyone. This self-imposed communicative suppression functions as a mechanism through which the janitors' voices are silenced. Daniela's comment about conflict suppression illustrates this point: "Pues a mi me gusta quedarme en mi esquinita. Pos no vale la pena meterse en problemas con nadie. Ahi botan a uno y se queda uno en la calle. A mi me gusta evitar problemas" [I like to stay in my little corner. It's not worth getting into trouble with anyone. They kick you out and there you are on the street. I like avoiding problems].

In line with LMX research, this finding suggests that constructive superior–subordinate relationships tend to be characterized by information breadth and depth in routine communicative exchanges (Olsson, 2017). Many janitors perceived a strong preferential treatment toward specific workers and that supervisors interacted with those workers more often, which reduces the breadth and depth of exchanges with other workers. According to several janitors, this experience caused them to perceive their relationships as low quality (Quade et al., 2020). The organization's leadership communicated that they perceived janitors as being expendable and, thus, treated them as low-valued commodities.

This communication climate within the superior–subordinate pair in organizations is vital for understanding overall organizational communication processes. In particular, this emphasis should be expanded to include relationships between people of different social identities (e.g., social class, race, ethnicity, immigration status, and occupation) and communication processes in the workplace: Many janitors expressed that the preferential treatment and poor communication they experienced was caused by their race/ethnicity (B. J. Allen, 2009). Ruben's comment vividly illustrates this point: "Quienes somos? Tu dime a mi; quienes somos? Somos los mas bajos de abajo. Si tu eres Latino e imigrante; vamos a ser honesto; tu eres comida de puerco para ellos" [Who are we? You tell me; who are we? We are the lowest of the low. If you are Latino and an immigrant, let's be honest, you are pig's feed to them]. This reality is difficult to address, though, because it has its roots in society at large, outside the organization itself.

Social Climate and Implications

Historically negative cultural views foment a climate in which people of Latin American descent are stripped of their humanity. The United States, however, needs the labor that people from Latin American countries provide (Grosfoguel, 2003; Navarro et al., 1984; O'Brien & Loach, 2000; U.S. Bureau of Labor Statistics, 2020). One of the main messages that emerged from the janitors' experiences is the idea that "we welcome the labor but not the laborer." Rodrigo's comment illustrates the disconnect that superiors display through their leadership approaches: "Estas gentes no piensan que estan manejando personas, pero maquinas. Es lo que te digo; muchas no tienen el nivel necesario para manejar a nadie. Estan ahí yo no se por que" [These people don't think that they are managing people, but machines. It's what I am telling you; many of them don't have the level needed to manage anyone. They are there I don't even know why].

The relationship between the core economic power (the United States) and the laborers from poorer Latin American countries can also be characterized as a tension between three forces. The first two forces are the need for the United States as a superpower to have the jobs done and, simultaneously, some host society members' desire to resent the people doing the jobs. The third force, which is in tension with the first two forces, is Latin American laborers' need and desire to work, to feel socially included, and to be treated with dignity and respect. Latin American immigrant janitors' interactions with their predominantly White male supervisors display the tensions between these forces.

Popular culture artifacts, such as the films *El Norte* (Navarro et al., 1984) and *Bread and Roses* (O'Brien & Loach, 2000), have also depicted the tensions among these three forces, by eloquently articulating a Latin American "subject" that exists in tension with fundamental social forces still operating in contemporary U.S. society. For instance, in his 2015 presidential campaign-launching speech, Donald Trump infamously said the following about people coming to the United States from Latin America, and Mexico in particular:

> When Mexico send its people, they're not sending their best. They're not sending you. They're not sending you. They're sending people that have lots of problems, and they're bringing those problems with us. They're bringing drugs. They're bringing crime. They're rapists. And some, I assume, are good people. (Phillips, 2017)

The fact that Trump got elected president, and continues to be popular with a significant segment of the population, is indicative of the extent to which racially prejudicial sentiments are still prevalent in U.S. society. Some of these social forces are shaped by historical relations of race, ethnicity, social class, and immigration, and also by the ways that these social differences play out in micro-level interactions (Ore, 2018).

Effects on Interpersonal Relationships

Latin American immigrant janitors' communication experiences with their supervisors seem to be mostly detrimental. This does not suggest that this situation is an epidemic, but it does suggest that some individuals have negative attitudes toward particular organizational actors. Such negative attitudes might be tied to the antecedents of interaction (i.e., socialization processes, racial prejudices, and biases). For example, it is probable that many White supervisors did not learn about Latin American immigrants experientially through interactions with them but, rather, through information that they obtain from social institutions, such as their families and the media (Nicolas & Skinner, 2017; Ore, 2018).

Not all supervisors were White, however, as several supervisors were people of Latin American descent. This situation caused serious cognitive dissonance for some janitors, as they wondered why that person, who is supposed to be one of them, would treat them so badly. This experience suggests that organizations tend to represent societal microcosms. For instance, most supervisors are White, and traditionally, many White U.S. Americans have displayed negative attitudes toward Latin Americans (specifically, toward Mexicans; Flores, 2018, 2020). This finding is not far removed from the lived experiences of many Mexicans and Mexican Americans in the United States. Fortunately for the Latin American immigrant janitors, coworkers act as buffers to cope with some of the daily hardships brought upon them by their supervisors' communicative behaviors.

Communicating With Coworkers

Latin American immigrant janitors indicated that they customarily have positive communication experiences with their coworkers. Janitors expressed that their coworkers are people with whom they interact the most during a typical workday. Though these relationships are not considered to be friendships, janitors routinely talked about topics such as social issues in their homelands, their sons and daughters, and religion, topics rooted in their common ground that act as a clear source of affinity in the face of supervisors acting in bad faith.

Seeking Refuge in Same-Language, Same-Culture Communities

Latin American immigrant janitors find safe havens in break rooms and hallways when they interact with their same-race coworkers. I experienced firsthand the camaraderie that coworkers displayed with each other. In the hallways and in the break rooms, coworkers were typically cheerful and pleased to be around one another. This cheerfulness is not surprising considering the language barrier and superior–subordinate communication issues that characterize RMU outside those insulated areas. In a work context where dominant language use is problematic and where superiors address their subordinates aggressively, reaching out to their peers is an obvious choice for many janitors.

Janitors believed that because of their language use challenges, they have more social constraints than does the average U.S. American. They perceived their Latin American immigrant coworkers as people who were in the same boat. Ricardo's comment illustrates this point: "Pues no, los veo igualitos a mi. Somos todos Latinos y por lo menos hablamos la misma lengua. Con los Asiaticos es diferente porque no nos podemos entender" [I see them as equal. We are all Latinos and at least we speak the same language. With the

Asians it is different because we can't understand each other]. Some of these social constraints are issues with the dominant language and race-ethnicity (with most janitors being non-English-speaking Mexicans). Therefore, janitors mostly rely on their peers for self-affirmative interactions. This situation has implications for language acquisition and sociocultural integration.

Some Latin American immigrants enter organizations with clear obstacles: Some of them are undocumented, some do not speak English, and their racial-ethnic identities are perceived disapprovingly in U.S. society. If janitors' interactions with supervisors and customers are sometimes marked by negativity (e.g., supervisors or customers being aggressive toward them), it makes sense that they would seek out affirming relationships with their same-culture/language peers. This situation poses both a blessing and a curse for janitors. First, janitors remain disconnected from U.S. culture and the organization, preventing them from integrating into U.S. society. As a result, many janitors expressed that their circumstances hurt their ability to move up the socioeconomic ladder. Manuel's comment highlights this point: "Pues yo quiero hablar mas con otras personas pero este Inglés se me ha hecho difícil. Y no me ayuda que na mas me la paso hablando con mis compañeros, oyendo el radio y mirando la tv en Español" [I want to talk more with other people, but this English has been difficult for me. And it doesn't help that I'm always talking with my coworkers, listening to the radio, and watching TV in Spanish]. Other janitors also indicated that they felt most comfortable with their coworkers because they are just like them. These narratives show that janitors' communication experiences relate to dominant language use and that supervisor communication causes them much stress. Coworkers' supportive communication thus allows janitors to cope with work-related stress (Etzion, 1984).

Janitors' communication experiences with coworkers are in line with research on supportive communication in the workplace (Brown & Roloff, 2015; Mikkola, 2020). According to communication scholars, supportive communication is a prevalent process that organizational members employ to cope with job stressors and burnout (Compton, 2016; Ray, 1987, 1991; Zhuang et al., 2019). Other scholars have argued that because people's lives revolve around work, it is important to examine social support in organizational settings (M. W. Allen, 1995; Brown & Roloff, 2015). For example, Brown and Roloff (2015) suggest that access to a network of support is vital for dealing with work-related stress. Regarding work-related problems, coworkers offer a unique type of emotional support (Ploeger-Lyons & Kelley, 2017). This is also an example of janitors' assertive accommodation orientation (Orbe, 2017), which is partially characterized by communication practices where non-dominant group members use intragroup networking to negotiate dominant social structures.

Janitors' narratives about coworker communication suggest that they receive social support from their coworkers. Most janitors stated that they mainly have collegial peers, and coworkers are people with whom the janitors have more in-depth interactions compared to their supervisors and customers. Having conversations with people provides a space where, at minimum, interactants can decide whether they want to continue engaging other people. As House (1981) observed, "Flows of social support occur primarily in the context of relatively stable social relationships rather than fleeting interactions among strangers" (p. 29). Therefore, it is not surprising that janitors find their relationships with coworkers as the most stable and positive ones in the workplace.

Managing Supervisor Treatment

Janitors' coworker communication experiences align with research about relationships between superior–subordinate and peer coworker communication (Kramer, 2017; Ploeger-Lyons & Kelley, 2017). Researchers have found that superior–subordinate differential treatment is related to coworkers' perceptions of themselves and others. For example, if coworkers perceive that a supervisor treats a coworker with preferential treatment, that employee can be cut off from the group (B. B. Jones, 2020). The janitors in this study indicated that supervisors blatantly showed preferential treatment toward some employees. This preferential treatment led to some common behavioral responses: gossip, banding together, and seeking support from each other.

Gossip

Supervisors seemed to strategically rely on employee gossip networks as a mechanism through which they stayed informed about issues, events, and situations in their work unit (Baumeister et al., 2004; Michelson et al., 2010; Tan et al., 2020). According to some janitors, gossiping occurred constantly among coworkers and between coworkers and supervisors. Johan's comment exemplifies this point: "Yo dije ya no quiero estar cerca de ellos porque no me trae nada bueno. Esa gente se la pasan chismeando acerca de otros. Todo el tiempo le digo" [I said no more, I don't want to be around them because it doesn't bring me anything good. Those people spend all their time gossiping about other people. All the time, I tell you].

Organizational gossip research shows that this type of informal communication happens with familiar, trusted coworkers and that it reinforces insider–outsider group dynamics (Mills, 2010; Tan et al., 2020). In general, organizational members engage in gossiping behaviors to entertain, inform, and influence each other (Rosnow, 1977). Some of the positive functions of workplace gossip are information sharing, enabling cultural learning in the organization, and encouraging the development of social networks (Doyle, 2000; Ellwardt et al., 2012). However, gossiping has also been criticized in scholarly and popular literatures because it affects employees' productivity, and when it is excessive and inappropriate, it can ruin people's reputations. Gossiping is also used to spread judgment and accusations about other people (Wu et al., 2018).

Research on gossiping explains some of the everyday communication practices of Latin American immigrant janitors in this organization. Specifically, most janitors viewed gossiping very negatively. Janitors perceived workplace gossiping to be dangerous and inappropriate and those who engaged in it as people to stay away from. Instead of viewing gossiping as a communication activity that maintained group identity and organizational culture (Fan et al., 2020), janitors felt that gossiping promoted attention-seeking, self-interest, and an inflated self-image through social comparison and discrediting others (Grosser et al., 2010; Wert & Salovey, 2004). Although research and popular literature have viewed gossiping as useful to maintaining employees' relationships during their free time (Feinberg et al., 2012), janitors in this study had a much different perspective.

Janitors' perspectives about gossiping might be a product of the toxic, defensive communication climate in which they worked. For example, janitors might view gossiping as a communication practice that was vital to maintaining the negative climate that exists within their work unit. According to most janitors, the negative gossiping was partially a by-product of supervisors' deliberate favoritism toward some employees. Gossiping seemed to provide supervisors with important information that enhanced their ability to orient differently toward employees. Gossiping became a communication resource that reinforced group norms and the organization's culture, as the supervisors conceived it. Supervisors might have used gossiping to know who was a foe and who was an ally, and subordinates might have used it to gain supervisors' deferential treatment. In other words, tapping into employee gossiping networks equipped supervisors with a strategic power and control mechanism (Wu et al., 2018). This control mechanism sustained a defensive communication climate that obstructed group cohesion among coworkers.

Banding Together in a Hostile Environment

Janitors' communication experiences with coworkers yield information that aligns with research on coworker communication, but this study's findings also illustrate how, in certain circumstances (i.e., when presented with communication adversities), individuals form particular relational bonds with similar others. The janitors demonstrated how communicative difficulty pushes people to form discursive enclaves in a hostile social environment. This environmental reality appears to compel Latin American immigrant janitors to pursue only certain types of jobs (i.e., where little communication is required) and to remain inside their same-culture and same-language circles, which can prevent them from getting access to a wider variety of jobs that could advance their socioeconomic status. These results also provide a type of rebuttal to arguments that Latin American immigrants cannot be assimilated (Amaya, 2007a, 2007b; Avila-Saavedra, 2010; Martínez & Gonzalez, 2020): Social systems sometimes have embedded mechanisms in place that keep them socially excluded and linguistically marginalized. Dominant social discourses about Latin American immigrants' inability to assimilate enter the U.S. social imagination, and people accept such discourses as taken-for-granted truths (L. R. Chavez, 2017; Jiménez Román & Flores, 2010).

Latin American immigrant janitors' choice to remain in their coworker enclaves within the boundaries of a predominantly White organization is not surprising, but the significance resides in the ways that complex social systems, such as groups and organizations, create and sustain marginalizing discursive mechanisms through micro-level interactions. Latin American immigrant janitors find themselves at a communicative disadvantage, and their coping mechanism is to rely on people who speak their language (e.g., through intragroup networking). This social survival mechanism simultaneously acts as an instrument for liberation and subjugation. Latin American immigrants get tangled up in a social web where doing jobs such as housekeeper, dishwasher, or janitor—for some permanently—is the only way to survive. Simultaneously, those occupations keep them marginalized and unable to advance socioeconomically.

Summary

This chapter outlined relevant information on workplace communication processes related to traditional organizational roles like superiors, subordinates, and coworkers. In general, superior–subordinate communication tends to be lopsided, as superiors tend to adopt role-taking stances that often lead to autocratic and transactional leadership styles. Additionally, superior–subordinate communication can also affect coworkers' interactions. Under highly autocratic supervisors, coworkers tend to see each other as equals and communicate for social support. Little communication research, however, has focused on communication between individuals in service occupations and their clients or customers. This research topic, thus, is ripe for further organizational studies.

CHAPTER 3

Communicating Co-Culturally

En cierta ocasion alguien me dijo "me das verguenza por el trabajo
que haces." Un estudiante y le dije yo no, le dije yo no te estoy
robando nada a ti. Le dije yo no te estoy robando a ti, y el penso que
yo no hablaba inglés. Yo le contesté, le dije yo no te estoy robando
a ti, yo hago un trabajo le dije, y esto es un sueldo y me siento
orgulloso de mi trabajo y le dije no tienes porque decirme eso.

[On one occasion someone told me, "I am ashamed of you
and the work that you do." A student, and I told him, me,
no, I told him I am not stealing from you. I told him I am not
stealing from you and he thought that I did not speak English.
I responded, and I told him I am not stealing from you, I do a
job here I told him, and this is a salary and I feel proud of my
work and I told him you have no reason to tell me that.]

—Manuel

Si, a veces se pone uno a platicar y dicen trata de aprender un poco
mas y yo le respondo, practica tu español conmigo, estudiantes
principalmente, principalmente estudiantes que trabajan aqui,
que son los estudiantes con lo que mas se comunica uno con
los que trabaja, entonces muchos tratan de aprender español,
pero a veces no quieren hablarlo porque dicen que no es bueno,
entonces les digo practica tu Español que yo practico mi Inglés.

[Yes, sometimes you start talking and they say try to learn
a little more and I respond, practice your Spanish with me,
students primarily, primarily students that work here, those are
the students that we talk the most with, the ones that we work
with, then many try to learn Spanish, but sometimes they don't
want to speak it because they say that it's not good, I then tell
them practice your Spanish and I practice my English.]

—Ofelia

THE PRECEDING narratives offer insights into the nuances of the exchanges that Latin American immigrant janitors had with majority-White students (or customers) in the workplace. Interpersonal communicative exchanges help people form and develop ideas about who they and others are (Goffman, 1963, 1967; Wilson et al., 1995). Co-cultural communication theory offers a conceptual framework for these exchanges. This framework classifies the ways that "dominant" and "nondominant" group members communicate and the choices that nondominant group members make when interacting with dominant group members (Orbe, 2017). According to co-cultural communication theory, the above exchanges show two types of communication practices. The first quote is an example of assertive separation—that is, when a nondominant group member communicates to create clear boundaries when communicating with dominant group members. The second quote is an example of assertive accommodation, which is when nondominant group members communicate to maintain both their identity and the dominant group members' (e.g., educating others about who they are).

In this chapter, I discuss the ways that these and other co-cultural communication practices play out in organizational settings in general and in the setting of this case study in particular: the communication experiences of Latin American immigrant janitors within a higher education organization. This study of service workers' narratives of their everyday communication provides an alternative perspective from that of traditional methodological frameworks (i.e., postpositivistic studies) by examining co-cultural workplace communication through an interpretive lens. The participants in my study are, in many ways, caught in the communicative effects of the intersections of their identities and their geographic and temporal locations. I therefore explore the extent to which intercultural communication complicates vertical, horizontal, and co-cultural communication practices involving people in "dirty work" (i.e., occupations that people typically associate with filth, such as housekeepers, garbage collectors, and janitors; see, e.g., Ashforth & Kreiner, 1999; Ashforth et al., 2007). Because I am interested in exploring relationships between organizational actors' social identities and their everyday communicative choices in their workplace interactions, it is crucial for my work to also account for intercultural dimensions of those interactions. As in the previous chapter on workplace communication, this chapter begins with key definitions and an examination of existing scholarship, then moves to excerpts from interview data and analysis of that data—this time in light of the combination of co-cultural and workplace communication.

Co-Cultural Communication Theory

In the context of U.S. social hierarchies, people of Latin American descent traditionally have been marginalized or perceived as a nondominant social group in relation to the dominant group (i.e., Whites). Working-class, lower-status employees also have been considered nondominant in formal organizational structures and communication systems. These combined, intersecting factors suggest that Latin American immigrant janitors' workplace communication could be better understood using Orbe's (2017) model of nondominant group members' communication practices and orientations. As Orbe and Spellers (2005) explain, "Co-cultural theory offers a framework to understand the process by which individuals come to select how they are going to interact with others in any given specific context" (p. 174). This model offers one perspective on the experiences of the Latin American janitors in this study, in terms of how they navigate workplace and co-cultural interactions—and, in some measure, the results of those interactions.

Foundational Theories

Co-cultural communication theory was founded on the central tenets of feminist standpoint theory and muted group theory (Kramarae, 1981, 2005; D. E. Smith, 1987). Muted group theory advances that societies have social hierarchies in which some groups are privileged over others, with the groups at the top of the hierarchies establishing the communication system of that society (E. Ardener, 1978; S. Ardener, 1975). Over time, these communication structures become (re)produced by both dominant and nondominant members' (routine) communication so that the dominant communication systems remain in place (Giddens, 1984). As Orbe (1998a) explains, "This process [of social reproduction] renders marginalized groups as largely muted because their lived experiences are not represented in these dominant structures" (p. 4). Co-cultural communication theory also holds that because asymmetrical power relations exist in all societies, there is always a muted group framework in place (Meares, 2017). Furthermore, people who have been "muted" often engage in certain communicative practices to resist the system's attempt to keep them muted.

Similarly, standpoint theory is the result of feminist scholars' work (e.g., Harding, 1987; Hartsock, 1983; D. E. Smith, 1987; Wood, 1992) and addresses the significance of acknowledging a special societal positioning and subjective perspective of people as they interact with the world. This theoretical framework is an epistemological stance that argues that all perspectives—not just the traditional White male one—are critical to fully understanding social phenomena (P. H. Collins, 1986). Moreover, standpoint theory argues that even though group membership provides some commonalities, not all group members have the same standpoint (B. J. Allen, 2000; Buzzanell, 1994). This framework suggests that for people to gain a deeper understanding of social phenomena, socially marginalized voices should be included (P. H. Collins, 1986), not least because marginalized groups are more able to identify instances of asymmetric power because of the greater effect of that asymmetry on their lives (Frankenberg, 1993, among others). According to Orbe (1998a), it is "through this process of inclusion [that] alternative understandings of the world that are situated within the everyday/every night activities of co-cultural and dominant group members can be revealed" (p. 235). Because all "truths," in essence, are standpoints, it is important to include and recognize various social actors' perceptions of their lived communication experiences.

These theories inform this book's analysis of everyday communication, which follows a line of theorizing from the margins that has deeply enriched communication theory and research (B. J. Allen, 2007; Alvarez et al., 2012; K. E. Bell et al., 2000; Blair & Liu, 2019; Ran, 2017). I theorize from the margins to foreground the communicative experiences of Latin American immigrant janitors in a society built to mute them.

Co-Cultural Communication Orientation

Co-cultural communication research has proposed that six factors serve as the basis of understanding and analyzing co-cultural groups' communication practices: (1) preferred interactional outcome, (2) field of experience, (3) situational context, (4) communication abilities, (5) perceived costs and benefits, and (6) communication approach. These factors, in turn, determine the orientations that co-cultural groups use to communicate within dominant cultural systems. Orbe (1998a) summarizes co-cultural communication theory's central idea as follows:

> Situated within a particular *field of experience* that governs their perception of the *costs and rewards* associated, as well as their *capability* to engage in various communicative practices, co-cultural group members will adopt certain *communication orientations*—based on their *preferred outcomes* and *communication approaches*—to the circumstances of a specific *situation*. (p. 19)

Co-cultural communication orientation refers to the communicative stance that nondominant group members adopt during everyday interactions with dominant group members. Co-cultural group members' communication orientations stem from a combination of their preferred interactional outcomes and communication approaches within particular situational contexts (Orbe, 1998a). Nondominant group members use certain communication orientations to assimilate, accommodate, or separate. People who prefer to assimilate employ communication behaviors that attempt to erase their cultural distinctiveness to fit in with the dominant societal structure. People who primarily choose to accommodate retain their cultural uniqueness with the goal of creating a pluralistic society that is accepting of cultural differences. Finally, people who employ separation communicative behaviors tend to resist forming any common ties with dominant group members and to advocate for the maintenance of cultural communities that reflect their values and norms.

In addition to these three preferred interactional outcomes, nondominant co-cultural group members employ three primary communication approaches when communicating with dominant group members: nonassertive, assertive, and aggressive (Razzante & Tracy, 2019). Nonassertive communicative behaviors display communicative inhibition and avoidance of confrontation. People who employ nonassertive behaviors tend to place others' needs before theirs. The opposite of nonassertive communicative behaviors are aggressive communicative behaviors that demonstrate highly expressive and controlling behavior. People who employ that style tend to put their needs before others' needs. In between nonassertive and aggressive communicative behaviors is assertive communication, where people use self-improving, expressive communication that includes the needs of both self and others. These communication approaches, paired with the preferred interactional outcomes, yield specific communication orientations and practices that co-cultural group members employ in their everyday interactions.

Co-cultural communication theory offers nine co-cultural orientations based on people's preferred interactional outcome (assimilation, accommodation, or separation) and communication approach (nonassertive, assertive, or aggressive): (1) nonassertive assimilation, (2) nonassertive accommodation, (3) nonassertive separation, (4) assertive assimilation, (5) assertive accommodation, (6) assertive separation, (7) aggressive assimilation, (8) aggressive accommodation, and (9) aggressive separation.

Nonassertive assimilation is when people use communicative practices that allow them to blend in with the dominant society. Communicative practices associated with this orientation are censoring the self and averting controversy in interaction. Nonassertive accommodation involves seeking out change nonconfrontationally. Communicative practices associated with this co-cultural orientation are strategically increasing visibility in social contexts and actively dispelling stereotypes. Nonassertive separation is when co-cultural group members use subtle communicative practices to stay distanced from dominant group members. People who employ nonassertive separation practices avoid places inhabited by dominant group members and maintain psychological barriers through both verbal and nonverbal cues.

People who use an assertive assimilation orientation also try to blend in to the dominant society, but these people adopt more proactive communication practices such as manipulating stereotypes, overcompensating, and preparing extensively prior to interaction. Those who employ an assertive accommodation orientation attempt to maintain a balance between their own needs and others' needs, with the goal of changing dominant societal structures. Assertive accommodation practices include communicating in an authentic and open way with dominant group members, as well as educating others about one's own cultural group. Finally, assertive separation is when people make a conscious attempt at sustaining communities that exclude dominant group members. People who use assertive separation communication practices typically exemplify their cultural group's strengths and embrace stereotypes to deepen the external sense of cultural identification.

Co-cultural group members who employ an aggressive assimilation orientation make proactive efforts to fit in with the dominant group. For those people, being considered as a dominant group member is very important. Communicative practices associated with this orientation are dissociating from one's cultural group, mirroring dominant group members' behaviors, and ridiculing self. An aggressive accommodation orientation involves co-cultural group members trying to become part of dominant structures to change them, using communicative practices such as confronting and gaining advantage over dominant group members. Finally, aggressive separation is a proactive orientation that people use when co-cultural segregation is the main goal. Communicative practices related to this orientation are attacking and sabotaging dominant group members to diminish their social privilege.

In summary, these communication orientations and practices illustrate how co-cultural communication theory attempts to develop an understanding of nondominant group members' communication with dominant group members. The following research overview exemplifies how scholars have used co-cultural communication theory to study communication phenomena in various social contexts, building a conceptual background central to the subsequent case study data analysis pertaining to the Latin American immigrant janitors.

Co-Cultural Communication Research

Since its emergence in the late 1990s, co-cultural communication theory (Orbe, 1998a) has been one of the most widely used theoretical frameworks in communication research. This theoretical framework draws its recognition from its applicability. It has expanded the perspectives that scholars and practitioners can adopt to study and understand intercultural communication in various social contexts. In this case, co-cultural communication theory provides useful language to describe and examine the janitors' communication experiences at work.

One study about international college students in the United States (Urban & Orbe, 2007) helps set the stage for exploration of how noncitizens' positionality as cultural outsiders, and thus as co-cultural group members, affected their communication experiences. Analysis of 62 international student essays yielded several significant themes. The first one, "assimilating into dreamland," showed how the international students felt pressured to assimilate into the "dreamland" that they had made the United States out to be before they arrived. Consequently, this idea encouraged the students to adopt U.S. customs, habits, and communication behaviors. The second theme was that the students had a skewed notion of life in the United States stemming from exposure to media messages, which made their transition more difficult because what they found once they arrived was far from what they expected. Another related finding was that the students thought that their language abilities would be enough to navigate U.S. culture, but they found that this was not the case for the most part.

Another salient theme from this study was the notion of educating self and others beyond the classroom. The international students felt that if they were going to be successful in accomplishing their educational objectives, they needed to be very knowledgeable and fully acquainted with their host culture. The students read everything American and immersed themselves in U.S. media. They also found themselves constantly educating others about their native countries and about themselves. The students saw each intercultural interaction as an opportunity to dispel stereotypes about foreigners and their countries.

Although the population samples are different, this study relates to the present analysis and speaks to the usefulness of co-cultural communication theory for understanding the communication experiences of Latin American immigrant janitors. For instance, in my analysis I examine how a group of people "foreign" to their cultural system negotiate their differences in everyday intercultural interactions. The international students in Urban and Orbe's

(2007) study felt a need to educate others about their native countries, language, and customs, but they were largely sojourners in the United States. The janitors with whom I worked are permanent residents and may be perceived differently by host-culture members.

In another study, Camara and Orbe (2010) examined how diverse groups of people respond to discriminatory acts based on their race, sex, age, sexual orientation, and disability status. These scholars surveyed 957 people of diverse race, sexuality, gender, age, and disability at two state universities. Their analysis indicated that people primarily respond to discriminatory acts by adopting certain communication orientations, such as assertive accommodation (51.5%), for example asserting a strong self-concept by pointing to discriminatory acts and alerting perpetrators that such acts would not be tolerated, and nonassertive assimilation (25%), such as remaining silent about discrimination and avoiding controversial subjects.

These examples illustrate how co-cultural communication theory is useful to understand processes whereby members of traditionally underrepresented groups enact communicative practices in contexts where membership in one or more social groups marks those people as nondominant (Orbe, 1994, 1996). This theoretical framework also is useful to understand participants' lived experiences because it focuses on their communication experiences within and outside of their co-cultural group membership.

Moreover, extant research using co-cultural communication theory has studied various groups, including non-Whites (Zirulnik & Orbe, 2019), women (Blair & Liu, 2019), gay, lesbian, and bisexual individuals (Ran, 2017), and people with disabilities (Cohen & Avanzino, 2010)—but these studies have not as often emphasized co-cultural perspectives such as immigration status and social class (for an exception, see Han & Price, 2018), which deserve more attention than they have received thus far in co-cultural communication analyses. In this organizational context, Latin American immigrant janitors represent nondominant group members as employees in a predominantly White organization. Therefore, I discuss janitors' communication experiences with customers through a co-cultural communication lens. In the following section, I present case study data and how they are connected to or distanced from extant co-cultural communication research.

Case Study and Research Implications

Janitors' narratives about their communication experiences with customers yielded divided responses, with some janitors opting to separate and others opting to accommodate customers (faculty, staff, and students). These responses varied even within the type of experience the janitors had (positive or negative), in part because of variations in how customers appeared to account for the janitors' perceived social identities.

Types of Interactions

Some janitors avoided interactions with the university's customers—primarily students—because those interactions were mostly harmful. In contrast, other janitors indicated that their interactions with students were very positive and considered many of them to be like their family. Janitors who cited consistent negative interactions with customers said that some people disregarded them, ran them over in public spaces, and insulted them. For instance, in the exchange depicted at the beginning of this chapter, a janitor stated that one student approached him and told him, "I am ashamed of you and the work that you do," to which the janitor responded, "I am not stealing from you." The janitor continued to explain,

> He thought that I did not speak English. I responded, and I told him I am not stealing from you, I do a job here I told him, and this is a salary and I feel proud of my work and I told him you have no reason to tell me that.

On the other hand, janitors who had positive interactions with customers stated that students wanted to learn about them and their cultural background. Furthermore, some students were interested in learning Spanish, and janitors enjoyed practicing their English with students. These results suggest that customers become a vehicle through which the janitors attempt to gain cultural capital (and to integrate socially into U.S. society).

Janitors who had negative experiences with customers disclosed that customers often dismissed or ignored them. Morelia's comment illustrates this point: "Le pasan por el lado y ni lo miran a uno. Uno trata de saludar o algo, pero mucha gente ni siquiera voltea la cabeza. Ellos si saben que uno esta ahí; ellos nos ven" [They walk by you and they don't even look your way. You try to greet them, but many people don't even bother to turn their heads. They know that you are there; they see us].

Janitors' experiences with public rejection may be the result of their social location as marginalized subjects in a context of White dominance. Janitors are also situated in a communication system that is dominated by Whites' control of communicative practices (both nonverbal and verbal). For instance, as Latin American immigrants, janitors' expectations of greeting behaviors might not be acknowledged by most Whites who walk by them (perhaps on purpose). It seems that some customers do not feel the need to give janitors the opportunity, or invite them, to interact with them. White customers' communicative stances may be related to perceptions that, due to their privileged social location, they do not need to reach out and connect with the janitors. In other words, many janitors perceived that some customers viewed them as people whose voice and presence were not to be acknowledged. This finding supports muted group theory's idea (Meares, 2017) that within any society there exist asymmetrical power relations and, thus, a muted group framework is in place. It is also within this dominant social structure that janitors enact communicative practices to cope with their environment (e.g., avoiding intergroup and preferring intragroup networking communication practices).

Customers perceive janitors as "muted," and their communicative responses toward janitors appear to produce a nonassertive separation communication orientation. Roberto's comment illustrates this climate: "Les repugnamos. Es como si le dieramos asco a ellos. Yo no entiendo porque tantos gringos se sienten de esa manera. Debe ser bien dificil llevar su vida asi. Per no nos beneficia a nosotros tampoco" [They find us repulsive. It's as if we are repugnant to them. I don't understand why so many Americans feel that way. It must be hard living their lives that way, but it doesn't benefit us either].

Co-cultural communication theory embodies some of the janitors' communicative practices with customers. Based on the janitors' narratives, their memberships in their racial-ethnic, immigrant, class, and occupational groups render them marginalized. Janitors perceived that customers viewed them negatively based on their social identities. Within this interactional context, both parties—nondominant and dominant group members—orient toward the other based on their field of experience (their knowledge about each other's cultural/ethnic backgrounds), so they have specific preferred interactional outcomes (separation, accommodation, or assimilation) when interacting with the other. Additionally, nondominant group members use specific communication orientations, which are shaped by the situational context and interactants' field of experience and communication abilities.

Janitors' Common Orientations

The janitors primarily employ two types of communication orientations—assertive accommodation and nonassertive separation—when communicating with customers. Janitors seem to have developed these interactional outcomes and communication orientations based on the feedback they received from customers and from their experiences in the organization. This finding suggests that janitors' interactional outcomes and communication orientations are not unilateral acts but acts co-constructed with their customers.

Janitors who had positive experiences with customers seemed inclined to accommodate and thus exhibited an assertive accommodation communication orientation, which focuses on maintaining cultural pride, keeping one's identity intact, and, simultaneously, communicating a competent self openly and honestly. Maria's comment exemplifies this communication orientation: "Pues si yo siempre les digo; mira yo te enseño Español y tu me enseñas Inglés. Asi pues aprendemos cada uno de nuestras culturas" [Well, yes, I always tell them, "Look, I teach you Spanish and you teach me English." That way we can learn about each other's culture].

Margarita's comment similarly demonstrates this approach: "Me gusta hablar con los que muestran interes en mi como persona. Pero yo siempre les sonrio y les hable muy cordialmente aunque no me miren. Con amabilidad y respeto todo se puede lograr" [I like to talk to the ones who show interest in me. But I always smile and talk to them very cordially, even if they don't look my way. With kindness and respect, we can achieve anything]. This finding shows that both nondominant and dominant co-cultural group members can make efforts to create a communication environment in which everyone has the opportunity to enact their voice. These interactional outcomes are mostly positive, with janitors feeling that some customers are like family members. Moreover, Maria's comment also exemplifies how some janitors have an assertive accommodation communication stance; in this case, Maria attempted to educate others about her language and culture.

The significance of the previous finding resides in janitors' narratives about their negative experiences with customers. Some of these experiences consist of constant feelings of disrespect and direct verbal insults. Approximately half of the janitors indicated that negative exchanges with customers compelled them to separate from them by adopting a nonassertive separation orientation. As Pedro said, "Yo ni los miro yo ya en los pasillos; y para que? Cada vez que trata uno de hablar con ellos na mas le responden con grocerias. Yo ya ni pa que; digo yo, no?" [I don't even look up when I am in the hallways; for what? Every time that you try to talk to them, they respond with rudeness. I said to myself, what's the point?]. These statements highlight the significance of expanding organizational studies research to more explicitly address low-status organizational members and their communication experiences.

Janitors' choice to separate from customers suggests that struggles with the dominant language and social identity intersections can create a communicative chasm between nondominant and dominant group members in organizational contexts. Organizational members' circumstances can sometimes create the illusion that communication barriers are impossible to overcome and are solely the result of a "bad attitude" or other dismissive label that does not attend to the challenging social and organizational structures in which the janitors find themselves.

The Effect of Janitors' Social Identity on Communication

Negative perceptions of social and cultural differences further exacerbate people's ability to reach across those differences and to have positive interpersonal encounters. Based on participants' narratives, it seems that their racial-ethnic and immigrant identities shape their younger, White, middle-class customers' perceptions. These observations suggest that janitors' communication experiences with customers perpetuate janitors' marginalized subject positions through mechanisms of social exclusion such as institutional racism and discrimination based on language use. For example, Ramona shared, "Los veo y ni les hablo . . . le hablan a uno como si fueramos basura y eso es cuando tiene la energia para dirigirse a nosotros" [That I see them and I don't talk to them . . . and they talk to you like you're garbage and that is when they have the energy to even address you].

Customers and supervisors' verbal mistreatment of janitors show how persistent negative attitudes get enacted in a social context. Discourses about social identity categories, especially those with visible markers, permeate social and organizational life. Negative communication choices can be especially damaging in organizations, where actions can have immediate and long-lasting repercussions. Janitors' narratives show that supervisors' and customers' communication choices offended them in significant ways, as Ramona's statement illustrates:

> Maltratada . . . si . . . porque . . . de la manera que le hablan a uno . . . nos miran como inferiores . . . porque, los supervisores y el otro siempre esta detras de nosotros chequeando . . . y este otro . . . tenia un supervisor que hablaba todo el tiempo, ¿Donde estas? ¿Que estas haciendo? ¿A donde vas? ¿Que vas a hacer? Tienes que hacer esto y lo otro . . . es injusto, injusto lo que hacen . . . y si hay maltrato de los supervisores a los trabajadores.

> [Mistreated . . . yes . . . because . . . the way that they talk to us . . . they see us as less than . . . because, the supervisors and the other one is always after us checking . . . and this one . . . I had a supervisor that was talking all the

time, Where are you? What are you doing? Where are you going? What are you going to do? You need to do this and that . . . it is unfair, unfair the things that they do . . . and yes there is mistreatment from the supervisors to the workers.]

These negative interactional outcomes (especially repeated ones, as Ramona references) can powerfully affect subsequent interactions at work. In fact, many janitors perceived that their race-ethnicity, immigrant, and occupational identities led people to address them in negative and prejudicial ways. For instance, Rodolfo expressed the following sentiment:

Si, he percibido discriminación por ser Latino. He percibido discrimación en el trabajo. Gente en las oficinas, estudiantes. No te saludan, no te demuestran nada. En el game room hay personas que trabaja ahi y para ellos ni existes. Cuando llegué aqui si percibí eso. Si he encontrado personas agradables, pero he percibído descriminación desde que comence a trabajar aqui y tuve mas contacto con las personas. Es dificil, no es raro.

[I have perceived racial discrimination for being Latino; I have perceived work discrimination. People in offices, students. They don't greet you, they don't show anything. In the game room there are people who work there and for them you do not exist. When I got here I did perceive this. Yes we have found affable people everywhere but I have perceived discrimination when I started working here, when I have closer contact with people. It's hard, it's not uncommon.]

These observations align with B. J. Allen's (in press) claims that, by default in U.S. society, people represent the social groups to which they obviously belong, whether they want to or not. Depending on the context, people need to communicatively negotiate with others the ascribed meanings associated with each of their social identities. In the case of Latin American immigrant janitors, they have to constantly negotiate their racial-ethnic, immigrant, and occupational identities with customers. In the institutional context (a predominantly White organization), these negotiations can be contested because social dominant group members may have preconceived negative attitudes toward nondominant group members, and vice versa. In such an interactional context, the burden almost always falls on the nondominant group member to accommodate dominant group members (Rudick et al., 2017; Zirulnik & Orbe, 2019). The findings indicate that many janitors choose to communicatively separate from dominant group members rather than to accommodate them.

The Effect of Marginalization on Communication Processes

These insights about customer–janitor communication highlight noteworthy communication processes. Dominant language use seems to have a critical function in janitors' everyday communication experiences. For instance, it appears that janitors' separation stance works against their ability to learn English, which has linguistic, social, and cultural implications. Janitors' communicative choices can deprive them from integrating socially and culturally and keep them linguistically marginalized.

Janitors' narratives suggest that they often felt communicatively impotent when interacting with dominant language speakers, as Daniela expressed: "Es desconcertante que uno no puede hablar con otras personas. Imaginese vivir en un lugar y estar rodeado de personas y que uno no puede hablar con ellas; es bien frustrante a veces" [It's discouraging not being able to talk with other people. Imagine living in a place surrounded by people and one can't talk to them; it's very frustrating at times].

This theme seems present throughout janitors' communication experiences: Social actors' communicative practices in public places feed a system that creates a communication chasm that gives the impression that reaching a point of cross-racial/cultural understanding is virtually unattainable. Such perceptions can produce feelings of public apathy where those who are most marginalized have the most to lose and experience the most feelings of hopelessness and powerlessness (Crocker & Major, 1989; Major & O'Brien, 2005).

For example, many janitors feel disrespected and dismissed; essentially, their humanity goes unacknowledged, as Raul's statement indicates:

Vamos a decir que eres Hispano o brasileño, lo que sea, pero que no eres blanco y por ejemplo yo estoy en mi oficina y tu entras y dices "Buenos dias señor" o "Perdón, voy a sacar la basura, ¿como esta hoy?" y es como si nadie habia entrado, ¿verdad? ¿Como lo tomarias eso? Te hago la pregunta. A eso es que me refiero; si, asi lo recibo, como racista; nos ven como si fueramos nada.

[Hey, let's say that you are Hispanic or Brazilian, whatever, but that you are not White and for example I am let's say in my office and you come in and you say "Good morning sir" or "Excuse me, I am taking out the garbage, how are you today?" And it's as if no one walked in, right? How would you take that? I ask you the question. That is what I am talking about, yes that's how I take it, as racist; they see us as nothing pretty much.]

The scenario that Raul asked me to imagine encapsulates the major issues the janitors in this study had in their communicative interactions at work with culturally different others. By their (non)interactions, verbal or nonverbal, the janitors' customers communicated that they ascribe limited value to low-status immigrants in their workplace. These results complement research that shows that individuals discursively create systems of communicative margin-alization (Callahan, 2006; Cruz, 2017; Hopson & Orbe, 2007). Those systems do not materialize from the ether: They are created and actively maintained by those who benefit from them most.

Co-cultural communication theory advances that nondominant group members sometimes employ nonassertive accommodation orientations and use practices such as "increasing visibility" (i.e., maintaining a "co-cultural presence" in the dominant social contexts that they inhabit). People who do not speak the same language as the dominant population in that society might be forced to decrease their visibility due to their inability to communicate in that society's dominant language. Under such circumstances, for example, immigrant janitors might have desired to seek accommodation, but their lin-guistic inability pushed them to adopt a separation communication orienta-tion instead. Mariela's experience reveals this issue:

> Pues tengo mas contacto si yo hablara inglés pudiera tener mas contacto, porque cuando menos con mis estudiantes, porque a ellos les gusta platicar conmigo y yo con ellos y no mas nos reimos, porque mas no se, no mas los saludo, good morning y asi, pero no mas, y a veces si me siento mal porque me hacen preguntas las niñas y no puedo contestarselas.

> [I have more contact if I spoke English I would have more contact, at least with my students, because they like to talk with me and I with them and we only laugh, because I don't know anything else. I only greet them, good morning and things like that, but not beyond that, and sometimes I feel bad because the girls ask me questions and I can't answer them.]

Language use adds a layer of complexity to the communication experiences of this co-cultural group that allows a view of co-cultural theory from an alter-native perspective.

Language use in everyday interactions illuminate how Latin American immigrant janitors' communicative choices play out in situations in which interactants do not speak the same language. The results lend important insights into such communicative negotiation processes. In this social context (the research site), it appears that the dominant language (English) trumps the communicative choices co-cultural communication theory implies that social actors possess. Results additionally show that dominant language use prohib-its the janitors from thinking that they have choices.

Pushing Back on Co-Cultural Communication

Latin American immigrant janitors' work experiences related to language use illuminate various issues embedded in co-cultural communication theory's main epistemological assumptions. First, co-cultural theory is founded on the idea that hierarchies exist in society that privilege the experiences of certain groups of people. The study shows that the lived experience of some social actors (e.g., nondominant language speakers) is less privileged than that of others who speak the dominant language. This scenario creates a context where those people who do not speak English are embedded in a social context where they are always already subaltern subjects (Butler, 1995). For instance, "dispelling stereotypes" (i.e., countering oversimplified generalizations about one's cultural group) is a type of communicative practice that co-cultural theory outlines. Many janitors are not able to engage in this practice due to their inability to speak English, and they inadvertently might reinforce dominant stereotypes about Latin Americans instead (e.g., we cannot speak English). Such a communicative disadvantage can shape perceptions of self and others. Consequently, nondominant/dominant co-cultural group members' routine communication can potentially (re)produce a linguistic hierarchy that tends to privilege dominant group members' lived experiences.

According to co-cultural communication theory, dominant societal members use their privileged positions to create communication systems that reflect and sustain their lived experiences. Some of the study's findings corroborate this assumption. Janitors overwhelmingly expressed that they felt that dominant language speakers appeared unwilling to linguistically accommodate them. Janitors perceived that the English speakers with whom they interacted felt that the non-English speaker needed to accommodate them in mundane interaction episodes. They describe many instances in which they sought linguistic accommodation from dominant language speakers, and in these instances, they found that this approach was not well received.

For example, according to most janitors, they constantly attempted to enact what Orbe (2017) called "assertive accommodation" practices, such as communicating self and educating others with customers. Mariela's comment shows this orientation:

> Ah, pues le hable en inglés para que mire que yo tambien tengo ese problema . . . de que no hablo inglés perfecto y el o ella no hable el español perfecto y entonces unas palabras que ella pueda ayudarme y yo ayudarle a ella.

[Ah, I talked to him in English so that he could see that I also have that problem that I don't speak English perfectly and he or she does not speak Spanish perfectly and then some words that she could help with and me help her.]

Mariela's comment exemplifies how many janitors attempt to communicate their authentic selves and also educate others about who they are.

Co-cultural communication theory's third assumption is that dominant communication structures hinder the progress of nondominant societal members. It appears clear that Latin American immigrant janitors' lived experience is not reflected in the dominant communication system. Janitors feel that their social location as nondominant language users keeps them from advancing socioeconomically. Many indicated that their inability to speak English prevents them from getting higher positions within the organization and from seeking out educational and other career opportunities. Those narratives illustrate that for those whose lived experience is not reflected in the dominant communication system, their ability to advance is negatively affected. The following comment illustrates these feelings: "Porque tenemos que aprender el idioma; es muy importante aqui. Estamos en otro lugar que no es el nuestro, que no es nuestra lengua. Y eso tambien ayuda a que nos esforcemos para aprenderlo y queramos salir adelante" [Because we have to learn the language; it is very important here. We are in a different place that is not ours, it is not our language, and that also helps us to work harder to learn and move forward]. Janitors' circumstances of not speaking the dominant language additionally compound their perceptions of themselves as people of no value within the dominant social structure.

Lastly, co-cultural communication theory assumes that co-cultural group members employ strategic communicative behaviors to negotiate their subject position within dominant societal structures. These behaviors are best illustrated through their communication experiences with customers. Janitors embraced a separation-preferred interactional outcome by enacting nonassertive separation communicative practices such as avoiding. According to several janitors, they embraced those approaches in response to constant verbal mistreatment and rejection from customers. In contrast, others indicated that they typically used assertive accommodation as interactional outcomes by enacting communicative practices such as communicating self and educating others. People who enact these practices attempt to present themselves in an authentic and open way, and, simultaneously, they attempt to teach dominant group members their cultural norms and values. Janitors also discussed how they employed some communication practices verbally as well as nonverbally.

For instance, avoiding behaviors were primarily enacted nonverbally, whereas communicating self and educating others were enacted verbally (typically in the janitors' native language—Spanish). Furthermore, assertive accommodation communication orientations were also enacted in the context of the immigrant dialogues mediated by an interpreter.

Summary

Understanding the communicative mechanisms of organizational and intercultural marginalization is key to fighting this marginalization. As people from diverse racial and ethnic backgrounds continue to join U.S. society, the likelihood that people will have culturally dissimilar neighbors, coworkers, spouses, and sons- and daughters-in-law will only rise (U.S. Census Bureau, 2020). The kind of discursive resistance the janitors in this study describe, especially to people who embody intersections of traditionally disadvantageous identities (e.g., recent immigrant, Latina, lower class, and service worker), will not subside on its own. As the United States shows signs of progress and moves forward with social justice issues, it must *not* simply revise its current systems of discrimination—whether based on language, race, or occupation. Therefore, works like this one must continue to emerge in order to foment deeper understandings of the diverse lived experiences that inhabit this nation.

Language use powerfully permeates janitors' communication experiences, and these experiences illustrate how linguistic hierarchies play out in U.S. society. Janitors' communication experiences also illustrate how dominant group members enact their privileged subject position through mundane interactions with nondominant group members. Such power dynamics hinder the progress of nondominant group members, which sometimes leads them to employ communication practices to survive within oppressive societal structures. This discussion of theoretical implications outlines how results expand and corroborate central tenets of co-cultural communication theory and research. These theoretical implications also show relationships between communication processes, power, and culture. Such relationships have implications for social identity research and theory.

CHAPTER 4

Communicating Social Identity

No le voy a decir que no, si porque recién llegado yo aquí habia uno hubieron personas que me atacaron muy feo asi de esa manera y como uno recien llegado no asimila muy bien la cultura aqui entonces este pero, pero como ha, poco a poco uno va conforme uno va quedandose aqui va conociendo va uno asimilando pero uno continua viendo el trato de otros y tu sabes que es porque tu eres imigrante Hispano.

[I'm not going to say no, yes because when I was recently arrived there was one, there were people who attacked very ugly that way and one as a recently arrived you are not assimilated very well to the culture here and then, but, but little by little one conforms, one starts staying here and you start to know and become assimilated, but you continue seeing the treatment of others and you know it's because you are a Hispanic immigrant.]

—Antonia

Afecta. Pues si, si influye porque pues si es una "custodian" de la limpieza lo peor de la limpieza. Pues si porque, porque pues tienes que limpiar las vomitadas, las pupus que, o sea, es trabajo que es honesto, pero sucio y yo creo que la gente piensa entonces que uno es sucio.

[It affects you. Yes, it influences because yes, you're just a "custodian" who cleans, the worst of the cleaning. Yes, because, because you have to clean vomit, feces that, I mean, it is honest work but dirty and I think people think then that we are dirty.]

—Isaura

Es sencillo pues la clase social a veces uno la da a, pues yo la doy
a conocer simplemente con el trabajo que hago. Se dan cuenta
a que clase social pertenesco; a la baja entonces por ahi, si es un
supervisor, si es un jefe grande administrativo, por ley me da a conocer
de quien soy yo. Si es un supervisor el no va a tomar una relacion
conmigo, un administrativo menos, un jefe menos, es sencillo que
tiene que aprender de mi entonces el estatus social, pues, al menos
yo me siento muy afectada, muy señalada, a manera directa pues
se siente la, la superioridad en su manera de ser que no deberia.

[It's simple because sometimes the social class one exposes it simply
with work that I do. They know to which social class I belong; the
lower one, so it's from there, if it is a supervisor, if it is a higher-up
administrative boss, by law they communicate to me who I am. If it is
a supervisor he won't have a relationship with me, an administrative
boss even less, a boss even less, it's simple what do they have to
learn from me therefore, social status, at least I feel very affected,
very out in the open, in a very direct way so you feel their sense of
superiority in their way of being and it shouldn't be the case.]

—Carlota

THESE NARRATIVES display various aspects of social identity that Latin American immigrant janitors perceive shape their everyday interactions with host society members in the workplace. These excerpts are also illustrative of meaningful connections between communication and pervasive meanings ascribed to particular social identity categories. This book advances social identity scholarship by emphasizing the work experiences of historically marginalized people in lower-status occupations. In this chapter, I discuss relevant research that highlights key issues and themes related to communication and social identity.

Although I address social identity in a separate chapter here, I am mindful that social identities and their attendant consequences for individuals' lived experiences cannot, and should not, be examined in isolation. I thus ground this analysis in the work of scholars who claim that it is necessary to produce scholarship grounded in intersectionality (e.g., considering race, gender, social class, sexuality, and ability status together as they [re]produce complex structures of oppression and discrimination; Crenshaw, 1991, 1992, 2017). I have also attempted to thread discussions of social identity throughout the previous chapters, especially where my participants indicated their identities' inextricability from their communication experiences, both positive and negative. Here I concentrate those discussions to explore how communication constitutes race, ethnicity, social class, immigrant status, and occupation for the janitors I interviewed at RMU. Lastly, I provide implications of both past research and my study's empirical data to show a broader picture of how communication practices relate to social identity categories for these janitors.

Communication and Social Identity Research

Researchers have proposed that significant relationships exist between social identity and organizational communication (e.g., B. J. Allen, 1995, 2017; Ashcraft & Allen, 2003; McDonald & Mitra, 2019; Mumby, 2010; Nkomo, 1992; Ochs, 1993; Parker, 2001, 2002); there are, too, clear patterns in how researchers have approached examining these relationships (Orbe & Allen, 2008). When studying race, a continuing scholarly emphasis is placed on Black and White people and their communication differences (Houston, 1997; Meng et al., 2016; Shuter & Turner, 1997). An underlying assumption of these studies seems to be that theories, concepts, and research findings (i.e., consisting primarily of White participants in white-collar occupations or as college students) are generalizable to other racial and ethnic groups. Furthermore, social identity research tends to isolate race from other identities (e.g., social class, gender, and sexual orientation; B. J. Allen, 2017).

Race and Ethnicity

Almost three decades ago, Nkomo (1992) claimed that race-related research in organizations "reflect[s] and reif[ies] particular historical and social meanings of race" (p. 487). Her pioneering work represents a call to action for researchers to study race in ways that move beyond superficial perspectives of race as biological. Specifically, Nkomo (1992) advanced that what was needed was "a 're-vision' of the very concept of race and its historical and political meaning . . . for rewriting 'race' as a necessary and productive analytical category for theorizing about organizations" (p. 487). According to Nkomo, research on race in organizational contexts has been "narrowly focused, ahistorical, and decontextualized"—and in it, "race is mainly treated as a demographic variable" (p. 497). A few years later, B. J. Allen (1995) claimed that "conducting research about race-ethnicity would allow us to confront a momentous social issue, while also providing insight and direction for developing and refining theory about organizational communication processes" (p. 144).

Unfortunately, since these scholars made these claims almost 30 years ago, there should have been more significant scholarly follow-up, especially in organizational communication research. Communication research and theory still largely espouse a Eurocentric bias that is narrowly focused and perpetuates one-dimensional perspectives for studying communication processes (Orbe & Allen, 2008). Consequently, these perspectives tend to exclude the experiences of nondominant, socially marginalized, and working-class people in service occupations. As I have emphasized in the prior chapters, it is paramount for communication research to amplify these experiences.

Scholars who *have* emphasized the need to centralize the experiences of marginalized social group members (e.g., K. E. Bell et al., 2000) present an interesting caveat: the need not only to centralize diverse voices but also to beware of continuing the practice of essentializing identities—and especially of essentializing race (K. E. Bell et al., 2000). For instance, Orbe (2000) argues that traditional theoretical and methodological frameworks "have fostered a 'universal iconography' for members of racial/ethnic minority groups whose intragroup diversity is ignored" (p. 604). In other words, essentialist views of race have engendered a level of superficiality that has negatively affected how communication scholars conceptualize and conduct research studies (Collier, 1991). Strine (1997) perhaps best articulated this issue:

> Efforts to adequately represent voice in scholarly discourse resist the reifying tendency of conventional social research. Under the guise of academic disinterestedness a typical research article suppresses individuating features of the researcher's voice while foregrounding protocols that signal methodological rigor. Similarly, the voices of informants or research subjects are reduced to predetermined categories for analysis or behavior variables for testing. (pp. 449–450)

Furthermore, much of the criticism about essentializing race centers on conventional epistemological and ontological assumptions that represent the foundation for how scholars conduct research in the social sciences. For instance, Mirande and Tanno (1993a) state that social scientific research has historically "stultified caricatures of ethnic cultures" (p. 152). The practice of ascribing identities keeps scholars bound to traditional conceptual frameworks. It is imperative to break away from such practices. This imperative is why this study emphasizes the experiential rather than the experimental; that is, it focuses on participants' direct lived experiences (e.g., Davis, 2018, 2019).

In social scientific research, race is often treated as a concept that operates in isolation from other social identity categories and is relevant primarily in conversations about cultural differences (Nicotera, 2020; Nicotera et al., 2009). This may be a reason why research shows a predisposition toward studying Blacks and Whites, given the historical relations between these two racial groups (Cox, 1993; Cox & Nkomo, 1990; Omi & Winant, 1986). I add to this claim that a ubiquitous reduction of race to a Black–White dichotomy in communication research further confounds important issues that deserve attention. An example of such an issue is the need to emphasize the extent to which various identities shape everyday interactions.

Therefore, this book advances the research that Orbe and Allen (2008) call "multifocal relational scholarship." This analysis aligns with Orbe and Allen's characterization of this type of scholarship specifically, with their call to conduct research that "engages in the process of discovery by exploring race as one of many aspects of a person's complex identity" (p. 211). Similarly, Berard (2005) found that social identity categories such as race, when studied in isolation, might not be as relevant as when they are analyzed in combination with other identities. As Berard claimed:

> Even when they are [identities such as race], their relevance cannot be properly understood without an appreciation for the multiplicity and diversity of identities which become relevant in particular contexts and courses of action. . . . Identity can be respecified more widely and more finely by situating identity within natural language use and social interaction. (p. 67)

These observations demonstrate the need to conduct research that emphasize not only race but also other identities that may be contextually significant for people's lived experiences. For this reason, I accept the calls to action by Nkomo (1992), B. J. Allen (1995), and other scholars (e.g., Houston & Wood, 1996; Mumby, 2010; Parker, 2001; Sanders & McClellan, 2015) to advance communication and social identity scholarship. One way that this book fulfills this mission is by employing methodological and theoretical frameworks (i.e., interpretive frameworks and co-cultural communication theory) that advance race-related communication scholarship by centralizing the experiences of a marginalized group: Latin American immigrant janitors.

Social Class, Immigration, and Occupation

The term *social class* has been defined generally as "an open (to some degree) stratification system that is associated with a systematically unequal allocation of resources and constraints" (Henry, 2001, p. 165). This definition suggests that social class is a concept that permeates people's lives because social class is reflected wherever hierarchical structures exist. For example, organizations are known to reflect society's hierarchies of race, gender, and social class (B. J. Allen, 2017; Parker et al., 2017). Still, research on organizational communication and social class is limited, at best. A review of relevant communication research yields two major topical areas: communication differences based on social class status (e.g., Schatzman & Strauss, 1955) and research examining individuals' social class prejudices based on others' linguistic abilities and communication (e.g., Giles & Sassoon, 1983).

Social Class and Communication Differences

Social sciences, such as sociology, anthropology, education, and psychology, have studied social class issues for decades (e.g., Bernstein, 1971, 1974; Jackman, 1979; Jackman & Sheuer-Senter, 1980; Willems et al., 2005). Some of the few significant treatments of organizational communication and social class are B. J. Allen's (in press) book *Difference Matters: Communicating Social Identity* and also Gibson and Papa (2000). In her book, Allen addresses, among other issues, how class status has had both discursive and material consequences within and outside of organizational structures.

Like that of B. J. Allen, Bernstein's (1971, 1974) earlier work on communication codes has influenced contemporary ideas about social class and everyday interpersonal interactions. Bernstein's theory of elaborated and restricted communication codes represents one of the best-known treatments of relationships between communication and social class. Bernstein famously advanced that individuals from different social classes tend to communicate using different types of codes: restricted codes have shorter sentences and simpler syntax, whereas elaborated codes generate meanings that are explicit, context-independent, and universal (Bernstein, 1971).

Bernstein's (1974) theory of elaborated and restricted codes has made a significant contribution to the study of human communication. The theory's tenets can be summarized by the following statement: "Social classes are reproduced largely as a consequence of the meanings, values, and significances of class life being transmitted through class-specific communication codes" (Huspek, 1994, p. 80). In other words, lower- and working-class people tend to reproduce their class status because they primarily have access to restricted codes, whereas middle- and upper-class individuals have access to both restricted and elaborated codes (Bernstein, 1971). A major implication of this work is that people who use elaborated codes are better equipped with the skills necessary to perform successfully in social contexts, such as school, work, or other places where elaborated codes tend to be preferred. However, Bernstein's work has been widely criticized because of how the theory stratifies individuals and overlooks how these codes are (re)produced in interaction among social classes.

Bernstein treated social classes as if they exist in isolation from each other (Bisseret, 1979; Gregersen, 1979). The theory did not consider that, although social class systems are systems of stratification, individuals interact across classes and meanings, and codes are highly dynamic and relationally driven (Hecht & Choi, 2012; Hecht et al., 2003; Hecht et al., 1993; R. L. Jackson, 1999). Additionally, that someone belongs to a lower class does not mean they are unable to linguistically deploy elaborated codes.

These criticisms have direct implications for this study. First, although Latin American immigrant janitors occupy traditionally lower-class organizational roles, they are not necessarily unable to use elaborated codes. For instance, several janitors came to the United States with postsecondary degrees and had the ability to understand and generate elaborated codes in their native language. Second, perceptions of people's social class status may lead middle- or upper-middle-class people who have attained a higher education degree to "code switch" to accommodate lower-class people. This scenario suggests that interclass communication is a dynamic process that is (re)produced in and through interaction.

Similar to traditional race research and its foci on Blacks and Whites, social class research has adopted a dichotomous approach to understanding relationships between communication and social class (Schatzman & Strauss, 1955). For instance, research has focused on investigating differences between lower- and middle-class individuals (e.g., Huspek, 1994). Although this line of research has been influenced primarily by Bernstein's work in the 1960s and 1970s, some earlier work focused on relationships between social class and communication. For example, Schatzman and Strauss's (1955) classic study of 340 lower- and middle-class people found several communication differences regarding number and types of perspectives taken when communicating with others. Findings revealed that middle-class people exhibited a greater ability to take a listener's role and to use communication styles to implement specific interactional strategies (e.g., information seeking). In Schatzman and Strauss's words, "differences between the lower and upper groups were striking" (p. 330).

Willems et al.'s (2005) meta-analysis of physician–patient interactions illustrates some of the ways social class shapes interpersonal interactions. The researchers found that patients from lower social classes received less positive socioemotional messages from their physicians and a more directive and less participatory consulting style. Physicians gave much less information to lower-class patients and gave fewer directions regarding future treatment. Physicians' communication styles were strongly related to their patients' communication styles. For example, patients from higher social classes communicated more actively and showed more affective expressiveness, eliciting more information from their doctors.

Conversely, patients from lower social classes were often disadvantaged because their physicians perceived that they had a lower desire and a lower need for information due to their asking fewer questions and showing less affective expressiveness. Willems et al.'s (2005) research suggests that there are clear communicative differences between people from high and low social classes, which presents lower-class people with disadvantages in various interactional contexts, such as in a health care organization. These linguistic and communicative differences, especially when they are marked, can lead to unequal treatment and prejudice.

The Language of Social Class and Prejudice

B. J. Allen's (in press) work on organizational communication and social class illustrate some of the central issues of prejudicial views based on social class. B. J. Allen (in press) advances that individuals form class-related ideas about who they and others are through their communication with self and others. In other words, people are constantly communicating social class. This observation is significant considering that communication systems tend to privilege the middle-class experience and subjugate the lower class (S. Ardener, 1975; Kramarae, 1981). These observations also have implications for organizations, as organizations are contexts in which individuals constantly communicate across social classes and so have daily opportunities to (re)produce larger societal class structures (Parker et al., 2017).

This previous research relates to this study because Latin American janitors work in traditionally lower-class organizational roles. Their occupation is riddled with ascribed meanings of social class status and thus some of the negative perceptions that come with such ascription. Those perceptions of social class are rooted in a historical hierarchy of social superiority. People perceive others negatively (or are prejudiced) because they feel that they belong to a higher class and consequently interpret lower-class people as being "less than" (Giles & Sassoon, 1983; Mallison & Brewster, 2005). Moreover, class prejudice based on communication style reflects a linguistic, class-based hierarchy where some people are perceived as being superior to others due to the so-called quality of their speech. For this study's participants, this issue becomes exacerbated due to their challenges with English. Their organizational narratives yield useful information about class status negotiation in everyday interactions, especially important because it comes from the perspective of a traditionally marginalized, lower class (Mills, 2002).

The contention that class prejudice based on people's communication abilities exists has been the subject of much research. For instance, Giles and Sassoon (1983) highlight the effects of speakers' accent, social class status, and communication style on listeners' social judgments about the speakers. The researchers exposed 120 college students who spoke "standard English," and who came from middle-class backgrounds, to audio recordings of persons who spoke in standard and nonstandard English. Students then rated both language style versions on 7-point rating scales that measured intelligibility, fluency, and standardness of the speaker's accent. The findings indicate, for one thing, that the students assigned lower-class membership to the speaker with the nonstandard accent. Significantly, the students were told in advance that the nonstandard speaker was of a middle-class background, but they still assigned them to a lower-class status based on the nonstandard utterances.

This research also implies that individuals tend to "read" people's communication styles vis-à-vis the sociocultural dominant communication style and then form negative assumptions and stereotypes about those people. Therefore, linguistic/communication hierarchies exist and tend to be replicated in organizational contexts. For instance, Mallison and Brewster (2005) examined how servers in a southeastern U.S. restaurant categorized patrons by drawing on racial and class stereotypes related to language use. The researchers conducted 15 in-depth, semi-structured interviews with restaurant servers who were all White and full-time employees; 13 servers had completed at least a year of college. The researchers found that servers talked differently about Blacks and "Bubbas" (White, lower-class "rednecks"). Their discourse about Blacks, as the servers categorized and stereotyped them, relied primarily on race, whereas "the servers' derogation of redneck patrons draws on many regional and/or class-based characteristics that are manifested in markers of cultural capital (such as linguistic behavior, table manners, and style of dress, which may be similar to class status markers)" (Mallison & Brewster, 2005, p. 799). This finding reflects a class and linguistic hierarchy in which the servers perceive themselves as being superior to the patrons, both in terms of language use and class status—regardless of their own social class, which was not specifically noted in the study.

People tend to symbolically create intraracial boundaries based on class status along economic and cultural lines, drawing on dominant discourses to form and develop stereotypes—in this case, about race and social class (Huffman, 2018). By "engaging in strategies to separate themselves sociopsychologically from stigmatized social groups, mark social distance from them, and emphasize positive characteristics about themselves, the servers create what Wodak (1997) calls a 'discourse of difference'" (Mallison & Brewster, 2005, p. 801).

The Latin American janitors in this study find themselves immersed in the discourse of difference created by their majority-White supervisors and customers due to the janitors' apparent race and class—both of which are often tied to their (actual or assumed) immigration status.

Immigration Status

Like social class, immigration status is a social identity that has not been explored in depth in organizational communication research (see, e.g., Alvarez, 2016; Amason et al., 1999); intercultural communication, media, health communication, and rhetoric scholars have done a better job of studying it (K. R. Chávez, 2009; Cisneros, 2008; Flores, 2020; Ginossar & Nelson, 2010). Immigration-related communication scholarship does reveal one broad category that is especially germane to this book: societal messages about immigration and (specifically) Latin American immigrants. Within this category, scholars have focused on issues related to language use and competence, communication experiences in a host society, and accessibility to interactions with host members (Y. Y. Kim, 1977, 1980, 2005). For example, Y. Y. Kim (2005) notes that adapting to a new society "occurs in and through communication activities" (p. 379). Because adaptation is directly linked to social and cultural capital (as well as, by extension, economic capital), workplace communication experiences are crucial to that process (Alkhazraji et al., 1997). Further,

> no matter how strongly motivated and fluent in English an immigrant is, [they] will find it difficult to form any meaningful relationship with Americans unless [they are] provided with some opportunity to approach or to be approached by Americans. (Y. Y. Kim, 1977, p. 70)

This observation suggests that even with linguistic abilities and motivation, it can be difficult for immigrants to create healthy relational bonds and adapt to their new society if they are isolated from other individuals or do not belong to any social networks.

Berg's (2009) study of core networks and Whites' attitudes toward immigrants is a good example of how people's communication within their interpersonal networks may be related to their communication with and about immigrants. Berg examined data from the General Social Survey (GSS) and the U.S. Census using a multilevel model to evaluate whether a network perspective predicted Whites' attitudes toward immigrants and immigration policy. The GSS draws a nationally representative sample of English-speaking adults, 18 years of age and older, currently residing in U.S. households, with the groups stratified by race and income selection. The findings showed that native-born Whites who are embedded in educated core networks (individuals and their close associates) with non-Whites are likely to hold pro-immigrant attitudes, whereas those who are embedded in older and tighter core networks are likely to hold anti-immigrant attitudes.

Additionally, educated core networks mediate the effects of perceiving immigrants as a threat and thereby mediate one's willingness to interact with immigrants. These outcomes suggest that interpersonal relational contexts (in people's private and work lives) and broader societal contexts may be related to attitude formation. Furthermore, Berg's study suggests that if people remain embedded in their racially similar networks, a good chance exists that they will not experientially learn new information about culturally different others. This result is true for both dominant and nondominant group members but has more significant negative ramifications for nondominant group members: Limited cultural knowledge and exposure can further perpetuate surface-level interactions and the continuity of negative dominant discourses and stereotypes. Those stereotypes can especially affect interpersonal interactions in contexts such as the workplace (Marra & Holmes, 2008; McDonald & Mitra, 2019)—a context already fraught with communicative difficulty. Other scholars have also focused on how those dominant mediated messages and macro-level societal discourses about Latin American immigrants have potential relationships with micro-level interactions (e.g., L. R. Chavez, 2017; Cisneros, 2008; Ono & Sloop, 2002).

The central finding of many of these studies is that if immigrants remain surrounded by culturally similar others in and out of the workplace, this isolation may obstruct their ability to learn the host society's dominant language. Even after many years of residence, immigrants may not possess the cultural knowledge that would allow them to become integrated into their new culture. It has been shown that if immigrants do not possess dominant linguistic abilities and if they do not have the motivation to interact with and access host society members, they probably will have a difficult time adapting to their new society and maintaining psychological well-being (Y. Y. Kim, 2017; Walsh et al., 2008). Immigrants' lack of motivation to adapt to their host culture also may function to feed persistent negative messages about foreign immigrants. These discourses especially tend to construct a Latin American "subject" who is perceived as un-American and as an outsider and thus cannot assimilate or be assimilated (Mastro et al., 2008).

Occupation

Any research in a workplace setting must attend to occupation, which is a perhaps untraditional social identity category but certainly one that intersects with others. As previously indicated, *occupation* is broadly defined as the formal role(s) that individuals enact within the structures of organizational bureaucracies. The word "enact" within this definition implies that an occupation is an inherently communicative construct (Ashcraft, 2017). For instance, occupation is intimately linked to other socially relevant constructs, such as economic and sociopolitical systems, as well as to individual and group categories of social difference such as gender, class, and race (Laliberte-Rudman & Dennhardt, 2008). For instance, a person's occupation often communicates to others their social class status, and it is also deeply linked to a person's self-identification. Further, people of a certain race and immigration status tend to be read as "belonging" to particular occupations, especially so-called dirty ones. The concept of occupation is one to which individuals, groups, and nations assign varied meanings; through those various meanings, social actors understand and talk about the world of work and their place in it.

Scholarship related to occupation is highly multidisciplinary, with key contributions made by social psychology, sociology, occupational therapy, and occupational science (e.g., Fine, 1996; Hebson, 2009; Kreiner et al., 2006; Laliberte-Rudman & Dennhardt, 2008; Meisenbach, 2008; Simpson & Simpson, 2018). Hughes (1951, 1962, 1971) and his research team at the University of Chicago were pioneers in advancing social scientists' understanding of the formation and functions of occupations in society. Hughes (1971) notably claimed that

> a man's work is one of the things by which he is judged, and certainly one
> of the more significant things by which he judges himself. Many people in
> our society work in named occupations. The names are tags, a combination
> of price tag and calling card. One has only to hear casual conversation to

> sense how important these tags are. . . . [I]t happens over and over that the people who practice an occupation attempt to revise the conceptions which their various publics have of the occupation and of the people in it. In so doing, they also attempt to revise their own conception of themselves and their work. (pp. 338–339)

In other words, occupation is a fluid social construction that can be "revised" through interactions in and out of the workplace—and people identify closely with their occupation (B. J. Allen, 2005; Berger & Luckman, 1966; Burr, 1995). In the United States, for example, one of the first questions asked of a new acquaintance is "What do you do?" One person's occupation tells another a lot about them, from their values to their social class.

The book contributes to research regarding the communicative aspects of occupations and how people in lower-status occupations (e.g., service workers) negotiate their occupational identities, examining a specific area that has been overlooked in occupational studies: understandings of occupational identities as they intersect with immigration status. Scholars in this area have focused on social identity categories such as race, social class, and gender, but not as much on immigration status (for exceptions, see Hsieh et al., 2017 and Villegas, 2019), though some have recognized that in the United States, occupation has historically been closely linked with a person's race (Meisenbach, 2008, 2017). In particular, occupation research yields two major categories: the relationship between sociocultural structures and occupation (Wilmers, 2019), and socially significant symbolic features of the occupation construct (Ashforth, 2019).

Society, Culture, and Occupations

Scholarship about occupation has devoted attention to how macro-level (e.g., cultural) and micro-level (e.g., organizational) contexts overlap to shape how societies and social actors create and use knowledge about occupations (Huws, 2006; Iwama, 2005; Simpson & Simpson, 2018; Whiteford & Wilcock, 2000). Research in this area suggests that cultures and societies are filled with complex competing social processes and meanings about what counts as the "truth" and which meanings are most pervasive and privileged. The communicative aspect of occupations, though, is implied but not explicitly explored. This book attempts to revise this trend by engaging communication as a unit of analysis within the workplace (especially occupation-related) experiences of janitors.

Adding to the groundbreaking work of Hughes (1971), Laliberte-Rudman and Dennhardt (2008) advanced a framework to connect sociocultural processes and occupational identity. These scholars used Kluckhon and Strodbeck's (1961) foundational research about cultural value orientations to illustrate the cultural underpinnings of the concept of occupation. Laliberte-Rudman and Dennhardt (2008) argued that the values of Western cultures are deeply embedded within contemporary conceptualizations of identity and that such conceptualizations are articulated through a variety of macro-level and micro-level processes (e.g., through how a specific culture views the person–nature relationship, time, activity, and relationships).

These conceptualizations are consistent with what Sokefeld (1999) attributed to the "Western" self (i.e., egocentric, autonomous, integrated, and able to pursue its goals). In other words, dominant cultural values, discourses, and ideologies permeate micro-level interactions. Laliberte-Rudman and Dennhardt's work has direct implications for organizational communication processes. For example, the janitors in this study largely originate from collectivistic cultures (typical of Latin American countries) where the needs of the group are emphasized over the needs of the individual, so their image of occupations might run counter to the individualistic Western self that Sokefeld (1999) described. In an individualistic culture such as the United States, a dominant discourse says that individuals are the "masters of their fate." As a consequence, people in certain undesirable occupations—and not the system in which they are bound—are blamed for creating their current circumstances (Meisenbach, 2017). In contrast, Awaad (2003) explained how in Middle Eastern culture the "interests of the clan are placed above interests of individuals, who subsequently have little autonomy" (p. 410). Additionally, Kashima et al. (2004) showed that the Japanese word for "self" means that the self is part of an interdependent whole. This culture–self relationship suggests that dominant cultural discourses about social constructs, such as occupation, shape people's understandings of self and others in embodied occupations.

The research that links culture and occupation, as exemplified by theoretical models, such as the one by Laliberte-Rudman and Dennhardt (2008), locates and reveals common assumptions and beliefs about how individuals and occupations are detached from social and cultural systems. This research enhanced scholars and laypeople's sensitivity toward the idea that there is a fundamentally interdependent relationship between culture and occupational selves (Haraway, 1991). The present analysis well illustrates the relationship between culture and occupation, as gaining a better understanding of how ascribed meanings of Latin American immigrant janitors intersect with organizational micro-level practices, such as routine interactions, is important to amplify ideas about the intersections of race, class, immigration status, and occupation. Additionally, "recognizing occupation-based knowledge as 'situated knowledge,' that is not separate from the social and cultural contexts in which it is produced, opens exciting perspectives on producing and sharing this knowledge" (Laliberte-Rudman & Dennhardt, 2008, p. 160).

The Symbolic Dimensions of Occupations

Research on occupations and occupational identity implies that this social construct is intrinsically and extrinsically symbolic. Occupation as a social construct creates many complex and overlapping meanings about categories of social identity, such as race, class, and gender. Sociologists' work on occupation and stigma exemplifies the inherent symbolism in the notion of occupation (Kreiner et al., 2006). This research area examines how social stigma shapes meanings about the people who perform "socially tainted" or "dirty" work (Simpson & Simpson, 2018; term first used by Hughes, 1951).

Beliefs and socially agreed-upon views about occupations within social structures are other aspects that give occupations a symbolic dimension. Fine (1996) argued that occupational rhetoric and occupational identities are communicatively negotiable. These two areas are, of course, conceptually interrelated. For instance, all social roles are discursively constructed and manifested through everyday interactions. Organizational members' views of such roles shape how they understand themselves and others within those roles. To inform how people view themselves in organizational roles, some researchers have studied occupations as "rhetorical" by looking at occupational identity negotiation (Holmer-Nadesan, 1996; Meisenbach, 2017). Regarding occupational rhetoric, Fine (1996) argued that organizational members define themselves in particular ways through a process of fitting work into a meaning system, which constitutes an occupational rhetoric.

This research suggests that people's worldviews of occupations (i.e., their occupational rhetorics) are diffused with their worldviews about other notions of who they are (e.g., father, mother, or pianist), and that these overlapping worldviews can play out in the workplace through interactions with others. In other words, people's "occupational rhetoric" gets enacted as they visualize and send messages that correspond with their self-schema vis-à-vis the occupation that they personify (Ashcraft, 2005; Gergen, 1991; Snow & Anderson, 1987). Within dominant societal views about certain occupations—janitors, for example—individuals are stripped of their agency to visualize themselves as being anything beyond "someone who cleans."

Identity negotiation research also has attended to issues related to power, control, and resistance in organizations (Alvesson, 2000; Ashcraft, 2005; Meisenbach, 2017; Mumby, 2010). Within the poststructuralist paradigm that seems dominant in this line of research, a focus on power and control processes makes sense. Identities "are developed in the context of power relations" (Alvesson, 2000, p. 1105) and are "partly a temporary outcome of the powers and regulations that the subject encounters" (Karreman & Alvesson, 2001, p. 63). The identity negotiation process also consists of two central pieces: identity regulation and identity work (Alvesson & Willmott, 2002). Identity regulation centers on how discourses engender and control individuals' self-identities, whereas identity work characterizes people's understandings and responses (such as resistance) to discourses. It would be noteworthy to assess whether salient discursive strategies exist that individuals use to position themselves as dominant or nondominant in micro-level interactions. As Alvesson and Willmott (2002) explained regarding identity negotiation in organizations, individuals constantly seek "opportunities for microemancipation as well as openings for 'new' forms of subordination and oppression" (p. 638).

I am partially interested in determining whether organizational actors' marginalized locations within organizations lead to the discovery of discourses of subordination and oppression. Such knowledge illuminates potential avenues for individuals' self-empowerment and disrupts systematic disempowerment in the workplace. Communication and social justice research is one avenue that communication scholars have embraced to address such issues of inequality (Frey, 1998; Frey et al., 2020; Huffman, 2018; D. Jackson et al., 2020).

Research on identity negotiation in organizations has generated knowledge that responds to questions about the lived experiences of organizational actors' identity negotiation processes. This research illuminates understandings of everyday micro-level practices in organizational contexts. Additionally, this line of research suggests that everyday workplace interactions are embedded within power relationships and overlap with larger societal discourses about who organizational actors are. The need to further understand identity negotiation processes when individuals embody traditionally marginalized occupations partially serves as the impetus for this study. Research that includes marginalized organizational members and their communication experiences is of increasing importance as the racial-ethnic diversity of the United States continues to rise. The topic is also important because, historically, large numbers of individuals who occupy a marginalized social location also occupy marginalized spaces within organizations. The following section illustrates how the major themes discussed in the previous sections emerged from the empirical data obtained in this study.

Case Study and Research Implications

Social Identity and Workplace Communication

According to most janitors in this study, their race, ethnicity, social class, immigration status, and occupation are more relevant with certain people than with others (e.g., customers). This finding aligns with the janitors' descriptions of their communication with customers. When asked whether race, ethnicity, class, immigrant status, and occupation are relevant to their interactions, janitors indicated that those social identities are relevant primarily when interacting with customers—that is, faculty, staff, and students. This finding suggests a consistency across participants' responses and how they perceive their communication experiences with specific organizational actors. Over half of the participants perceive that many host-society members in the research site often communicatively orient toward them in hostile ways, likely because of their superficial characteristics.

Additionally, more participants perceive race-ethnicity as being a greater issue than social class, immigration status, or occupation. This finding reinforces extant research on race-ethnicity—specifically research indicating that race-ethnicity as a social identity category fundamentally structures people's lived experiences in U.S. society (McIntosh, 1998; Mercer, 2019; Ore, 2018; Shen et al., 2018). In this section, I discuss the findings related to race-ethnicity and workplace communication experiences. Subsequently, I follow with a discussion of findings related to social class, immigration status, occupation, and janitors' communication experiences.

Race, Ethnicity, and Workplace Communication

According to Frankenberg (1993), systems of racial separation shape the experiences not only of the oppressed but also of the people in dominant positions. The Latin American immigrant janitors' narratives show instances of how perceptions of race-ethnicity shape how some people communicatively orient toward them. Rodolfo's comment suggests that he perceives that some of his negative exchanges with people result from how others perceived him based on his race-ethnicity: "Tiene que ser eso; yo no me puedo imaginar que mas puede ser. Si tu tienes un intercambio con ellos y continua pasando regularmente; que mas puede ser? Ellos no me conocen a mi y yo no los conozco a ellos" [It must be that [racial prejudice]; I can't imagine what else it could be. If you have an exchange with them and it continues happening regularly, what else could it be? They don't know me and I don't know them].

Workplace experiences such as Rodolfo's highlight the need for investigations that explicitly address service workers' interactions at work. In this regard, this project advances knowledge about communication between service workers and customers (Callahan, 2006; K. Kim & Baker, 2019; X. Wang & Wang, 2017). Communication scholars could expand their knowledge about the types of interactions that individuals in marginalized spaces have with dominant group members and specifically those who embody marginalized racial-ethnic identities in tandem with immigration status, social class, and occupational identities.

The presence of people of Latin American descent is scant in studies of organizational communication and race-ethnicity (for exceptions, see C. W. Choi & Berhó, 2016 and Guerra, 2019). In her study of Latinas in public relations firms (another exception to this lack of research), Pompper (2007) found that Latina public relations agents have to negotiate their racial and gender subject positions with White men who view them as unqualified for their job and Latino men who view them as sex objects. The results show that Latinas perceive themselves as having low status or no power, navigating identity crises or dealing with self-contained opposites (i.e., enacting both oppressive and resistance behaviors).

The present study's findings are revealing in light of Pompper's (2007), as, according to Deitch et al. (2003), "Even people who are strongly motivated not to be racist are subject to automatic cognitive activation of stereotypes that can unconsciously influence behavior" (p. 1317). These stereotypes and (perhaps unconscious) prejudicial behavior led to the janitors feeling verbally and nonverbally discriminated from both other Latin Americans and Whites alike. Roberto's comment shows how many janitors experienced their race-ethnicity through communication: "Yo nunca voy a entender porque los gringos nos tratan asi. ¿Pues que le hemos hecho? Yo no se; tal vez es porque no fui a la escuela, pero te tratan refeo a veces. Te hablan como pura basura" [I'll never understand why Americans treat us that way. What have we done to them? I don't know; maybe because I didn't go to school, but they treat us pretty bad. They talk to us like pure garbage].

The results support the idea that marginalized social actors view communication processes from a unique perspective compared to dominant social group members (Halpern, 2019). Janitors feel "muted" because they embody a racial-ethnic category that is undesirable in U.S. society (Meares, 2017). In the context of a predominantly White organization, janitors perceive that the identities they represent are viewed as marginal and that those perceptions guide people's communicative behaviors. This result proposes that the idea that the United States is in a post-racial period may be nothing more than a social imaginary (Jiménez Román & Flores, 2010). This social imaginary perpetuates the idea that racism primarily has to do with overt communicative behaviors (e.g., overt racist comments and slurs). However, this type of overt racial prejudice is less socially accepted today, so people now engage in new, less conscious forms of interpersonal prejudice (Payne et al., 2017). These new forms of prejudice still display negative attitudes toward traditionally marginalized social group members (e.g., verbal dismissal or neglect and hostile nonverbal behaviors; Chaney & Sanchez, 2018). Some of the janitors' narratives illustrate that these new subtle ways of enacting prejudicial behaviors are present in U.S. society.

The results reveal that Latin American supervisors exhibit discriminatory communicative behaviors toward Latin American immigrant janitors. When scholars address race-ethnicity from nondominant groups' perspectives, we should not assume that Whites are the primary perpetrators of racist behaviors. Individuals become socialized to believe that their race-ethnicity is inferior to Whites', especially in a society immersed in White supremacy ideologies. This internalized belief acquired through socialization experiences is known as internalized oppression (Uzogara, 2019). Internalized oppression can be enacted through mistreatment of same-race others in various social contexts. For instance, many janitors expressed that their Latin American supervisors mistreat them worse than any other person, as Pedro's comment shows: "Ese hombre era una bestia con los Latinos; y era Mexicano el. Todos sabiamos que ese señor no tenia nada de respeto por su propria gente. ¿Y digame usted, como explica eso usted? No tiene nada de sentido" [That man was a beast toward Latinos, and he was Mexican. We all knew that he did not have respect for his own people. You tell me, how do you explain that? It doesn't make any sense].

Half of the janitors who said that race-ethnicity is an issue in their daily interactions also said that same-race individuals are the principal sources of racially discriminatory messages. The significance of this finding resides in that most of those Latin American supervisors were janitors prior to reaching supervisory roles. Therefore, some janitors could not understand why someone who looks and sounds like them would verbally mistreat them regularly. Several janitors reported that this phenomenon caused much cognitive dissonance and they thought that it should be further explored. For instance,

Ricardo stated: "La situacion se puso fuera de control en el sentido que esa persona abusaba de los trabajadores Latinos. Simplemente nos hablaba como animales y nadie hacia nada; uno se sentia como si fueramos animales y a nadie le importaba" [The situation got out of control in the sense that that person abused Latino workers. He would simply talk to us like animals and no one did anything. We felt like animals and no one cared]. This finding lays important groundwork for future research in organizations that addresses the notion of internalized oppression and how behaviors associated with that concept are communicatively enacted in everyday institutional interactions.

Relationships between participants' race-ethnicity and communication experiences cannot be divorced from other social identities (i.e., social class, immigration status, and occupation). For instance, the janitors who indicated that race-ethnicity is relevant to their communication experiences also said that the other social identities are relevant. Across the board, those janitors say that they perceive race-ethnicity, social class, immigration status, and occupation strongly shape customers', same-race peers', *and* supervisors' communication orientations toward them.

As a collective, findings related to race-ethnicity and janitors' communication experiences suggest that race-ethnicity is still a significant social problem in the United States. For this reason, studies that focus on how individuals deploy messages to racially different others in organizations are still ripe for investigation. In addition to race-ethnicity, the current research project focuses on whether race-ethnicity intersects with other social identities to shape Latin American janitors' communication experiences (i.e., social class, immigration status, and occupation). The results suggest that race-ethnicity does overlap with other marginalized identities to shape janitors' workplace interactions.

Social Class, Immigration, Occupation, and Workplace Communication

Latin American immigrant janitors' responses to questions about their social class, immigration status, and occupation show that racial-ethnic identity overlaps with the first three aspects of identity. The janitors who indicated that one social identity is relevant to their everyday communication experiences also indicated that the other three were as well. For example, 11 of 25 janitors expressed that social class, immigration status, and occupation are relevant to how other people communicated with them. These findings indicate that focusing research agendas on specific social identities in isolation is counterproductive. Scholars must, therefore, address outcomes related to how multiple identities are communicatively negotiated to address issues related to communication and social differences (B. J. Allen, in press). For this reason, in this discussion of research findings related to social class, immigration status, and occupation, I address these social identities as a cluster. I support my claims with pertinent scholarly literature and the data obtained from the janitors' narratives.

Historically, in the United States, a pervasive rationale for oppression and discrimination has been a person's ability. Ability has been used as a vehicle to discriminate against and oppress groups of people based on their race-ethnicity and gender, for example. This investigation's results are noteworthy because they highlight how people orient toward others whom they potentially perceive as "unable" based on the intersections of identity that those people embody. Results show that janitors' marginalized identities overlap to produce "unintelligible" bodies (Butler, 1995). Furthermore, the janitors' inability to speak English adds another layer of "incompetence" that seems to render them as "disabled" in the eyes of many.

For instance, this situation may be related to janitors' observations that they oftentimes feel dismissed by customers in offices and in hallways. Janitors' perceptions of their social class, immigration status, and occupation as being connected to each other suggest that those identities work in tandem to produce complex meanings about who the janitors are. Janitors' perceptions align with basic assumptions of social construction, specifically that individuals make meaning with and about each other from dominant sociocultural discourses about their identities (Langman & Shi, 2020).

Research and theory demonstrate that janitors' lack of cultural capital may be related to host society members' negative perceptions of them (Y. Y. Kim, 2017). This finding has direct implications for immigrants' encounters with host society members because many immigrants come to this country unable to speak English, and this situation creates a communication chasm that requires people to compromise and accommodate. This finding is additionally significant because according to Huspek (1994), "social classes are reproduced largely as a consequence of the meanings, values, and significances of class life being transmitted through class-specific communication codes" (p. 80). In other words, individuals (re)produce social class through their use of elaborated and restricted codes (Bernstein, 1974). In the case of the present study's participants, they lack access to the societal linguistic currency (i.e., English). For this reason, janitors are mostly qualified to be in occupations where communicative codes of any kind (i.e., restricted or elaborated) are minimally needed.

Janitors' lack of ability to speak English often leads to perceptions of lack of intellectual ability. In a society where ability matters, being perceived as lacking intellect primes others to perceive the message target negatively. Aurelia's comment expresses such sentiment: "Creen que uno es bruto porque no habla Inglés. Yo pues no tengo mucha educación, pero no es que soy retardada mental tampoco. Me molesta como le hablan a uno porque no sabe uno inglés" [They think that you are dumb because you don't speak English. I don't have much education, but I am not mentally retarded either. It bothers me how they talk to you because you don't speak English].

When we consider social class, immigration status, and occupation in addition to language use in the context of Aurelia's comment, we could be in the presence of a new underclass that lives in the shadows of America's social classes. Case in point, many of the Latin American immigrant janitors bear the "burden" of not speaking English as one of their marginalized identities. This situation relates to research on social class, which illustrates that people who use elaborated codes tend to orient toward people who use restricted codes differently than they orient toward other elaborated code users (Bernstein, 1974; Huspek, 1994).

This study's results parallel previous findings about social class and communication (e.g., Cha et al., 2020; Mallison & Brewster, 2005; Willems et al., 2005). For instance, supervisors and customers' communication style used with janitors may have been shaped by their perceptions that the janitors do not want to engage them (due to their inability to speak English). In this case, it seems like all interactants should try to accommodate to the other person. Based on the janitors' narratives, the problem seems to be that those in a privileged linguistic position are oftentimes unwilling to accommodate to the person in a less privileged position. Making different communication choices can bring about a social shift in which humans resist systems of social inequality where classism and occupationalism sustain imbalanced power dynamics.

As microcosms of the society in which they exist, "most organizations reflect the class system of society" (B. J. Allen, in press, p. 108). If this is true, then it could also be true that they reflect immigration, racial, occupational, and language systems. Janitors' narratives substantiate how systems of oppression might operate in workplaces. For example, Mirella stated: "Yo no creo que es porque yo soy Latino nada mas; es otras cosas tambien. Yo limpio para ellos, la ropa delata mi nivel social. Soy salvadoreña; no soy de aqui. Son muchas cosas las que influyen" [I don't think it's only because I am Latina; it's other things as well. I clean for them; my [work] clothes reveal my social status. I am Salvadoran; I am not from here. A few things are influential]. This comment supports the idea that this organization reflects various social hierarchies present in U.S. society, hierarchies that uphold systems of oppression that are discursively formed and sustained.

Furthermore, according to B. J. Allen (in press), a linguistic class-based hierarchy—and, I add, immigration status–based hierarchy—exists where bodies are, indeed, stacked up in ways such that those on "top" are more privileged than those at the "bottom." Based on these findings, it is evident that dominant language use functions as a catalyst for discrimination that permeates various social life activities. This observation further implies that research that includes traditionally marginalized groups also should include analyses of language use and how it might sustain systems of inequality. This investigation indicates that a language hierarchy could be an instrument for marginalizing people and sustaining systems of inequality (see, e.g., Ayllon, 2016; Pertúz, 2017; Pujiastuti, 2017; Shi et al., 2018).

Social class is a complex phenomenon that affects immigrants in a unique way because it relates to issues of linguistic hierarchies. As the janitors' narratives show, social class cannot be divorced from immigration status and occupation. Many immigrants from Latin America tend to be uneducated and lower class, which primarily gives them access to lower-status occupations in the United States. These findings contribute to understandings of how social identities have material consequences for persons who embody marginalized identities (Cranford, 1998; Segal, 2002). In the case of Latin American immigrant janitors, intersections of immigration status, social class, and occupation seem to locate them in a disadvantaged social position that becomes exacerbated by their lack of cultural capital. This lack of cultural capital appears to be closely connected to their status as immigrants and their sociocultural and economic integration into U.S. society.

For instance, Latin American immigrant janitors' communicative isolation functions to prevent them from acquiring the dominant language, which hurts their chances to fully immerse themselves into U.S. social life. The following comment by Rodolfo illustrates this point: "Todo me trae ansiedad porque no puedo hablar inglés. Ir de compras al supermercado me trae ansiedad porque no sabe uno si va a poder constestar alguna pregunta. Es bastante frustrante; no puede uno formar parte del entorno social" [Everything causes me anxiety because I can't speak English. Going to the supermarket causes me anxiety; you don't know if you'll be able to answer a question. It's very frustrating; you can't become part of the social environment].

Latin American immigrant janitors learn, through their interactions, that their immigrant status is not well received by many, which causes some of them to lose motivation to learn English and further integrate socially, which perpetuates feelings of anxiety. Rodolfo's comment illustrates this: "Le tengo que preguntar todo a mi esposa; que aprendio un poco de inglés. Que es esto/ aquello? Cuando voy al centro comercial tengo que estudiar lo que voy decir. Es un estado bien critico hermano" [I have to ask my wife about everything; she learned a little bit of English. What is this/that? When I go to commercial centers I have to study what I'm going to say. It's a critical state, brother].

Many janitors expressed feeling anxiety similar to Rodolfo's. Janitors' lack of cultural capital seems to have created feelings of paranoia where they feel like they are stuck in the middle of a permanence–impermanence tension. In this context, workplace interactions become significant for janitors because their outcomes yield feelings of belonging or rejection. Conversely, positive workplace interactions can strengthen a sense of belonging and social integration (Jian, 2012).

The Latin American immigrant janitors, when offered the opportunity, do learn about the culture and the English language (i.e., acquire cultural capital) through communication experiences with customers (mostly students). Their communicative experiences drive immigrants to create their own discursive cultural spaces. These discursive cultural spaces become subsystems that prevent sociocultural integration and perpetuate systems of linguistic and cultural separation.

Additionally, discursive acts of separation and rejection do not necessarily happen based on one salient identity but on intersections of identities, which contributes to the idea that communication constitutes interlocking systems of subjugation (Soto Vega & Chávez, 2018). For instance, 44% of the participants said that their occupation does shape how others communicatively orient toward them. Lucia's comment demonstrates how those participants perceived those interactions: "Los estudiantes a veces le faltan el respeto a uno. Yo creo que si es porque uno trabaja de limpieza aqui. Tal vez se creen mejores que uno porque uno les esta limpiando a ellos" [The students are disrespectful sometimes. I think so because we work cleaning. Maybe they feel that they are better than us because we clean after them]. Janitors who perceived that occupation shapes how others communicate with them also feel that their immigrant status and social class are germane. The news of this finding is the janitors' descriptions of supervisors and customers' hostile verbal and nonverbal communicative behaviors.

Carlota's comment is an example of such behaviors: "Le digo que mucha de esta gente lo ven a uno como menos de basura y porque irian a tratar a uno como gente. Le digo ese supervisor se dirigía a nosotros como si no fueramos gente. Y los estudiantes ni mas; peor le hablan a uno" [Many of these people see us as less than garbage so why would they address us like people. That supervisor addressed us as if we weren't human. And the students, forget it;

they talk to us even worse]. In the pages that follow, I discuss the findings related to communication and occupation informed by the participants' narratives and pertinent scholarly literature.

About half of the janitors stated that their occupation shapes their interactions with other social actors in the organization. Maria's comment exemplifies how janitors viewed others' perceptions of them in their organizational role: "Juntan el trabajo con la persona. Pues si el trabajo es sucio la persona tambien. ¿Pues que hace uno? Limpiar lo sucio; lo que quiere decir que uno esta sucio tambien y miran a uno como eso" [They mix the work with the person. If the work is dirty, the person is as well. What do we do? We clean what's dirty, which means that we are also dirty and they see you as such].

Latin American immigrant janitors perceived that their occupation cannot be divorced from other overlapping social identities—most salient in this context, social class and immigrant status. The consistency across those three social identities suggests that participants view them as interconnected. Research on dirty work advances that people who do this kind of work are perceived as degrading by the larger society and as subjects who do socially tainted work (Ashforth, 2019; Ashforth et al., 2017). Based on this research, I would add that participants' immigrant status works in concert with their occupation to construct a socially tainted subject. This hyper-subaltern (Butler, 1995) subject position can thus structure janitors' everyday workplace interactions.

Janitors' narratives reflect awareness of their position as subaltern subjects who occupy lower ranks of organizational and societal hierarchies (i.e., cleaning staff and Latin American immigrants). Ramona's statement shows such awareness: "Nunca pense que alguien me veria de esa manera pero es verdad, el Latino no es nada en este pais. Pero imaginate tu no solamente Latino pero Latino y trabajando en limpieza" [I never thought that people would see me this way but it's true; Latinos are nothing in this country. Imagine, not only are we Latinos but we also work cleaning].

Janitors' sense of themselves in their occupation suggests feelings of repulsion about the work that they do. Janitors believe that people value them primarily because of their labor. Artemia's comment highlighted this sentiment: "No les importa la persona para nada. Mientras hayan dos manos para limpiar que importa si la persona esta bien o no. A ellos no les importa. Somos maquinas pues" [They don't care about the person at all. Although there are two hands to clean, it doesn't matter if the person is okay or not. They don't care; we are machines]. This comment illustrates how the janitors have a kind of contextual signification. In other words, their body has different value-laden meanings in different social contexts. This comment also shows how some people might perceive others based on dominant sociocultural meanings attached to individuals in lower-status occupations and furthermore attached to race-ethnicity, social class, and immigrant status.

This situation suggests that in different social spheres the signifier (the person) embodies various historically devalued signifiers—mediated by social identities such as race-ethnicity, gender, and class—that shape their material realities and lived experiences (Butler, 1995). Additionally, when janitors crossed cultural boundaries (migrated to the United States), they involuntarily interpellated the current meanings associated with people who have membership in that immigrant group (A. J. Aldama & Aldama, 2020; F. L. Aldama & González, 2018). When janitors entered into U.S. territory, their unintelligible identities automatically became imbued with their localized cultural meanings. Consequently, social actors' communicative behaviors toward Latin American immigrants shifted to reflect that society's dominant values in how it regards those identities.

Occupations are classed, gendered, raced—and I would like to add "immigrant-ed"—within the society and culture in which they exist. Janitors' narratives about occupation suggest a relationship between their status as immigrants and the work that they do. They realize that as adult immigrants, they had obstacles that prevented them from learning English (e.g., a lack of education opportunities, the need to work, and families to support) and, thus, they perceived that they only had access to certain types of jobs. In that situation, immigrant status, dominant language use, and occupation became inextricably linked.

Summary

In this chapter, I discussed how social identities (e.g., race-ethnicity, social class, immigration status, and occupation) structure Latin American immigrant janitors' communication experiences. Over half of the janitors said that race-ethnicity shaped their communication experiences. Some of the main reasons offered were that people (including faculty, staff, and students) often did not acknowledge the janitors' presence, which the janitors attributed to people's negative attitudes toward Mexican immigrants. Overall, it is noteworthy that the janitors who said that race-ethnicity shaped their communication experiences also perceived that social class, immigrant status, and occupation were relevant factors in their everyday interactions.

CHAPTER 5

Encounters With Strangers

If you don't connect with people you'll never know what impact they'll
have on your life or you'll have on theirs, and that's the whole point.

—Anthony Hull (*In Passing*; Genao-Homs & Hull, 2010)

I ARRIVED IN *Nuebayol* over 25 years ago, and now I arrive to the occasion
of writing this *capitulo*[1] (i.e., enacting my voice). I have had some time to
reflect on this journey, on the lessons I have learned, and on important themes
that resonate with both my personal and professional experiences. During my
journey, several themes have surfaced that I interweave throughout the narrative of the final two chapters. These themes have common threads running
through them: immigration, language, communication, and sociocultural
integration. The first theme is arriving, which usually means reaching a place
at the end of a journey or a juncture. Arriving also means that a person has
accomplished a goal that they have set for themselves. Coming to this chapter
embodies both of those meanings for me. However, as I have learned since my
arrival in *Nuebayol* many years ago, arriving means much more to me and to
many other Latin American immigrants. For instance, at this moment, I have
arrived at a place where I can use the opportunities that life has given me not
only to enact my own voice in self-empowering ways but also to empower
others. While writing this book, I have had time to reflect on the many (Latin
American) immigrants who have not yet arrived—or may never arrive—to
materialize their "American Dream."

---

1. Word for "chapter" in Spanish.

To illustrate what I mean by arriving, consider a dichotomy between the physical, entering the United States, and the metaphysical, gaining the ability to enact voice. Clearly the Latin American immigrants who participated in this research have physically arrived in the United States. They arrived with the intention of bettering their lives, and, in many ways, they have. Holding a job with benefits in this country constitutes a major success for most of them. Simultaneously, arriving has to do with having a presence in the metaphysical sense. For example, many janitors felt that they had arrived physically but had not transcended their physical or material presence. Arriving means having the power to present oneself in a way that one's presence is acknowledged and valued and has at least the potential to influence others.

Arriving is enacted in the form of compelling discourse that lets the world know that "I am here." Such a compelling discourse plays out in micro-level contexts (everyday talk) and macro-level contexts (mass mediated interaction). For many immigrants, including myself, simply arriving physically is not enough; we must also "arrive" discursively so that we feel that we are part of our sociocultural environment. For instance, based on this investigation's findings, it appears that most of the Latin American immigrant janitors do not feel they have arrived, and language is the main reason for their liminality or "layover" along the way. All those years ago when my uncle anxiously expressed to me, "Tu tienes que aprender inglés" [You have to learn English], he appeared to be asking me to move beyond just the realm of the physical and to arrive in the sense of becoming an acknowledged member of U.S. society. My uncle was referring to the importance of learning English to integrate into U.S. society and to augment my ability to perform discursively in my everyday life. As an immigrant, my uncle knew that arriving meant being on a certain type of life track.

My immigrant life track in the United States has been education. My immigrant story began the very moment my father and uncle asked me to register for school. Many immigrants commonly receive an invitation to find a job (often doing hard labor) when they arrive to the United States. I was fortunate to receive an unusual invitation by my uncle and father: Please go to school. For me, that request was momentous, and it placed me on a life track that would lead to my consequent "arrival." My arrival at this present moment has been dictated by my takeoff.

My father and uncle's invitation to consider education instead of work served as the catalyst that propelled me to a place different from that of the Latin American janitors with whom I worked in this investigation. Getting encouragement from my family to advance my education in the United States to learn English shaped my immigrant life track because it gave me the ability to enact voice in ways that the janitors in this project cannot do. For many Latin American immigrant janitors, arriving has not been an option; it never has been. This situation presents them with a future that is much different than mine. Many of them may never have the opportunity to arrive in the United States in this sense. Language still remains an obstacle in their path to getting there.

In this study, I examined the everyday communication experiences of Latin American immigrant janitors at a large public university in the United States. My primary goal was to gain a deeper understanding of janitorial workers' mundane communication with other organizational members—specifically, supervisors, coworkers, and customers (i.e., students, faculty, and staff)—from their standpoints. I found that their co-cultural communication experiences are inextricable from their workplace communication experiences and that their social identities are at the root of both. This chapter addresses these complexities by interweaving narratives of salient themes that emerged during the research journey. These themes highlight common threads in the janitors' lived experiences and my own: language, immigration, and sociocultural integration.

The (English) Language Dilemma

It is well established that language is linked to national identity and group membership (F. L. Aldama & González, 2018; L. R. Chávez, 2017; Jiménez Román & Flores, 2010). Though immigrants may be motivated to learn their new culture's language, that society and its main social institutions (including host society members) must also have a positive attitude and the willingness to support those immigrants' desires to learn the dominant language. In a country like the United States, which fervently values its dominant language, "outsiders" or "foreigners" who speak a language other than English are often viewed as people trying to acquire something that belongs to "us." Past and current public discourse in the United States, such as the "English Only" movement, communicate that many host society members are unwilling to consider integration to be complete (or even begun) without immigrants' commitment to learning English and speaking only English in public places. Latin American immigrant janitors' communication experiences show some of the complex dynamics that inform these kinds of experiences in a new country. In particular, the janitors in this investigation appear to continuously find themselves in situations that might diminish their opportunities and desire to learn English. In sum, many immigrants' desire to learn English must be matched by the new society's willingness to have mechanisms in place that aid in that language acquisition process.

In line with existing research, Latin American immigrant janitors perceive that their inability to speak English is a major problem that affects their communication experiences in and out of the workplace. The janitors shared that not speaking English impedes them from forming and establishing meaningful relationships at work and beyond. For instance, as Daniela's previous comment illustrates, janitors' frustration with acquiring the dominant language spoken in the United States: "Es desconcertante que uno no puede hablar con otras personas. Imaginese vivir en un lugar y estar rodeado de personas y que uno no puede hablar con ellas; es bien frustrante a veces" [It's discouraging not being able to talk with other people. Imagine living in a place surrounded by people and one can't talk to them; it's very frustrating at times].

For Latin American immigrant janitors, proficient language use is the basis for their ability to communicate in the workplace. The inability to speak English has shaped their social life from the moment that they entered U.S. society. Language barriers become a serious social and communicative barrier. For instance, salient outcomes stemming from language use (in)ability include Latin American immigrants' reliance on interpersonal networks to find jobs (S. S. Smith, 2010), challenges with everyday communicative exchanges, the creation of safe linguistic zones for social survival, the constant need for host society members to communicatively adapt and accommodate to their communication needs, and sociocultural and economic transition and adaptation.

The Language–Interpersonal Network Connection

Language use is a major communication problem for Latin American immigrant janitors *before* they enter a U.S. organization. Most janitors indicated that they found their current job through a close friend, romantic partner, or family member (i.e., their interpersonal networks). Juana's comment exemplifies this situation: "Pues si, mi cuñada me dijo que venga a aplicar que estaban cojiendo gente y yo vine a postular" [Yes, my sister-in-law told me to apply, that they were taking people, and I came and applied].

It is not news that people in the United States rely on their interpersonal networks to find jobs. However, for socially marginalized people (e.g., racially minoritized people, low-status organizational members, and immigrants), these networks are much more significant (S. S. Smith, 2010). Due to pervasive social hierarchies in the United States, power imbalances that place underrepresented people at the bottom of organizational hierarchies persist (Anderson et al., 2020; Avgar et al., 2018; Fitzgerald, 2019). As a result, Whites occupy the large majority of middle- and upper-management positions in organizations, meaning that immigrants have direct contact and access to associates in mostly the lower levels of organizations. Consequently, their job pipelines (people in their interpersonal/social network) are people who typically hold positions in the lower levels of organizations. Furthermore, Latin American immigrants might struggle to expand their social networks in any significant way because many of them never learn English and, consequently, remain within their reduced and oftentimes under-resourced social networks. In other words, if, after an immigrant arrives in their new country, people with cultural capital receive the immigrant, then the immigrant would quickly have access to human resources that would potentially provide access to those other people's cultural capital. Cultural capital could translate to further extended social networks and access to additional opportunities. Without it, immigrants often end up in circumstances where (usually poor and uneducated) Latin American immigrants remain in the same low-level job for decades.

The types of jobs to which Latin American immigrant janitors have access when they enter the United States further demonstrate the language–interpersonal network relationship. Most janitors expressed that janitorial work is not as harsh on their bodies as were previous jobs they held, such as being a landscape worker, factory employee, hotel housekeeper, and restaurant dishwasher. Comparing her current janitor role with her previous factory worker position, Ramona said: "Pues es mas suave en el cuerpo. En el otro tabajo era rapido, rapido, rapido y si uno no producia lo echaban" [It's much easier on the body. In the other job, it was fast, fast, fast, and if you didn't produce, they would kick you out].

The list of jobs that janitors have held reveals an interesting common theme: little to no requirement to communicate regularly with people, which means the people holding the jobs do not need to be fluent in English to execute them effectively. These jobs represent what I refer to as communicatively superficial and/or isolated occupations. Many of the jobs that janitors mentioned typically exist within organizational structures where communication is minimal. Those occupations tend to have night shifts, and the daily tasks associated with those jobs are predominantly routine and monotonous. There is no need for receiving complex instructions or giving explanations, such as reciting a high-end restaurant menu or discussing a detailed procedure.

Whether individuals choose these occupations, end up there circumstantially, or are actively blocked into them, there is a strong stereotype of Latin American immigrants performing "dirty work." This seemingly traditional matching of Latin American immigrant bodies with communicatively isolated jobs is socially significant because such practices contribute to perpetuating public perceptions that some jobs belong with certain bodies (e.g., janitors, landscapers/gardeners, hotel housekeepers, construction workers). Further, labor-intensive jobs that do not require regular interpersonal communication or a high communication skill level subtly perpetuate an unequal social system in which certain people (e.g., uneducated and working-class immigrants) tend to occupy those jobs. This situation suggests that a person who does not speak English fluently can only aspire to hold certain stigmatized positions within U.S. organizations, creating an environment in which the dominant language becomes a highly valued social commodity.

As U.S. society continues to change, due to shifts in internal demographics and immigration patterns, the upper end of the social system (i.e., people who hold most of the economic and political power) develops other ways to discriminate against social groups that moves beyond race-ethnicity or gender. The language–interpersonal network relationship and its consequences exemplify the reconfiguration of a social system that gives Latin American immigrants specific (and few) choices in job opportunities. As a result, the inability to communicate in English permeates every sphere of the janitors' social life. This reality is also evident in the challenges that immigrants encounter with mundane interactions once they enter U.S. workplaces.

Routine Communication

For Latin American immigrant janitors, their inability to speak English is a significant problem because mundane verbal exchanges become a constant, oftentimes unavoidable challenge. For example, Juan discussed his experiences with the simple task of giving directions to customers: "Algunas veces no puedo dar direcciónes en Inglés. Se me hace bien difícil porque no tengo las palabras para explicar los sitios y como decirles a las gentes como llegar a ellos" [Sometimes I can't give directions in English. It becomes really difficult because I don't have the words to explain the places and how to tell people how to reach them]. Furthermore, another janitor shared that she was not interested in moving up the organizational ladder because she would need to fill out forms to order supplies and talk with the people who bring the supplies, which she could not do because she could not speak English.

For these reasons, most janitors perceive that learning English is virtually impossible because everyday communication is often very difficult for them. Maria's comment illustrates most janitors' beliefs about the impossibility to learn English: "Ya no aprendo; tengo la cabeza muy dura. Son cincuenta y nueve años que tengo y muchos años en Estados Unidos. Se me ha hecho muy duro aprender" [I can't learn; my head is too hard. I already am 59 years old and I have many years in the United States. It has been very hard to learn [English]].

Janitors' communication challenges, coupled with a lack of education (for some) and contact with host society members (for many), plant and foment a seed in their minds that learning English is simply too demanding. Most janitors stated that not knowing English and lacking a formal education led them to believe that their current job is the best occupation to which they can aspire. The consequences of such beliefs are that janitors distance themselves from English speakers, a communicative stance that prevents them from forming and developing relationships at work. The janitors thus use avoidant communicative behaviors to maintain their distance from dominant group members.

Language use issues also obstruct nondominant group members' ability to select verbal strategies to negotiate dominant social structures. The people with whom the janitors have positive relationships are typically their same-language and same-ethnicity coworkers. In many cases, those coworkers are the people who brought them to the organization. Janitors' interpersonal networks oftentimes get transported to the workplace, and their opportunity to learn English is lessened because they do not have much contact with English speakers.

The transplantation of janitors' interpersonal networks from the private to the public sphere (the workplace) illustrates a cultural and language-based fluidity that may seem positive but that, under the surface, yields negative outcomes. In other words, janitors' communicative practices cultivate a context that strengthens their ethnic identity and pride, as well as their native linguistic vitality, by remaining in close contact with their friends and family members in and out of the workplace. However, janitors' disconnect from host society members and from the cultural capital they could obtain from those people is due to partly self-imposed linguistic boundaries.

I noticed janitors' distance from host society members during my time working with them. Janitors actively approached and engaged their same-language coworkers, whereas the opposite occurred with people who did not speak their language. Janitors' cultural and linguistic relocation to and from their private and public spheres seems to hinder their opportunities to learn English and to form and develop relationships with host society members. Therefore, the janitors' choice to remain culturally embedded is simultaneously advantageous and damaging. A possible alternative response to this situation would be adopting an accommodating communication orientation

(Orbe, 2017) by making a more concerted effort to learn English and to learn about U.S. culture, even as they maintain strong cultural roots. However, for this scenario to transpire, host society members must display a willingness to accommodate and reciprocate Latin American immigrants' eagerness to learn about them and integrate into U.S. society, a willingness many of my participants noticed their customers lacked.

Janitorial Work and Communicative Isolation

The nature of janitorial work is related to janitors' communicative superficiality and isolation. This finding suggests that the nature of janitorial work contributes to a system that maintains Latin American immigrant janitors in a discursively suppressed space (Harlos & Pinder, 1999). Ramona describes the phenomenon this way: "Mire, vengo, hago mi trabajo y me voy. La verdad es que no hablo mucho con nadie; hay mucho que hacer" [Look, I come, do my job, and leave. The truth is that I don't talk much with anyone; there is too much to do]. It seems that significant relationships exist between organizational structures and janitors' communicative agency within those structures. This communication climate engenders a complex system in which several elements operate to discipline Latin American immigrant janitors (though they blame it on the work itself).

Janitorial work has given the janitors the stability that they sought when they arrived in the United States. This reality produces an allure of freedom from past almost slave-like occupations. Janitors often cited "job benefits" as the main reason for their feelings of stability. However, at the same time, janitorial work continues their trend of working in communication-deprived occupations. Latin American immigrants become catalysts for perpetuating social structures that confine their own and other people's future socioeconomic opportunities. This (re)production of the social system perpetuates existing constraints (Giddens, 1984). By settling or comfortably staying put in jobs that do not encourage them to learn English, transition and adapt to the United States, and move up the socioeconomic ladder, immigrants' presence in those jobs complements pervasive images of Latin Americans as the personification of service work in the United States.

Latin American immigrants' ability to integrate socioeconomically becomes hindered by the "choice" to remain in occupations such as janitorial staff. Based on the participants' narratives, it is evident that many of them desire to be in jobs other than janitor. Some janitors said that limited English skills and low education level are the two main barriers that prevent their lack of upward social movement. Many janitors perceive that their communicative seclusion in the workplace is of their own design, and many even said that they do not interact with people because they prefer it that way. Raul's comment demonstrates this point: "Que mejor para uno pues? Aqui no le piden a uno que hable el inglés mucho. Uno no estudio pues; nos quedamos brutos. Para mucho de nosotros este trabajo es como mandado del cielo porque no hablamos la lengua" [What would be better for us? Here they don't ask you to speak much English. We didn't study; we stayed illiterate. For many of us this job is like a godsend because we don't speak the language]. For Latin American immigrant janitors, communicative isolation becomes part of a process for which their work environment is the outcome. When janitors have a perceived and real need to do work that keeps them communicatively isolated, a job where communicating in English is not required becomes very enticing.

Janitorial work's appeal becomes evident when I learned that the janitor position is highly coveted in this organization, especially by Latin American immigrants. Janitors primarily have positive interactions with people who speak the same language, are on the same organizational level, and belong to a similar cultural/ethnic background. This reality illustrates a system of quasi-seclusion where the participants, perhaps because of their identity intersections and lack of cultural capital, remain in a space of a little cross-language communicative activity.

In other words, janitors' subject positions and inability to speak the dominant language create a "perfect storm" that contributes to everyday communication experiences of superficiality and isolation from English-speaking organizational actors. The complex interlocking of organizational actors' negative attitudes toward Latin American immigrants and the communicative enactment of such attitudes, the nature of janitorial work, and janitors' inability to speak English functions as a barrier that obstructs janitors' sociocultural integration. This reality shapes janitors' perceptions about the attainability of substantial social progress. Such perceptions are reflected in Manuel's comment:

Mira, yo hize un quinto grado en Mexico. Vine aqui mayorcito ya. El inglés se me ha hecho difícil. Sin inglés y sin educación la verdad es que mas crees que vaya a hacer? Me gustaria abrir mi business de landscaping, pero eso es todo ya; no mas de ahi.

[Look, I completed the fifth grade in Mexico. I came here [the United States] older. It's been difficult learning English. Without English and an education the truth is what else can I do? I would like to start a landscaping business but that's it; no more after that.]

It was as a result of this comment and others like it that I examined how janitors themselves perceive that individual characteristics (e.g., race-ethnicity and immigration status) influence their workplace communication.

Achieving Communicative Integration

As complex systems made up of individuals who contribute with their unique qualities and skills, organizations should constantly seek to foster those individuals' skills and overall development. In the case of Latin American immigrant janitors, their experiences signal that this particular organization functions in a way that does not support their English language skill development. This type of organizational culture communicates that some organizational members are more valued than others. Achieving communicative integration is thus a multidimensional process that requires the engagement of various stakeholders, including the janitors themselves.

The Role of the Host Society

In the case of the university in my study, organizational structures and host society members appear openly unsupportive of the janitors' inclinations to learn English (in these janitors' experiences). For instance, work overload not only keeps the janitors from forming and sustaining substantive relationships with people outside of their same-language coworker group but also impedes them from learning English. Some janitors expressed that the institution attempts to support them by offering once-weekly one-hour English classes. Considering this type of institutional "opportunity," it is important to note that they have to purchase supplies and it also requires additional time outside of work, which is already scant. Overall, the small amount of resources invested in janitors' language acquisition reflects minimal effort from a large public university in the United States.

It would be appropriate for this organization, as a higher education institution, to make a greater effort to provide educational opportunities for its service workers. For example, currently, this institution has a strategic plan called "Flagship 2030" in which the university outlines a set of initiatives to improve its long-term standards and goals. One of the seven "core initiatives" states the following: "7. LEARNING FOR A DIVERSE WORLD. We will develop, implement, and assess university strategies to improve the diversity of faculty, students, and staff, as well as to foster a supportive, more inclusive community for all" (University Website). Based on the janitors' experiences, it appears that their work experiences do not match this organization's self-professed value for diversity, which means the organization is not addressing the needs of all its stakeholders. This situation additionally suggests that the institution privileges students and faculty and *not* nonadministrative staff members. The lack of resources that the university puts into the development of its service workers offers some evidence to substantiate this claim.

Second, janitors' narratives about their communication experiences suggest that many of the people with whom they interact are not interested in engaging nondominant language speakers. This uncooperative communication orientation could potentially discourage immigrants from attempting to learn the new language because they might perceive that language acquisition is too difficult due to incessantly mundane communication challenges. Results imply that host society members should appear more inclined to meet non-English speakers halfway. The foreign-language speakers might then feel that their efforts to learn the language are welcomed and supported.

This situation suggests that within social systems, all stakeholders are in some way responsible for perpetuating foreign-language speakers' lack of English-language skills. Host society members' communicative orientation toward non-English speakers should communicate to them that host society members are interested in the new members' well-being and progress. I propose that one small but influential way in which everyone can accomplish the goal of promoting all stakeholders' progress is by reaching out to them when in mundane interpersonal encounters. This reaching out can take the form of simple exchanges whereby people leave the encounter feeling better about their chances to learn English. For example, a simple exchange could be a brief teaching moment in which words are exchanged and interpreted into English or could be one in which the other person's native language might prove useful. Host society members' attitudes toward immigrants' English language acquisition efforts can also have significant consequences for immigrants' interpersonal and social networks.

Language acquisition is partially an interdependent process in which a society depends on social actors to sustain its linguistic vitality, but, at the same time, social actors depend on social structures to support their linguistic practices. For the Latin American immigrant janitors, becoming embedded in this interdependent social process has significant ramifications.

The Role of the Immigrant in Communicative Integration

Regardless of their social antecedents, Latin American immigrants have some agency to shape how their U.S. experience unfolds. These immigrants can make strides toward acquiring the English language, and thereby they could possibly place themselves in a position where they would be prepared to take advantage of educational and work opportunities. Making such moves is critical for the immigrant's ability to move up the socioeconomic ladder. Some ways that Latin American immigrants can accomplish this forward movement are by exposing themselves to English-language media, signing up for free weekend English courses offered by community organizations, and finding conversational partners with whom they feel safe talking.

Based on the janitors' narratives, it is clear that they are aware of the negative outcomes that not speaking English causes in their social lives. However, many of them appear not to have taken tangible steps to move in a direction where they become semi-fluent or fluent in English. This reality also illustrates why a person's interpersonal/social network is indispensable. Some of the participants, for instance, may not have been aware of available opportunities and, thus, they provide insufficient reasons as to why they cannot improve their English-language skills.

Furthermore, many janitors who participated in this study remain transnational citizens even after many years of residence in the United States. They remain connected to their countries of origin and somewhat disconnected from U.S. culture and society. This circumstance further affirms that immigrants have some agency in the choices that they make to shape their lived experiences. Although many janitors indicate that they want to learn English, they also disclosed that they rarely watch English-language television, listen to the radio, or read anything in English. Consequently, this lack of action helps to structure their current social reality.

Unlike European, African, and Asian immigrants, Latin American immigrants are in close hemispheric proximity to their countries of origin and, therefore, have easier access to their familiar cultural products and artifacts, as well as having close proximity to their native language. With the exception of some "tropicalized" spaces (Aparicio & Chávez-Silverman, 1997) like Miami and parts of New York City and Los Angeles, for example, Latin Americans who do not learn English tend to remain on the social, cultural, and economic fringes of U.S. society. It can thus be concluded that context is highly relevant to Latin American immigrants' communication experiences. In the case of the janitors in this research, the overlapping historical, institutional, and relational contexts are not conducive to their English-language development and, consequently, do not support their social and economic integration into U.S. society.

Due to their status as transnationals, for many Latin American immigrants, linguistic segmentation appears more sustainable. This means that not only their close geographic distance to their home countries but also several other factors contribute to their sustained inability to learn English. These factors might be the core communities (e.g., immediate interpersonal networks) that receive them in the United States, the formation of ethnic co-communities (e.g., New York's Washington Heights neighborhood, Miami's Little Havana, and Chicago's Humboldt Park neighborhood), and advanced transportation systems. These combined social factors function to convey to Latin American immigrants that they can build a life in the United States without much knowledge of and proficiency in the English language.

Latin American immigrants who live in ethnic co-communities are primarily exposed to the media of their native countries, and work in places and jobs where they primarily interact with same-language people. Latin American immigration, coupled with anti-immigrant and specifically anti–Latin American sentiment, may potentially lead to a bilingual state similar to the Quebec model, in which there could be conflict around issues of identity and around access to resources, with language at the center of such a conflict. These situations play out through social actors' mundane communicative exchanges in public spaces such as the workplace.

Summary

The janitors in my study reinforced that not speaking the dominant U.S. language fluently is a significant communication impediment in various social contexts, and several conclusions can be drawn from this finding. First, Latin American immigrants' motivation to learn English must align with U.S. society's desire and social structures to promote immigrants' language acquisition. The presence or absence of these structures has important implications for immigrants' interpersonal networks. Second, linguistic ability and social and cultural integration are inextricably linked. If host-society members are unwilling to engage new cultural members, then cultural neophytes will have a difficult time integrating into that society. Third, because social actors' actions are interdependent with how that society is structured, nondominant group members often bear the burden of responsibility to proactively adjust to or shift the social status quo to be able to participate in that society.

CHAPTER 6

Research Implications, Advocacy, and Future Directions

AS I COME to the end of this book, I want to place the work presented in the previous chapters back into conversation with the literature and with productive opportunities for change. In particular, I want to explore this study's implications for communication theory, research, and practice in institutional settings. First, it demonstrates how other branches of communication theory can be employed strategically to highlight some of the complex relationships between communication and social identity present in work life. For example, co-cultural communication theory is useful to elucidate lower-status service workers' experiences. Second, it illustrates some of the intricacies involved in conducting research with marginalized people. Lastly, it shows how Latin American immigrant janitors' subpar access to developmental resources such as language programs, educational opportunities, and advanced job placement does not align with the organization's professed commitment to diversity, equity, and inclusion.

Theoretical Implications

Communication theories are useful to advance understandings of communication processes and social identity in modern organizations. Particularly, co-cultural communication theory (Orbe, 2017) is valuable to understand work experiences such as non-White service workers' communication in a predominantly White institution (PWI). The primary goal of co-cultural communication theory is to develop understandings of traditionally marginalized people's communicative practices. Social identity intersections also appear relevant to understand routine communication experiences. Therefore, this study contributes to understandings about social identity intersections' material consequences for social actors in routine interactions (e.g., verbal mistreatment and discrimination). Finally, this study highlights relationships between culture, power, and communication. Critical lenses could, thus, be helpful to advance knowledge about the work experiences of historically marginalized organizational actors.

Social Identity Intersectionality

Intersectional communication studies are still limited decades after scholars like B. J. Allen (1995) and Crenshaw (1992) argued that this research is necessary to inform humanistic and social scientific scholarship and organizational practices. This study's results suggest that those calls to action are still relevant. Latin American immigrants' narratives of their communication experiences show that identity intersections can function to shape societal members' direct lived experiences. As the United States' dominant discourses continue to shape residents' perceptions of social difference, research that informs how those perceptions might be outwardly enacted by social actors is highly significant for research and practice. This work has highlighted four specific identities and their intersections in a workplace communication context: race-ethnicity, social class, immigration status, and occupation.

Latin American immigrant janitors' communication experiences in a PWI show significant complexities in communication and social identity. Findings include janitors' perception that their social class and immigration status work in tandem with their occupation to hypermarginalize them, a result that reinforces Crenshaw's (1991) observations about how different identity categories interrelate to form and sustain systems of oppression, or what hooks (1989) called "interlocking systems of oppression." This finding also suggests that these social identity categories do not necessarily act in isolation from the other categories but are instead equally significant and interconnected.

The data also show relationships between power dynamics and communication. Within U.S. hierarchies of social class, immigration status, and occupation, communication plays a key role in sustaining or eradicating these hierarchies (B. J. Allen, in press). Latin American immigrant janitors' work experiences show how these hierarchies are communicatively sustained. For instance, janitors' situations make it difficult for them to advance socioeconomically. Their inability to speak English makes it challenging for them move up socioeconomically and attain higher-status occupations. The data also display the everyday political "games" played in (especially organizational) social contexts, which center on power and privilege based on social identity.

Critical Theory

Data show that it would be useful to continue building on this study's findings through the use of critical theory frameworks. The aim of critical theory is to identify and eradicate existing uneven power structures to emancipate subaltern subjects' socially constructed realities (Deetz, 2005; McDonald, 2017; Mumby, 1993, 2004, 2010). Critical theoretical frameworks are useful to gain a deeper understanding, and, potentially, to change the organizational experiences of nondominant group members.

Power is enacted and negotiated through everyday communicative encounters, and those encounters can function to suppress persons' communication, and, thus, their ability to enact voice (Deetz, 1992; McInnes & Corlett, 2012; Musson & Duberley, 2007). In the context of the present study, the way that janitors showed resistance in a dominant communication system, where their voices were disadvantaged, was by engaging in avoidance behaviors. They remained distant and thereby separated themselves from this system. Critical theoretical approaches can be employed to study how organizational structures perpetuate systems of powerlessness and inequity (B. J. Allen, 2010; Alvesson, 2000; Ashcraft, 2017; Mumby, 2016). This study shows that supervisors use aggressive communication styles to discipline and control their subordinates. The defensive communication climate to which the supervisors' communication styles contribute additionally support a workplace where subordinates avoid dissent and conflict. These types of structures, where voice and agency are suppressed, become exacerbated by situations where social actors lack the ability to speak the dominant language.

This institutional analysis contributes to critical theory by examining how subaltern subjects negotiate their various marginalized subject positions in an organizational structure. The findings illuminate issues of language and oppression, marginalization, and discrimination. Language surfaced as a contentious factor that positions some people in a more powerful and privileged position. This analysis also highlights a somewhat neglected cultural group in critical communication theory—people of Latin American descent. Critical analyses can improve the institutional experiences of Latin American immi-grant service employees by creating spaces where they have opportunities for institutional advancement.

Practical Implications: Institutional Advocacy

Organizations benefit from having practices and processes in place that pro-mote intercultural understanding and the development of *all* stakeholders. This study shows that organizations could do a better job at promoting inter-cultural understanding and the development of all staff members across hier-archies. This analysis highlights the need to continue conducting research about higher education institutions' dynamics related to communication and social difference. In traditional organizational communication research, this type of organization seems to take a back seat to other organizational contexts (e.g., corporate and other types of nonprofits). This examination reveals that the complexities of higher education contexts provide a rich arena in which to study communication processes related to leadership, difference, and group interaction. Third, this study elucidates the importance of considering inves-tigations that focus on the work experiences of low-status employees. Applied communication research seems particularly well suited to address issues related to improving communicative practices involving service employees.

The organization at the center of this study can and should display a stronger commitment to the personal and occupational development of Latin American immigrant service workers. The institution represents a complex social system in which all stakeholders are responsible for the systems' out-comes. An important issue for organizational leaders to consider is the extent to which they act upon the values to which the university is committed (e.g., diversity and education for all community members). For example, most jani-tors indicated that they do not perceive that administrators emphasize their occupational and personal development. This suggests a different orientation toward the janitors than toward other members of the organization. Accord-ing to the janitors, they receive little to no attention from the administration, which translates to lesser benefits and less emphasis on their development (Magolda, 2016).

A stronger commitment by the administration toward service workers' development would be reflected in more opportunities for learning English and advancing their education. However, this institution is not alone in its leaders' lack of commitment toward providing occupational and personal development opportunities for service workers. I conducted a search for educational or occupational opportunities for janitorial workers at various universities, and I could not produce any specific practices that were tailored to assist service workers in their professional and personal development. This analysis illuminates the need to pay attention to the work experiences of low-status employees. Many of those employees are immigrants and, thus, may require special attention regarding opportunities to learn English. This investigation exposes the administrators' lack of commitment to developing all of their employees, regardless of their location in the organization hierarchy.

This study highlights the need to study education settings and low-status employees' communication experiences. Organizational practices that address the occupational development needs of these workers are virtually nonexistent. The benefits of focusing our research on higher education settings are that we can advance practices that would benefit all stakeholders. Moreover, researchers could act as whistleblowers regarding unjust practices that affect particular groups of people in organizational settings. For instance, if an organization's leadership claims that it has a particular mission or value, and they do not appear to fulfill it regarding some stakeholders, then it is our duty to raise questions about how that organization is addressing those persons being left out. This study reveals that service workers are not reaping the rewards of being part of an organization with ample resources. The lack of attention toward janitors' occupational development suggests that the leadership places less emphasis on those organizational members than it does on other members.

In organizational systems, stakeholders are responsible for the well-being of each other, as well as for the well-being of the organization. Paying attention to the issues that I address in this research yields benefits for organizational stakeholders across hierarchies. One way that the leadership would show a stronger commitment toward its stakeholders is by making the most out of its human capital (e.g., members' expertise) to address important internal issues such as the ones that I indicate in this study.

For example, the research site has one of the top-rated communication departments in the country. Furthermore, this university's leaders could engage with its ethnic studies department for expertise about cultural groups' experiences and interethnic understanding. One of the practical implications of this study is that it has produced information regarding how service workers perceive their experiences working at this institution. Bringing its resources to bear would mean for the organization to conduct a thorough self-study where it analyzes in depth work practices across organizational units—for instance, surveying janitors, supervisors, and customers to better understand what can be done to improve how supervisors and customers communicate with the janitors. The university's communication and ethnic studies departments can be consulted to provide expert advice on matters related to interethnic/racial communication.

Several participants perceived that administrators are not concerned with their well-being. Janitorial employees continually cited *time* as a factor that prevented them from pursuing educational opportunities (Hood, 1988; Müller, 2020; Rabelo & Mahalingam, 2019). One way that the organizational leadership could address employees' developmental needs is by making room for them to pursue those opportunities. However, according to many janitors, the main issue might be lack of resources. Janitorial workers have to cover a lot of ground in a small amount of time, and this work structure impinges on their ability to pursue developmental opportunities.

Organizational leaders introduced a strategic long-term plan to develop the university's ability to meet organizational goals. The administration outlined a long-term vision to make this organization one of the leading higher education institutions in the 21st century. With this plan, university leadership hopes to create a place that "exemplifies the power and promise of diversity, intercultural understanding and community engagement" (University Website). Although this strategic plan has outlined diversity as one of its main goals, the plan does not address service workers and their long-term needs. This reality prompts me to raise the question, What is the strategic plan for that employee population? The university leadership appears to address students and faculty in this strategic vision, but what about other staff members, including lower-status employees? How will their work experiences be met in the next quarter century? This exception suggests that those employees are not as important as other organizational members. These observations reveal why it is important to focus communication research on higher education settings.

Developing our knowledge of organizational practices in higher education institutions benefits scholars, practitioners, and organizational stakeholders, and applied communication research is well suited to address some of the issues raised in this investigation (Cissna, 2000). Applied communication research is when communication scholars use methodological and theoretical tools and resources to alleviate or solve a practical, communication-related social problem (Buzzanell & Houston, 2018; High & Young, 2018; Villanueva et al., 2017); this area's goal is to create spaces where individuals can empower themselves to deal with problems in the context where they occur. The continuum of observation–intervention applied research symbolizes the work of applied communication researchers (Frey & SunWolf, 2009). Observational applied communication research is conducted when scholars describe, interpret, explain, and, sometimes, critique a communication problem in a specific communication site, with the purpose of informing other scholars, practitioners, and the public. The current study falls on this side of the continuum. On the opposite end of this continuum is intervention-oriented scholarship, which takes a more involved and engaged approach to doing applied research. Interventionists come into research sites with the intention of creating tangible changes that help people to deal with a communication problem (e.g., Artz, 1998; Kahl, 2017; Villanueva et al., 2017). Although this study represents the observational type, its topic has great potential for intervention-oriented research.

Interventionists provide practical implications and ensure that the stakeholders apply the tools that they have been given and that some visible changes result from the application (e.g., Hartnett, 1998, 2018). One component of the intervention-oriented side of the continuum is the communication activism for social justice approach. A social justice approach produces knowledge that attempts to change dominant discourse into discourse where underrepresented individuals have an equal voice. This type of scholarship also attempts to change the grammars that, historically, keep individuals in a socially dominant position. In the communication activism approach, researchers not only point to a group of people who are socially, politically, and culturally marginalized but also take a vigorous and direct approach to producing positive change in the contexts that they study (Frey et al., 2020). Embracing these conceptual tools has clear practical implications.

Although this study falls on the observational end of the applied communication continuum, it could move toward the intervention side when the findings are presented to organizational administrators. The goal is to start courses of action to improve service workers' work environments. I believe that sharing the findings with key administrators can lead to action regarding, for instance, how supervisors communicate with their subordinates. Workshops to address interpersonal communication skills could be implemented to improve communication between supervisors and subordinates. Supervisors' communicative practices can be changed if organizational leaders take particular actions to remedy such problems.

Administrators' possible lack of interest in the janitors' occupational and personal development might translate to other organizational members' orientations toward them. Janitors' comments regarding how supervisors and customers verbally mistreated them led some of them to view themselves as inferior to others. Furthermore, the janitors constantly questioned why others perceived them negatively. According to their narratives, the answers reside in their race-ethnicity and their occupation. Those perceptions appeared to lead to questions such as, "Why would anyone be interested in a janitor?" Janitors' mundane interactions with other organizational members illuminate the reasons why, in addition to considering higher education as an organizational context, scholars and practitioners should also focus on understanding low-status employees' experiences.

Systemic issues are also present regarding how immigrant service employees are treated in organizations. Administrators' lack of attention to janitors' occupational development, their treatment of janitors, and the janitors' negative experiences with customers suggest that there is a systemic problem. The problem may be that janitors are perceived as unimportant to the organization, its leadership, and other organizational members. The organization's lack of commitment to create opportunities (e.g., accommodating janitors' time constraints) and to ensure that the janitorial staff supervisors have the appropriate interpersonal skills to deal with their subordinates leads to this conclusion. In short, it appears that many of the problems that janitors encountered regarding customers' verbal mistreatment reflect systemic issues surrounding public perceptions of Latin American service workers.

In sum, the findings suggest that administrators lack a commitment to promoting janitors' personal and occupational development. Although the organization had some practices in place (e.g., English as a second language classes), those practices are more superficial than a real effort to improve the janitors' conditions. Consequently, it would be beneficial for organizational scholarship, practitioners, and stakeholders to emphasize higher education as an organizational setting that matters. The issues that janitors face in the workplace suggest that researchers' familiarity with their experiences is somewhat limited and that learning more about them is important to advance organizational theory, research, and practice. Finally, in addition to advancing organizational practices and studying higher education contexts, learning about lower-status employees' experiences would benefit organizational scholars, practitioners, and stakeholders. Lower-status organizational actors have been overlooked in research, which emphasizes upper-level middle-class employees, such as White managers and supervisors. These practical implications illuminate the need to continue studying particular communication experiences (e.g., traditionally marginalized cultural group members) in organizational settings such as higher education institutions.

Practical Recommendations

In this section, I offer practical recommendations to improve organizational practices. One of the main conclusions that surfaced from this investigation is that the organizational leaders do not promote a supportive communication climate. These leaders should address some of the problems that surfaced with factions of its leadership (e.g., janitorial staff supervisors). Administrators could also take tangible steps to display that they are committed to including and developing lower-status employees. I also offer particular practical recommendations for the janitorial staff. Finally, organizations should support specific units and departments that serve roles beyond classroom instruction. At universities, in particular, a department such as ethnic studies serves the key purpose of educating the campus community on issues that deeply affect traditionally marginalized organizational and societal members. If organizational leaders engage in these practices, they would greatly benefit janitorial workers, faculty, staff, and students.

A major advantage that a higher education institution has in relation to other organization types is that it possesses rich human capital in the form of intellectual capital. For this reason, academic leaders could tap into this capital to reach organizational goals. For instance, administrators could tap into the communication and ethnic studies departments whereby faculty experts could present workshops to organizational leaders about the benefits of promoting supportive communication climates, showing commitment toward subordinates, and showing commitment to cultural sensitivity issues. Furthermore, university leadership can maximize its use of other units, such as the Center for Multicultural Affairs, Women's Resource Center, Human Resources, and world languages academic departments. In short, it seems that the administration at RMU is not maximizing their resources to ensure that stakeholders such as janitors receive the best work experience possible.

Furthermore, organizations' human capital can be put into use to offer knowledge that could be used by other staff members to train supervisors on interpersonal and intercultural skills (e.g., information-seeking, requesting feedback, and the importance of listening to foster positive relationships). This study's results reflect top leadership's managerial decisions. If the administration makes serious efforts to capitalize on its own human resources to raise awareness of the internal issues that affect its functioning, and if it implements practices to address these issues, then the institution would be displaying a commitment to all of its stakeholders and not just to those at the top of its hierarchy.

The administration could engage in regular practices that communicate to service workers that they are valued community members. The administrative leadership can accomplish this goal by offering educational, occupational, and personal advancement opportunities. Although the university offers the participants English courses, these courses are brief, once a week for one hour, and do not provide a real opportunity for language acquisition. I am aware of some of the impediments present to achieve such goals: Many janitors could not read or write, which hinders their development from the start. For this reason, organizations should offer some opportunities for educational development that include reading and writing courses at the janitors' levels. Creating such opportunities would communicate to janitorial workers that the administrators care about their development. Language acquisition classes are useful, but these classes should be more intensive than one hour a week lessons. Classes could be offered during off hours to accommodate work schedules. Obtaining basic English reading and writing skills would create a stronger foundation for the service workers to envision better occupational opportunities. Many janitors expressed that they felt hopeless due to their inability to speak English and/or read and write.

In addition to basic English acquisition, reading, and writing opportunities, the administration should invest more resources into advancing educational and career opportunities. For example, a noble attempt to support service workers is the School of Education's efforts to temporarily offer bilingual courses that led to high diploma equivalency credits. However, this opportunity is not oriented toward gaining the social and cultural capital that comes with learning English; it also ignores the immigrants who may come with education from their home country and simply need to learn English. I suggest that the university's priorities need to shift: Once there are opportunities in place to help service workers learn how to read and write in English, then there should be opportunities for them to continue to advance their formal education and career paths. The university could also provide vouchers for the janitors to take college courses as part-time degree-seeking students. Those opportunities would give the janitors hope that they can improve their current conditions—in other words, the institution would display a social justice orientation. Once stakeholders like the service workers in this investigation attain a GED, they can pursue college and the occupational opportunities that come with attaining a college degree. Those skills would prepare the service workers for advancement within or outside of the organizational hierarchy. But the starting point has to be teaching and learning English.

Perhaps one of the main issues discovered in this analysis regarding organizational practices is that an environment of ethnic intolerance still exists at this university. The cross-cultural dialogues that take place at the organization are, in theory, useful to foster intercultural understanding. However, this practice appears to be insular, and I propose expanding it to the entire campus community. The dialogues that happen in the residence halls are tailored to the experiences of residence hall janitors and the students who live there. Janitors in other areas such as Facilities Management and Recreation Services, for instance, should also be part of those dialogues.

Campus-wide dialogues should also be advertised and implemented every semester to show service workers that the organization's administration is committed to their well-being. In the context of a PWI, dialogues would be highly beneficial for all community members. Many universities apply inter-group dialogue approaches, but these approaches tend to focus on students, some faculty, and upper-level staff (see Schoem & Hurtado, 2001). Institut-ing such practices would help create a climate of intercultural understanding and an awareness of different lived experiences. The aforementioned organiza-tional practices would enhance Latin American immigrant janitors' workplace experiences and beyond, into other spheres of their social lives.

Finally, higher education institutions should show a genuine commitment to supporting campus departments and units such as the department of eth-nic studies and centers for multicultural affairs. These units should not merely represent good public relations: They should become a central part of the uni-versity culture and community. Moreover, ethnic studies departments tend to be active by exposing the plight of less privileged societal members through panel discussions, documentary film showings, and on- and off-campus com-munity involvement. Those departments' role is important because it educates stakeholders (the campus community), and, thus, holds people accountable for their actions. I suggest that organizational leaders should encourage all campus units and departments, such as ethnic studies departments, to maxi-mize and diversify the ways in which they apply department members' intel-lectual resources to address issues pertaining to "isms" and intolerance—for example, through encouraging faculty to engage in community outreach and diversity-related curricular development (e.g., Alvarez et al., 2015) by assign-ing greater value to those efforts for purposes related to tenure and promo-tion. This approach displays a commitment to broader communal values and efforts beyond highly criticized traditional ways of being in the "Ivory Tower" (i.e., public perceptions of these institutions as "elitist" and "self-absorbed").

Higher education organizations could perform practices that show a commitment to all and not just to some stakeholders. From a social justice and equity standpoint, some of the practices that I discovered analyzing this institution should be of some concern to all stakeholders (i.e., faculty, staff, students, administrators). For example, the university privileges the experi-ences of faculty and students, and it downplays staff members' experiences and needs. In the context of this implicit hierarchy, lower-status employees receive less attention than other staff members due to their social meanings and status. Organizational practices should reflect the administration's commitment to stakeholders across the organizational hierarchy. Within many U.S. organizations, and within society as a whole, the United States' claim is that its citizens support justice and equality for all. Apparently, this is not the case for the janitors in this study.

I posit that how people treat less privileged others reflects their dominant values. People like Latin American immigrants are not "free" in the United States. As a society, we can take tangible steps toward rectifying this inequity. Organizational members, and citizens in general, can help change the status quo by looking inward and taking concrete steps to create social justice in their own backyards.

Shifting My Positionality: From Watching to Doing

After a long, challenging, and rewarding journey writing this book, its ending is bittersweet. In this reflection, I share some lessons learned from this experience. I reflect on my experience as a researcher, but also on the people at the center of this study, the people whose lived experiences prompted me to embark on this journey. I organize this reflection in two parts. First, I turn the lens inward and reflect on my assumptions and subject positions at the outset. Second, I share my thoughts and feelings about the people who are the heart of this investigation—the Latin American immigrant janitorial workers whose voices and experiences give life to this study, and who eternally inspire me to live to serve others—especially those less fortunate than me.

Watching from a distance, as I did before I embarked on this journey, did not give me a complete picture of the people I watched. I watched and made assumptions about who they were and what their work lives were like. Those people were Latin American service workers. At the time, I was not aware that I was looking at them through my privileged, middle-class, and educated lenses. I was somewhat unaware of my social locations in relationship to theirs. I just contemplated from a distance the question, "How miserable must they be?" and, at the same time, I wondered what it was like to be them. These were the thoughts running through my mind because I simultaneously perceived myself as being one of them, but in reality, I was *not* one of them. Many of them had to go through harrowing experiences to get to that place where our lives converged. I had arrived at that moment propelled by the privilege that my status as an educator afforded me. As I watched from a distance, I thought that I was one of them, and I could easily have been one of them. However, I was not a service worker but, instead, an educator who wanted to understand what it meant to work and communicate with others from overlapping spaces of hypermarginalization.

The main lesson I learned from this journey is never to assume that the lenses through which people see others are accurate. Accuracy has nothing to do with perception and has everything to do with subject position. In this sense, I learned a valuable lesson about subject positionality. I was not certain why I had the thoughts I did about the service workers, but now I feel that my subject positions had something to do with it. I perceived them to be miserable compared to me and to where I was positioned. The reality was that, considering their antecedents and the difficult pasts that most of them had experienced, their jobs at the organization symbolized for them not only progress but also stability and relief. As I learned, being a janitor was not a misery but a satisfaction to many of them. Having a stable job with benefits meant that they at least had an opportunity to live a decent life. I quickly learned that the janitors were much more complex than I imagined, even before I uttered a single word to any of them.

Watching people from a distance may give us a certain impression about who they are. In the case of the janitors, anyone could have easily thought that they simply were uneducated people who clean buildings for a living. Among many other things, I learned that when I watched them, I only got a superficial view of these highly multidimensional and complex human beings. It was no different with the janitorial workers who accompanied me in this journey. I learned that, although they did not have the letters "PhD" after their names, they were as complex, funny, witty, theoretical, practical, and interesting as any of the degree-holders I met at the university.

My observations also inspire me to continue devoting my time to listening to the voices of immigrants in the United States. This is important work because immigrants are often perceived as undeserving or as robbers of the American Dream, especially those who entered the United States without documents. Immigrants tend to be negatively perceived and are often mistreated. How we treat those who got to this country last constitutes a measuring stick of this country's values and humanity. Those who live in a country that boasts about being a beacon of freedom and equality for all must not give life to hypocrisy through the mistreatment of immigrants, especially if they work in occupations that are stigmatized but essential to the functioning of organizations. For these reasons, Mirella, Ofelia, Morelia, Isaura, Maria, Daniela, Juan, Ricardo, Roberto, and Rodolfo (pseudonyms) inspire me to continue writing for them, to continue giving them opportunities to enact their voices, because they and others perceive that they are not heard and are simply dismissed.

Finally, before beginning this project, I perceived myself as being culturally similar to the janitors. I learned that my perceived similarities were challenged during our interactions. This result illustrates the complexity of people's humanity. My perception of the janitors as similar, and my realization of our differences, highlights the need to move beyond watching into doing. I learned that when people engage in doing, glimpses of hope surface. Brief encounters with people who are perceived as different can provide people with a lifetime of hope and inspiration about how far they might go regarding their ability to make connections with other people. Through my experience with Latin American immigrant janitors, I moved from watching to doing. Because I did this, and did not just watch, those janitors have provided me with a lifetime of hope and inspiration, and I take this with me to pass on to others.

Limitations

This organizational analysis has several limitations. First, although this study is about the communication experiences of Latin American immigrant janitors, the majority of the janitors in the study are Mexican nationals. Second, I focused my analyses on particular social identity categories, such as race and social class, to the exclusion of other categories like gender. This is an important analytic category that deserves attention in similar future studies. Third, I offer a unilateral perspective that does not include the voices of supervisors, culturally and linguistically dissimilar coworkers, and customers concerning their perceptions of their communication experiences with the janitors. Also, janitors' perceptions of their interactions with students, faculty, and staff were not parsed out. Fourth, because the focus of this case study was the subjective knowledge of Latin American immigrant janitors, I relied on a primary research method (interviewing). Research method triangulation could yield comprehensive and robust findings about the organizational experiences of lower-status, blue-collar immigrant workers. Finally, as a case study, this project focuses on the experiences of a particular group of people in one organization, and it would be useful to do an interorganizational comparative study to look at communication experiences in different organization types.

Mexican nationals make up the majority of the janitors, primarily because the study took place in a heavily Mexican-populated state in the southwestern United States. Furthermore, Mexicans compose the majority of self-identified Latin Americans living in the United States. Still, the mostly Mexican population sample might not have yielded a comprehensive perspective of the work experiences of Latin Americans in the United States. As a heterogeneous ethnic group, Latin Americans come from different countries and customs, and they have had different immigration experiences in the United States. Nevertheless, this work offers useful insights into the workplace dynamics involving non-native English speakers in lower-status occupations.

Driven by my expertise and research interests, in this study, I sought to analyze and explain the ways in which race, ethnicity, immigrant status, and occupational identities shape the janitors' everyday communication experiences. As a result, other potentially insightful identity categories shaping those experiences were excluded. Particularly, for example, this study did not emphasize gender as an analytic category that could have deepened the study's insights and findings. In future parallel studies, this is an identity category that deserves close attention. This is especially important if the number of research participants in empirical studies include comparable numbers of men and women.

This book focuses on the standpoints of Latin American immigrant janitorial workers and, thus, I interviewed this population only. My choice poses a limitation to the claims made about janitors' communication experiences, because those claims are based on just this one occupational population within the social system. Also, janitors' perspectives regarding customers were mostly about students, and janitors' communication experiences with students were not analyzed in relation to interactions with faculty and staff. Additional analysis would benefit by including the voices of supervisors, culturally dissimilar coworkers, and university staff, faculty, and students.

Although this analysis partially includes participant-observation data, these data were mainly incorporated to contextualize the study. For instance, I worked as a janitor for several months, and this information could have been employed in more depth to reinforce the research claims. Furthermore, due to schedule conflicts, I did not conduct ethnographic participant-observation at some of the Dialogues on Immigrant Integration. Adding this component to the research process would have enhanced interpretations of the janitors' communication experiences.

Finally, this investigation focused on one organization. Although doing so is not a major limitation in qualitative research, conducting a multiorganizational analysis would have augmented the findings. Studying multiple organizations would have potentially yielded a wider window into how different work structures, for instance, complicate Latin American immigrant janitors' everyday communication experiences. This is not to say that these experiences are consistent across the board in similar organizations or even in this one, but this is a chief reason why the present research could benefit from multiorganizational studies that explore differences and similarities in cultural manifestations, such as leadership styles and communication climate. Such studies could enhance researchers' ability to advance knowledge about immigrant populations' workplace experiences.

Directions for Future Research

This research produced several avenues for future research. Future inquiries could focus on the perspectives of the organizational members with whom Latin American immigrants interact (i.e., supervisors, coworkers, and customers). Also, multiple organizations could be studied to appraise any salient convergence and divergence in regard to relationships between organizational cultures and communication experiences. Another exciting line of inquiry related to the topic of this book would be to explore the communication experiences of Latin American immigrants in both lower-status and higher-status occupations. Lastly, it would be useful to examine the communication experiences of immigrants from other historically marginalized world regions, such as Southeast Asia and Africa.

Future similar studies could collect the narratives not only of immigrant organizational members but also of the people with whom they interact. More than one organization can also be studied to explore how differences in organizational structures shape Latin Americans' communication experiences. One of the main limitations of this research is that it includes only the voices of the janitors' self-reports and, thus, other voices are excluded. Conducting studies that are inclusive of all elements within the communication system could constitute one way to address this limitation. Such studies could take the form of longitudinal ethnographies. Comparative studies of various organizations could bring in evaluations of differing organizational cultures and structures, which could deepen knowledge about communication processes.

Continuing with this line of inquiry, it would be interesting to explore everyday interactions of Latin Americans who work in lower-status and higher-status occupations (e.g., project managers, doctors, and other highly regarded organizational roles). These studies could further be supplemented by studies of immigrants from other parts of the world. This line of research could be constructive because it would serve to deepen our understanding of organizational actors across hierarchies and work experiences. Moreover, such work would contribute to the work originated in this book, which is partially about understanding how immigrant identities are communicatively negotiated in the workplace. In general, such a line of inquiry offers further insights into the communication experiences of immigrant employees who occupy a lower status in the socially constructed hierarchies of the industrialized First World.

Closing Thoughts

Racial and occupational groups deemed as belonging to the fringes of U.S. society have had to endure a long history of symbolic violence through practices such as ascribed negative labels and popular culture representations, urban segregation, institutional stigmatization, and discrimination. Communication researchers claim to be at the forefront of addressing socially significant communication-related issues (Frey et al., 2020). Many of these issues demand action to reconfigure long-standing unequal power dynamics within U.S. social structures. This organizational case study contributes to the research, theory, and practice about the communication experiences of historically marginalized social groups—in this case, immigrants, people of Latin American descent, and service workers. In the rapidly changing 21st-century U.S. sociocultural landscape, fostering these conversations is not just useful to understand those neglected lived experiences, but a social imperative that has the potential to radically improve their lives, and as a result, reshape complex systems such as organizations and society.

Interview Guide

HELLO, MY NAME IS Wilfredo Alvarez. I appreciate you taking your time to be here with me today. The reason for this meeting is for us to have a conversation about your work experiences. The information gathered from our conversation is to be used for a research project. My aim in talking with you is to gain an understanding of your communication with other people at work. Please share as much as you feel comfortable sharing and know that this information will strictly be used for this research and you will have complete anonymity in the written report. Thank you again for agreeing to participate in this study.

First, let me get a little bit of information about you (demographics):
1. *What is your race-ethnicity?*
2. *How long have you lived in the United States?*
3. *How old are you?*
4. *What is your marital status? Any children? How many?*
5. *Native/First language?*
6. *What is your highest level of education attained?*

Now, let's talk a little bit about work, and your job:
1. *Where are you working right now?*
2. *How long have you been there?*
3. *What do you do in that job?*

Now let's talk about your relationships and everyday talk with other people at work . . .

Workplace Interactions

1. Please tell me about your everyday experiences with other people at work:
   a. *During most of your workdays (or nights), who do you talk to regularly? (Prompt: supervisor, coworkers; titles, names)*
   b. *[For each person:] How often do you talk?*
   c. *What do you usually talk about?*
   d. *Is there anyone at work with whom you do not talk (or rarely talk with)? If so, why not?*
   e. *If ESL, do you ever talk in your native language? (If yes, probe for details.)*
2. Describe the relationships you have developed at work and with the people we've just discussed. *(Prompt: Supervisor? Coworkers? Customers?)*
   a. *Why do you think those relationships have formed and developed that way? (Probe for each.)*
   b. *How do you feel about those relationships at work? (Probe for each.)*
3. Has anyone at work ever asked for your suggestions about work-related tasks, problems, situations?
   a. *If yes, how did you respond?*
4. Have you ever offered suggestions to anyone at work on your own about work-related tasks, problems, situations?
   a. *Why or why not? If yes, please explain.*

I'd like you to tell me more about the people you interact with at work . . .

1. Of the people with whom you talk/come in contact with at work, who seems similar to you in any way? (Describe further how if co-researcher needs more information.)
   a. *[For each person:] Tell me who they are, their positions, talk a bit about their background. How is _____ [each person] _____ similar to you?*
2. How would you describe your communication with these people who you perceive as similar?
   a. *Please provide some specific examples of what your everyday interactions are like.*
      i. *What is it like talking with this person / these persons?*
      ii. *How do they tend to respond to you when you talk?*
      iii. *How do you tend to respond to them?*

    iv. As you think about conversations with people like you at work, do any particular conversations/events stand out in your mind? (Ask to role-play if necessary.)

3. Of the people with whom you talk/come in contact with at work, who seems different from you?

    a. For each person, please tell me who they are, their positions, talk a bit about their background. How is each person different from you?

4. How would you describe your communication with these people who you perceive as different from yourself?

    a. Please provide some specific examples of what your everyday interactions are like.

      i. What is it like talking with this person / these persons?

      ii. How do they tend to respond to you and you to them when you talk?

      iii. Any particular conversations/events that stand out in your mind? (Ask to role-play if necessary.)

As you continue to reflect on your communication with others at work, I now want to ask you about your sense of how others respond to who you are as an individual . . .

Organizational Communication and Social Identity

1. Do you perceive that there is anything about you as an individual that influences how you interact with others and how others talk with you at work?

    a. (Probe:) How others perceive you; their impression of you and vice versa as related to:

    b. Race/ethnicity: Influence how you communicate with supervisors, coworkers, and customers? If yes, why do you think this is case? Can you please provide some examples?

    c. Immigration status: Influence how supervisors, coworkers, and customers communicate with you at work and you with them?

    d. Social class status: Influence how supervisors, coworkers, and customers perceive and communicate with you at work?

2. Have you ever felt that anybody mistreated you /you were treated unfairly at work? (*Probe: supervisors, coworkers, customers*)

    a. If yes, please tell me about it.

3. Have you ever felt that someone at work treated you with preference over others?

    a. If yes, why do you think that happens?

    b. Can you please describe some of these experiences?

Final Questions

1. Do you think that your workplace relationships and interactions affect your quality of life outside of work? If so, how?

2. Are there any changes that you would like to see regarding the way anyone at work talks to you? If yes, who? What would these changes be?

3. Are there any changes that you would like to see regarding how you talk to anyone at work? If yes, who? What would these changes be?

4. Have we missed anything that would be important for me to know about your work experiences regarding how people communicate with you at work? If so, whom and what? Have we missed anything that would be important for me to know about your work experiences regarding how you communicate with people at work? If so, whom and what?

Farewell Statement

That concludes our conversation, _____. I want to thank you very much for your candor, time, and attention. I want you to know that this information will be used with much integrity and also that I will not use your name in any written reports related to this research. I can give you a copy of the final report if you so desire. Once again, thank you for your time and have a good day.

Guía de Entrevista

HOLA, MI NOMBRE ES Wilfredo Alvarez. Gracias por tomar su tiempo para entrevistarse conmigo. La razón por esta entrevista es para nosotros tener una conversación acerca de sus experiencias comunicándose con otras personas en el trabajo. Esta información solamente será utilizada para el propósito de este proyecto, el cual se enfoca en entender sus experiencias comunicándose con otras personas en sus experiencias diarias de trabajo. Por favor, comparta toda la información que se sienta cómoda/o compartiendo conmigo. Sepa que usted tendrá anonimidad total en el reporte final. Gracias por participar en este estudio.

Primeramente, déjeme hacerle unas preguntas preliminares:
1. *¿De cual raza o antecedente étnico se considera parte?*
2. *¿Cuanto tiempo ha vivido en los Estados Unidos?*
3. *¿Cual es su edad?*
4. *¿Cual es su estatus marital? ¿Tiene hija/os? ¿Cuantos?*
5. *¿Cual es su primer idioma?*
6. *¿Cual es el nivel mas alto de educación que ha obtenido?*

Gracias, y ahora vamos a hablar un poco acerca de su trabajo:
1. *¿Donde trabaja corrientemente?*
2. *¿Cuanto tiempo tiene trabajando ahí?*
3. *¿Descríbame que tipo de tareas hace en ese trabajo?*

Ahora hablemos un poco acerca de su comunicación y relaciones con otras personas en el trabajo. . . .

Comunicación en el Trabajo

1. Por favor, hábleme un poco acerca de sus experiencias diarias con otras personas en el trabajo:

   a. *Durante la mayoría de su día de trabajo, con quien usted habla mas regularmente? (Por ejemplo—supervisor, compañeros de trabajo, clientes. Puede nombrar títulos y nombres si quiere.)*

   b. *¿Que tan frecuentemente ustedes hablan?*

   c. *¿De que tipo de temas ustedes hablan?*

   d. *¿Hay alguna persona con la cual usted no habla o casi nunca habla? ¿Por que si o no?*

   e. *Si inglés es su segunda lengua: ¿usted alguna vez habla en su idioma nativo en el trabajo? (Hablar de los detalles.)*

      i. *¿Que tan bueno usted cree es su inglés?*

      ii. *¿Usted cree que el uso del idioma afecta su comunicación diaria con otras personas? ¿Si aplica, como afecta? ¿Si no aplica, por que no afecta?*

      iii. *¿Cuándo habla usted inglés con otras personas en el trabajo?*

      iv. *¿Alguna vez habla español en el trabajo? ¿Si aplica, con quien? ¿De que tipo de cosas hablan usualmente? ¿Como se siente hablando en español en su trabajo?*

      v. *¿Alguna vez personas que no hablan español como primera lengua le hablan a usted en español? Si aplica, deme un ejemplo por favor. Cuando esto ocurre, como usted se siente cuando esta persona(s) le hablan en español? Cuando esa persona(s) le hablan a usted en español, usted usualmente responde en español o en inglés? Por que si/no?*

      vi. *A usted le gustaría que mas personas alrededor suyo en el trabajo hablaran su idioma nativo? Por que si/no?*

2. Por favor describa los tipos de relaciones que usted ha podido desarrollar en el trabajo con las personas que hemos discutido hasta ahora (Ejemplo—supervisores, compañeros de trabajo, o clientes)

   a. *Por que usted cree que esas relaciones se han formado y desarrollado de esa manera? (Discuta cada relación individualmente.)*

3. Alguna vez alguien le ha pedido su sugerencia/opinión acerca de tareas, problemas o situaciones relacionada con el trabajo?

   a. *¿Si aplica, como usted ha respondido?*

4. Alguna vez ha ofrecido su sugerencia/opinión acerca de tareas, problemas o situaciones relacionada con el trabajo sin que nadie se la pida?

    a. *¿Por que si/no? Si aplica, por favor expliqueme . . .*

Ahora hábleme un poco acerca de las personas con las cuales usted interactua en el trabajo . . .

1. ¿De las personas con las cuales usted tiene contacto diario en el trabajo, a quien usted percibe como similar a usted?

    a. *[Por cada persona:] Por favor digame quien es, sus posiciones, sus antecedentes. ¿Como es cada persona similar a usted?*

2. Como usted describiria su comunicación con estas personas que uste percibe como similares a usted?

    a. *Me puede proveer algunos ejemplos de sus interacciones diarias con estas personas:*

        i. *¿Como se hablan el uno al otro?*

        ii. *¿Como ellos tienden a responderle a usted y vice versa?*

        iii. *¿Hay algunas conversaciones o eventos en particular que resaltan?*

3. ¿De las personas con las cuales usted tiene contacto diario en el trabajo, a quien usted percibe como diferente a usted?

    a. *[Por cada persona:] Por favor digame quien es, sus posiciones, sus antecedentes. ¿Como es cada persona diferente a usted?*

4. ¿Como usted describiria su comunicación con las personas que uste percibe como diferente a usted?

    a. *Me puede proveer algunos ejemplos de sus interacciones diarias con estas personas:*

        i. *¿Como se hablan el uno al otro?*

        ii. *¿Como ellos tienden a responderle a usted y vice versa?*

        iii. *¿Hay algunas conversaciones o eventos en particular que resaltan?*

Ahora me gustaría que hablemos de como usted percibe como otras personas le responden a usted como individuo. . . .

Comunicación Organizativa e Identidad Social

1. Usted percibe que hay algo acerca de usted como individuo que influye como otras personas se comunican con usted y vice versa en el trabajo?

    a. Por ejemplo—como otras personas lo/la perciben a usted; la impresion que ellos/ellas tienen de usted y vice versa relacionado con su:

        i. *Raza/grupo étnico: ¿Usted cree que su raza influye como otras personas se comunican con usted y vice versa? (Supervisores, compañeros de trabajo, clientes) Si aplica, por que usted cree que eso pasa? ¿Me puede dar algunos ejemplos?*

        ii. *Estatus como imigrante: ¿Usted cree que es porque usted es un imigrante Latino, esto influye como supervisores, compañeros de trabajo, o clientes se comunican con usted y vice versa?*

        iii. *Clase social: ¿Usted cree que su clase social influye como otras personas, incluyendo supervisores, compañeros de trabajo y clientes, lo/la perciben y se comunican con usted en el trabajo y vice versa?*

        iv. *Ocupacion: ¿Usted siente que su ocupacion como trabajador de servicio influye como otras personas se comunican con usted y vice versa?*

        v. *¿Como usted consiguio su trabajo como trabajador de servicio/conserje?*

        vi. *¿Como se siente con su trabajo?*

2. Alguna vez ha percibido que alguien lo/la ha maltratado o lo/la ha tratado injustamente en el trabajo? (Por ejemplo—supervisores, compañeros de trabajo, clientes)

    a. *Si aplica, por favor hábleme un poco acerca de esta(s) experiencia(s).*

3. Alguna vez ha sentido ha lo han tratado con favoritismo en el trabajo.

    a. *¿Si aplica, porque usted cree que este ha sido el caso?*

    b. *Puede describir alguna(s) de esta(s) experiencia(s) por favor.*

El Lugar de Trabajo (Estructuras y Cultura en la Organización)

1. ¿Que tan frecuentemente usted interactua con personas mas altas en la organizacion? (Ejemplo—los jefes de su jefe)

    a. *Si no frecuentemente, ¿le gustaría? ¿Usted siente que tener contacto con estas personas es importante? ¿Por que si/no?*

2. Como usted percibe la Universidad como lugar de trabajo? ¿Es importante para usted que trabaja en una Universidad? ¿Como compararia la Universidad con otros lugares en que ha trabajado?

3. ¿Como percibe su departamento (Housing and Dining Services, Facilities Management, SU [Student Union], Student Recreation Center) como lugar de trabajo?

a. *¿Usted sabe acerca de otros trabajadores de servicio y sus relaciones/comunicación con otras personas en esos departamentos?*

b. *¿Como se compara(n) con la suya aqui en su departamento?*

4. Me puede describir los lugares donde usted pasa su tiempo en un día tipico de trabajo?

   a. *¿Áreas que tiene que limpiar?*

   b. *¿El cuarto o sala de recreo?*

5. ¿En un día tipico de trabajo, cuanto tiempo pasa en estas áreas?

6. Usted siente que el tipo de trabajo que usted hace influye con quie usted habla y que tan frecuentemente? ¿Como?

7. ¿Le gustaría tener mas contacto con otras personas en el trabajo? Por que si/no?

Preguntas Finales

1. ¿Sus relaciones con otras personas en el trabajo afectan su calidad de vida fuera del trabajo? ¿Si aplica, como?

2. ¿Hay algunos cambios que usted le gustaría ver en cuanto al modo como otras personas se comunican con usted en el trabajo? ¿Si aplica, quien? ¿Cuales serian los cambios?

3. ¿Hay algunos cambios que usted le gustaría ver en cuanto al modo como usted se comunica con otras personas en el trabajo? ¿Si aplica, quien? ¿Cuales serian los cambios?

4. ¿Hay alguna(s) otra(s) cosa(s) que seria(n) importante que nosotros hablemos de ellas relacionadas con sus experiencias de comunicación en el trabajo? ¿Si aplica, por ejemplo, que? ¿Con quien?

Declaracion de Despedida

Aqui concluye nuestra conversación, Sra./Sr._____. Muchas gracias por su tiempo y atención. De nuevo, esta información será usada solamente para esta investigación y su nombre no será usado en el reporte final. Le puedo proveer una copia del reporte si asi lo desea. Finalmente, muchas gracias por su tiempo; tenga un buen día.

REFERENCES

Abu Bakar, H., Mohamad, B., & Mustaffa, C. S. (2007). Superior–subordinate communication dimensions and working relationship: Gender preferences in a Malaysian organization. *Journal of Intercultural Communication Research, 36,* 51–69. https://doi.org/10.1080/1747575070126528

Abu Bakar, H., & Mustaffa, C. S. (2008, May). *An investigation of the mediating role of superior-subordinate communication practices on relations between LMX and commitment to work-group in a Malaysian organization* [Paper presentation]. International Communication Association meeting, San Diego, CA, United States.

Acker, J. (1990). Hierarchies, jobs, bodies: A theory of gendered organizations. *Gender & Society, 4,* 139–158. https://doi.org/10.1177/089124390004002002

Adkins, L., & Lury, C. (1999). The labour of identity: Performing identities, performing economies. *Economy and Society, 28,* 598–614. https://doi.org/10.1080/03085149900000020

Agarwal, V. (2020). Patient communication of chronic pain in the complementary and alternative medicine therapeutic relationship. *Journal of Patient Experience, 7*(2), 238–244. https://doi.org/10.1177/2374373519826137

Al-Amer, R., Ramjan, L., Glew, P., Darwish, M., & Salamonson, Y. (2015). Translation of interviews from a source language to a target language: Examining issues in cross-cultural health care research. *Journal of Clinical Nursing, 24*(9–10), 1151–1162. https://doi.org/10.1111/jocn.12681

Al-Amer, R., Ramjan, L., Glew, P., Darwish, M., & Salamonson, Y. (2016). Language translation challenges with Arabic speakers participating in qualitative research studies. *International Journal of Nursing Studies, 54,* 150–157. https://doi.org/10.1016/j.ijnurstu.2015.04.010

Aldama, A. J. (2001). *Disrupting savagism: Intersecting Chicana/o, Mexicana/o, and Native American struggles for representation.* Duke University Press.

Aldama, A. J., & Aldama, F. L. (Eds.). (2020). *Decolonizing Latinx masculinities*. University of Arizona Press. https://www.jstor.org/stable/j.ctv13xprdp

Aldama, F. L., & González, C. (2018). *Latinx studies: The key concepts*. Routledge.

Alkhazraji, K. M., Gardner, W. L., Martin, J. S., & Paolillo, J. G. P. (1997). The acculturation of immigrants to U.S. organizations: The case of Muslim employees. *Management Communication Quarterly, 11*, 217–265. https://doi.org/10.1177/0893318997112003

Allen, B. J. (1995). "Diversity" and organizational communication. *Journal of Applied Communication Research, 23*, 143–155. https://doi.org/10.1080/00909889509365420

Allen, B. J. (1996). Feminist standpoint theory: A Black woman's (re)view of organizational socialization. *Communication Studies, 47*, 257–271. https://doi.org/10.1080/10510979609368482

Allen, B. J. (2000). "Learning the ropes": A Black feminist standpoint analysis. In P. M. Buzzanell (Ed.), *Rethinking organizational & managerial communication from feminist perspectives* (pp. 177–208). Sage.

Allen, B. J. (2005). Social constructionism. In S. K. May & D. K. Mumby (Eds.), *Engaging organizational communication theory & research* (pp. 35–53). Sage.

Allen, B. J. (2007). Theorizing communication and race. *Communication Monographs, 74*, 259–264. https://doi.org/10.1080/03637750701393055

Allen, B. J. (2009). Racial harassment in the workplace. In P. Lutgen-Sandvik & B. D. Sypher (Eds.), *Destructive organizational communication: Processes, consequences, and constructive ways of organizing* (pp. 164–183). Routledge.

Allen, B. J. (2010). A proposal for concerted collaboration between critical scholars of intercultural and organizational communication. In T. K. Nakayama & R. T. Halualani (Eds.), *The handbook of critical intercultural communication* (pp. 585–592). Wiley. https://doi.org/10.1002/9781444390681

Allen, B. J. (2017). Diversity. In C. Scott & L. K. Lewis (Eds.), *The international encyclopedia of organizational communication*. Wiley. https://doi.org/10.1002/9781118955567

Allen, B. J. (in press). *Difference matters: Communicating social identity* (3rd ed.). Waveland Press.

Allen, M. W. (1995). Communication concepts related to perceived organizational support. *Western Journal of Communication, 59*(4), 326–346. https://doi.org/10.1080/10570319509374525

Allen, T. D., McManus, S. E., & Russell, J. E. A. (1999). Newcomer socialization and stress: Formal peer relationships as a source of support. *Journal of Vocational Behavior, 54*, 453–470. https://doi.org/10.1006/jvbe.1998.1674

Alvarez, W. (2016). The Latino/a immigrant myth and the (im)possibility of realizing communal appreciation. In S. K. Camara & D. K. Drummond (Eds.), *Communicating prejudice: An appreciative inquiry* (pp. 64–73). Nova Science.

Alvarez, W. (2017). Phenomenology of cultural communication. In Y. Y. Kim (Ed.), *International encyclopedia of intercultural communication*. Wiley. https://doi.org/10.1002/9781118783665

Alvarez, W. (2018). Disciplining the immigrant body through collective bullying. In R. West & C. Beck (Eds.), *The handbook of communication and bullying* (pp. 64–69). Routledge.

Alvarez, W. (2021). A historic first: The president of the United States as/is a cyberbully. In L. R. Salazar (Ed.), *Handbook of research on cyberbullying and online harassment in the workplace* (pp. 216–241). IGI Global.

Alvarez, W. (2022). Bad hombres! do-nothing Democrats! and . . . oh yes, Mexico: Donald J. Trump's myth-making machine and overcoming a politics of division in the age of Twitter. In L. M. Chao & C. Wang (Eds.), *Communicating across differences: Negotiating identity, privilege, and marginalization in the 21st century* (pp. 19–44). Cognella.

Alvarez, W., Bauer, J. C., & Eger, E. K. (2015). (Making a) difference in the organizational communication undergraduate course. *Management Communication Quarterly, 29*(2), 302–308. https://doi.org/10.1177/0893318915571352

Alvarez, W., Orbe, M. P., Urban, E. L., & Tavares, N. A. (2012). Transnational Dominican culture through phenomenological analysis. In A. Kurylo (Ed.), *Inter/cultural communication: Representation and construction of culture in everyday interaction* (pp. 214–221). Sage.

Alvesson, M. (2000). Social identity and the problem of loyalty in knowledge-intensive companies. *Journal of Management Studies, 37*, 1101–1123. https://doi.org/10.1111/1467-6486.00218

Alvesson, M., & Willmott, H. (2002). Identity regulation as organizational control: Producing the appropriate individual. *Journal of Management Studies, 39*, 619–644. https://doi.org/10.1111/1467-6486.00305

Amason, P., Watkins-Allen, M., & Holmes, S. A. (1999). Social support and acculturative stress in the multicultural workplace. *Journal of Applied Communication Research, 27*, 310–334. https://doi.org/10.1080/00909889909365543

Amaya, H. (2007a). Latino immigrants in the American discourses of citizenship and nationalism during the Iraqi war. *Critical Discourse Studies, 4*, 237–256. https://doi.org/10.1080/17405900701656841

Amaya, H. (2007b). Performing acculturation: Rewriting the Latina/o immigrant self. *Text & Performance Quarterly, 27*, 194–212. https://doi.org/10.1080/10462930701412320

Ambrose, M. L., Harland, L. K., & Kulick, C. T. (1991). Influence of social comparisons on perceptions of organizational fairness. *Journal of Applied Psychology, 76*, 239–246. https://doi.org/10.1037/0021-9010.76.2.239

Anderson, L. B., Ruiz-Mesa, K., Jones-Bodie, A., Waldbuesser, C., Hall, J., Broeckelman-Post, M. A., & Hosek, A. M. (2020). I second that emotion: A collaborative examination of emotions felt in course administration work. *Journal of Contemporary Ethnography, 49*(2), 201–228. https://doi.org/10.1177/0891241619873130

Aparicio, F. R., & Chávez-Silverman, S. (1997). *Tropicalizations: Transcultural representations of Latinidad.* University Press of New England.

Ardener, E. (1978). Some outstanding problems in the analysis of events. In G. Schwinner (Ed.), *Yearbook of symbolic anthropology* (pp. 103–121). C. Hurst.

Ardener, S. (Ed.). (1975). *Perceiving women.* Wiley.

Artz, L. (1998). African-Americans and higher education: An exigence in need of applied communication. *Journal of Applied Communication Research, 26*, 210–213. https://doi.org/10.1080/00909889809365502

Ashcraft, K. L. (2005). Resistance through consent? Occupational identity, organizational form, and the maintenance of masculinity among commercial airline pilots. *Management Communication Quarterly, 19*, 67–90. https://doi.org/10.1177/0893318905276560

Ashcraft, K. L. (2007). Appreciating the "work" of discourse: Occupational identity and difference as organizing mechanisms in the case of commercial airline pilots. *Discourse & Communication, 1*, 9–36. https://doi.org/10.1177/1750481307071982

Ashcraft, K. L. (2017). "Submission" to the rule of excellence: Ordinary affect and precarious resistance in the labor of organization and management studies. *Organization, 24*(1), 36–58.

Ashcraft, K. L., & Allen, B. J. (2003). The racial foundation of organizational communication. *Communication Theory, 13*, 5–38. https://doi.org/10.1111/j.1468-2885.2003.tb00280.x

Ashforth, B. E. (2019). Stigma and legitimacy: Two ends of a single continuum or different continua altogether? *Journal of Management Inquiry, 28*(1), 22–30. https://doi.org/10.1177/1056492618790900

Ashforth, B. E., & Kreiner, G. E. (1999). "How can you do it?" Dirty work and the challenge of constructing of positive identity. *Academy Management Review, 24,* 215–235. http://www.jstor.org/action/showPublication?journalCode=acadmanarevi

Ashforth, B. E., Kreiner, G. E., Clark, M. A., & Fugate, M. (2007). Normalizing dirty work: Managerial tactics for countering occupational taint. *Academy of Management Journal, 50,* 149–174. https://doi.org/10.5465/amj.2007.24162092

Ashforth, B. E., Kreiner, G. E., Clark, M. A., & Fugate, M. (2017). Congruence work in stigmatized occupations: A managerial lens on employee fit with dirty work. *Journal of Organizational Behavior, 38*(8), 1260–1279. https://doi.org/10.1002/job.2201

Avgar, A., Boris, M. B., Bruno, R., & Chung, W. (2018). Worker voice and union revitalization: The role of contract enforcement at SEIU. *Labor Studies Journal, 43*(3), 209–233. https://doi.org/10.1177/0160449X18756739

Avila-Saavedra, G. (2010). A fish out of water: New articulations of U.S.–Latino identity on *Ugly Betty. Communication Quarterly, 58,* 133–147. https://doi.org/10.1080/01463371003773416

Awaad, T. (2003). Culture, cultural competency and psychosocial occupational therapy: A Middle Eastern perspective. *British Journal of Occupational Therapy, 66,* 409–413. http://www.cot.org.uk/Homepage/Library_and_Publications/British_Journal_of_Occupational_Therapy_(BJOT)

Ayllon, M. (2016). *Understanding the experiences of Latino/a non-academic employees at the University of Missouri* [Unpublished doctoral dissertation]. University of Missouri.

Babalola, S. S. (2016). The effect of leadership style, job satisfaction and employee–supervisor relationship on job performance and organizational commitment. *Journal of Applied Business Research, 32*(3), 935–946. https://doi.org/10.19030/jabr.v32i3.9667

Bakar, H. A., Mohamad, B., & Herman, I. (2020). Leader–Member exchange and superior-subordinate communication behavior: A case of a Malaysian organization. *Malaysian Management Journal, 8*(1), 83–93.

Barreto, A. A., & Lozano, K. (2017). Hierarchies of belonging: Intersecting race, ethnicity, and territoriality in the construction of U. S. citizenship. *Citizenship Studies, 21*(8), 999–1014. https://doi.org/10.1080/13621025.2017.1361906

Bartoo, H., & Sias, P. M. (2004). When enough is too much: Communication apprehension and employee information experiences. *Communication Quarterly, 52,* 15–26. https://doi.org/10.1080/01463370409370175

Baumeister, R. F., Zhang, L., & Vohs, K. D. (2004). Gossip as cultural learning. *Review of General Psychology, 8,* 111–121. https://doi.org/10.1037/1089-2680.8.2.111

Bell, K. E., Orbe, M. P., Drummond, D. K., & Camara, S. K. (2000). Accepting the challenge of centralizing without essentializing: Black feminist thought and African American women's communicative experiences. *Women's Studies in Communication, 23,* 41–62. https://doi.org/10.1080/07491409.2000.11517689

Bell, R. A., Tremblay, S. W., & Buerkel-Rothfuss, N. L. (1987). Interpersonal attraction as a communication accomplishment: Development of a measure of affinity-seeking competence. *Western Journal of Speech Communication, 51,* 1–18. https://doi.org/10.1080/10570318709374249

Berard, T. J. (2005). On multiple identities and educational contexts: Remarks on the study of inequalities and discrimination. *Journal of Language, Identity, and Education, 4,* 67–76. https://doi.org/10.1207/s15327701jlie0401_4

Berg, J. A. (2009). Core networks and Whites' attitudes toward immigrants and immigration policy. *Public Opinion Quarterly, 73,* 7–31. https://doi.org/10.1093/poq/nfp011

Berger, P. L., & Luckman, T. (1966). *The social construction of reality: A treatise in the sociology of knowledge.* Anchor Books.

Bernal, D. D. (2002). Critical race theory, Latino critical theory, and critical raced-gendered epistemologies: Recognizing students of color as holders and creators of knowledge. *Qualitative Inquiry, 8,* 105–126. https://doi.org/10.1177/107780040200800107

Bernstein, B. (1971). *Class, codes, and control: Vol. 1. Theoretical studies towards a sociology of language.* Routledge.

Bernstein, B. (1974). *Class, codes, and control: Vol. 4. Structuring of pedagogical discourse.* Routledge.

Bisel, R. S., Messersmith, A. S., & Kelley, K. M. (2012). Supervisor-subordinate communication: Hierarchical mum effect meets organizational learning. *The Journal of Business Communication, 49*(2), 128–147. https://doi.org/10.1177/0021943612436972

Bisseret, N. (1979). *Education, class language, and ideology.* Routledge and Kegan Paul.

Blair, M., & Liu, M. (2019). Ethnically Chinese and culturally American: Exploring bicultural identity negotiation and co-cultural communication of Chinese-American female adoptees. *Journal of International and Intercultural Communication,* 1–19. https://doi.org/10.1080/17513057.2019.1649710

Bogel-Burroughs, N. (2019, August 9). "I'm the shooter": El Paso suspect confessed to targeting Mexicans, police say. *The New York Times.* https://www.nytimes.com/2019/08/09/us/el-paso-suspect-confession.html

Bourdieu, P. (1987). What makes a social class? On the theoretical and practical existence of groups. *Berkeley Journal of Sociology, 22,* 1–18.

Bourdieu, P. (1991). *Language and symbolic power.* Harvard University Press.

Bridgewater, M. J., & Buzzanell, P. M. (2010). Caribbean immigrant discourses: Cultural, moral, and personal stories about workplace communication in the United States. *Journal of Business Communication, 47,* 235–265. https://doi.org/10.1177/0021943610369789

Brown, L. A., & Roloff, M. E. (2015). Organizational citizenship behavior, organizational communication, and burnout: The buffering role of perceived organizational support and psychological contracts. *Communication Quarterly, 63*(4), 384–404. https://doi.org/10.1080/01463373.2015.1058287

Burr, V. (1995). *An introduction to social constructionism.* Routledge.

Butler, J. (1995). Contingent foundations for a careful reading. In S. Benhabib, J. Butler, D. Cornell, & N. Fraser (Eds.), *Feminist contentions: A philosophical exchange* (pp. 35–57, 127–143). Routledge.

Buzzanell, P. M. (1994). Gaining a voice: Feminist organizational communication theorizing. *Management Communication Quarterly, 7,* 339–383. https://doi.org/10.1177/0893318994007004001

Buzzanell, P. M., & Houston, J. B. (2018). Communication and resilience: Multilevel applications and insights–a Journal of Applied Communication Research forum. *Journal of Applied Communication Research, 46*(1), 1–4. https://doi.org/10.1080/00909882.2017.1412086

Caillier, J. G. (2017). The impact of high-quality workplace relationships in public organizations. *Public Administration, 95*(3), 638–653. https://doi.org/10.1111/padm.12328

Callahan, L. (2006). English or Spanish?! Language accommodation in New York City service encounters. *Intercultural Pragmatics, 3,* 29–53. https://doi.org/10.1515/IP.2006.002

Camara, S. K., & Orbe, M. P. (2010). Analyzing strategic responses to discriminatory acts: A co-cultural communicative investigation. *Journal of International and Intercultural Communication, 3*(2), 83–113. https://10.1080/17513051003611602

Campbell, K. L., Martin, M. M., & Wanzer, M. B. (2001). Employee perceptions of manager humor orientation, assertiveness, responsiveness, approach/avoidance strategies, and satisfaction. *Communication Research Reports, 18,* 67–74. https://doi.org/10.1080/08824090109384783

Carter, N. M., & Pérez, E. O. (2016). Race and nation: How racial hierarchy shapes national attachments. *Political Psychology, 37*(4), 497–513. https://doi.org/10.1111/pops.12270

Cha, M. K., Yi, Y., & Lee, J. (2020). When people low in social class become a persuasive source of communication: Social class of other donors and charitable donations. *Journal of Business Research, 112,* 45–55. https://doi.org/10.1016/j.jbusres.2020.02.039

Chaney, K. E., & Sanchez, D. T. (2018). The endurance of interpersonal confrontations as a prejudice reduction strategy. *Personality and Social Psychology Bulletin, 44*(3), 418–429. https://doi.org/10.1177/0146167217741344

Chávez, K. R. (2009). Embodied translation: Dominant discourse and communication with migrant bodies-as-a-text. *Howard Journal of Communications, 20,* 18–36. https://doi.org/10.1080/10646170802664912

Chávez, L. R. (2008). *The Latino threat narrative: Constructing immigrants, citizens, and the nation.* Stanford University Press.

Chávez, L. R. (2017). *Anchor babies and the challenge of birthright citizenship.* Stanford University Press.

Cho, J. (2014). Impacts of information-providers' perceived cultural backgrounds on information-seeking behaviors: Investigation of American employees' information-seeking behaviors in a Korean multinational corporation in the U.S. *International Journal of Intercultural Relations, 41,* 66–79. https://doi.org/10.1016/j.ijintrel.2014.05.003

Choi, C. W., & Berhó, D. (2016). Ethnic identity maintenance within the Latino-American church: A structuration perspective. *Journal of Intercultural Communication Research, 45*(2), 91–107. https://doi.org/10.1080/17475759.2015.1086811

Choi, J., Kushner, K. E., Mill, J., & Lai, D. W. (2012). Understanding the language, the culture, and the experience: Translation in cross-cultural research. *International Journal of Qualitative Methods, 11*(5), 652–665. https://doi.org/10.1177/160940691201100508

Cisneros, J. D. (2008). Contaminated communities: The metaphor of "immigrant as a pollutant" in media representations of immigration. *Rhetoric & Public Affairs, 11,* 569–602. http://doi.org/10.1353/rap.0.0068

Cissna, K. N. (2000). Applied communication research in the 21st century. *Journal of Applied Communication Research, 28,* 169–173. https://doi.org/10.1080/00909880009365563\

Ciszek, E. L. (2017). Advocacy communication and social identity: An exploration of social media outreach. *Journal of Homosexuality, 64*(14), 1993–2010. https://doi.org/10.1080/00918369.2017.1293402

Clair, R. P. (Ed.). (2003). *Expressions of ethnography: Novel approaches to qualitative methods.* State University of New York Press.

Clark, L., & Chevrette, R. (2017). Thick description. In J. Matthes, C. S. Davis, & R. F. Potter (Eds.), *The international encyclopedia of communication research methods.* Wiley. https://doi.org/10.1002/9781118901731

Cohen, M., & Avanzino, S. (2010). We are people first: Framing organizational assimilation experiences of the physically disabled using co-cultural theory. *Communication Studies, 61*(3), 272–303. https://doi.org/10.1080/10510971003791203

Colbert, A. E., Bono, J. E., & Purvanova, R. K. (2016). Flourishing via workplace relationships: Moving beyond instrumental support. *Academy of Management Journal, 59*(4), 1199–1223. https://doi.org/10.5465/amj.2014.0506

Collier, M. J. (1991). Conflict competence within African, Mexican, and Anglo-American friend-ships. In S. Ting-Toomey & F. Korzenny (Eds.), *Cross-cultural interpersonal communication* (pp. 132–154). Sage.

Collins, B. J., Burrus, C. J., & Meyer, R. D. (2014). Gender differences in the impact of leadership styles on subordinate embeddedness and job satisfaction. *The Leadership Quarterly, 25*(4), 660–671. https://doi.org/10.1016/j.leaqua.2014.02.003

Collins, P. H. (1986). Learning from the outsider within: The sociological significance of Black feminist thought. *Social Problems, 33*, S14–S23. https://doi.org/10.1525/sp.1986.6.03a00020

Collins, P. H. (2000). *Black feminist thought: Knowledge, consciousness, and the politics of empow-erment* (Rev. ed.). Routledge.

Compton, C. A. (2016). Managing mixed messages: Sexual identity management in a changing U.S. workplace. *Management Communication Quarterly, 30*(4), 415–440. https://doi.org/10.1177/0893318916641215

Cox, T. H. (1993). *Cultural diversity in organizations: Theory, research, and practice.* Berret-Koehler.

Cox, T. H., & Nkomo, S. M. (1990). Invisible men and women: A status report on race as a vari-able in organizational behavior research. *Journal of Organizational Behavior, 2*, 419–433. https://doi.org/10.1002/job.4030110604

Cranford, C. (1998). Gender and citizenship in the restructuring of janitorial work in Los Ange-les. *Gender Issues, 16*, 25–51. https://doi.org/10.1007/s12147-998-0009-x

Cranmer, G. A., & Myers, S. A. (2015). Sports teams as organizations: A leader–member exchange perspective of player communication with coaches and teammates. *Communica-tion & Sport, 3*(1), 100–118. https://doi.org/10.1177/2167479513520487

Crenshaw, K. W. (1991). Mapping the margins: Intersectionality, identity politics, and violence against women of color. *Stanford Law Review, 43*, 1241–1299. https://doi.org/10.2307/1229039

Crenshaw, K. W. (1992). Gender, race, and the politics of Supreme Court appointments: The import of the Anita Hill/Clarence Thomas hearings: Race, gender, and sexual harassment. *Southern California Law Review, 65*, 1467–1476.

Crenshaw, K. W. (2017). *On intersectionality: Essential writings.* The New Press.

Crocker, J., & Major, B. (1989). Social stigma and self-esteem: The self-protective properties of stigma. *Psychological Review, 96*, 608–630. https://doi.org/10.1037/0033-295X.96.4.608

Cruz, J. M. (2017). Invisibility and visibility in alternative organizing: A communicative and cul-tural model. *Management Communication Quarterly, 31*(4), 614–639. https://doi.org/10.1177/0893318917725202

Dansereau, F., Graen, G., & Haga, W. J. (1975). A vertical dyad linkage approach to leadership within formal organizations. *Organizational Behavior and Human Performance, 13*, 46–78. https://doi.org/10.1016/0030-5073(75)90005-7

Davis, S. M. (2018). Taking back the power: An analysis of Black women's communicative resis-tance. *Review of Communication, 18*(4), 301–318. https://doi.org/10.1080/15358593.2018.1461234

Davis, S. M. (2019). When sistahs support sistahs: A process of supportive communication about racial microaggressions among Black women. *Communication Monographs, 86*(2), 133–157. https://doi.org/10.1080/03637751.2018.1548769

DeChaine, D. R. (2009). Bordering the civic imaginary: Alienization, fence logic, and the Min-uteman Civil Defense Corps. *Quarterly Journal of Speech, 95*, 43–65. https://doi.org/10.1080/00335630802621078

Deetz, S. A. (1992). *Democracy in an age of corporate colonization: Developments in communica-tion and the politics of everyday life.* State University of New York Press.

Deetz, S. A. (2005). Critical theory. In S. K. May & D. K. Mumby (Eds.), *Engaging organizational communication theory & research* (pp. 85–111). Sage.

Deitch, E. A., Barsky, A., Butz, R. M., Chan, S., Brief, A. P., & Bradley, J. C. (2003). Subtle yet significant: The existence and impact of everyday racial discrimination in the workplace. *Human Relations, 56,* 1299–1324. https://doi.org/10.1177/00187267035611002

Delgado, F. (2009). Reflections on being/performing Latino identity in the academy. *Text and Performance Quarterly, 29,* 149–164. https://doi.org/10.1080/10462930902774858

Denzin, N. K., & Lincoln, Y. S. (Eds.). (2017). *Handbook of qualitative research* (5th ed.). Sage.

Doyle, J. (2000). *New community or new slavery? The emotional division of labour.* Industrial Society.

Drzwiecka, J. A. (2000). Discursive construction of differences: Ethnic immigrant identities and distinctions. In M. J. Collier (Ed.), *Constituting cultural difference through discourse* (pp. 241–270). Sage.

Dyer, J., & Keller-Cohen, D. (2000). The discursive construction of professional self through narratives of personal experience. *Discourse Studies, 2,* 283–304. https://doi.org/10.1177/1461445600002003002

Ehala, M. (2015). Ethnolinguistic vitality. In K. Tracy (Ed.), *The international encyclopedia of language and social interaction.* Wiley. https://doi.org/10.1002/9781118611463

Eilon, E. (1968). Taxonomy of communication. *Administrative Science Quarterly, 13,* 266–288. http://www.jstor.org/action/showPublication?journalCode=admisciequar

Ellwardt, L., Labianca, G. J., & Wittek, R. (2012). Who are the objects of positive and negative gossip at work?: A social network perspective on workplace gossip. *Social Networks, 34*(2), 193–205.

Etzion, D. (1984). Moderating effect of social support on the stress–burnout relationship. *Journal of Applied Psychology, 69,* 615–622. https://doi.org/10.1037/0021-9010.69.4.615

Ezzy, D. (2002). *Qualitative analysis: Practice and innovation.* Routledge.

Fairhurst, G. T. (1993). The leader–member exchange patterns of women leaders in industry: A discourse analysis. *Communication Monographs, 60,* 321–350. https://doi.org/10.1080/03637759309376316

Fairhurst, G. T., & Chandler, T. A. (1989). Social structure in leader–member interaction. *Communication Monographs, 56,* 215–239. https://doi.org/10.1080/03637758909390261

Fairhurst, G. T., Rogers, L. E., & Sarr, R. A. (1987). Manager–subordinate control patterns and judgments about the relationship. In M. McLaughlin (Ed.), *Communication yearbook* (Vol. 10, pp. 395–415). Sage.

Falcione, R. L., McCroskey, J. C., & Daly, J. A. (1977). Job satisfaction as a function of employees' communication apprehension, self-esteem, and perceptions of their immediate supervisors. In B. Ruben (Ed.), *Communication yearbook* (pp. 363–375). Sage.

Fan, Z., Grey, C., & Kärreman, D. (2020). Confidential gossip and organization studies. *Organization Studies,* 1–14. https://doi.org/10.1177/0170840620954016

Fay, M. J., & Kline, S. L. (2011). Coworker relationships and informal communication in high-intensity telecommuting. *Journal of Applied Communication Research, 39*(2), 144–163. https://doi.org/10.1080/00909882.2011.556136

Feinberg, M., Willer, R., Stellar, J., & Keltner, D. (2012). The virtues of gossip: Reputational information sharing as prosocial behavior. *Journal of Personality and Social Psychology, 102*(5), 1015–1030. https://doi.org/10.1037/a0026650

Fine, G. A. (1996). Justifying work: Occupational rhetorics as resources in restaurant kitchens. *Administrative Science Quarterly, 41,* 90–115. http://www.jstor.org/action/showPublication?journalCode=admisciequar

Fitzgerald, L. (2019). Unseen: The sexual harassment of low-income women in America. *Equality Diversity and Inclusion, 39*(1), 5–16. https://doi.org/10.1108/EDI-08-2019-0232

Fix, B., & Sias, P. M. (2006). Person-centered communication, leader member exchange, and employee job satisfaction. *Communication Research Reports, 23,* 35–44. https://doi.org/10.1080/17464090500535855

Flores, L. A. (2003). Constructing rhetorical borders: Peons, illegal aliens, and competing narratives of immigration. *Critical Studies in Media Communication, 20,* 362–387. https://doi.org/10.1080/0739318032000142025

Flores, L. A. (2018). Laboring to belong: Differentiation, spatial relocation, and the ironic presence of (un)documented immigrants in the United Farm Workers "Take Our Jobs" campaign. *Rhetoric & Public Affairs, 21*(3), 447–480.

Flores, L. A. (2020). Stoppage and the racialized rhetorics of mobility. *Western Journal of Communication, 84*(3), 247–263. https://doi.org/10.1080/10570314.2019.1676914

Flynn, M. (2018, November 2). An "invasion of illegal aliens." The oldest immigration fear-mongering metaphor in America. *The Washington Post.* https://www.washingtonpost.com/nation/2018/11/02/an-invasion-illegal-aliens-oldest-immigration-fear-mongering-metaphor-america/

Foucault, M. (1977). *Discipline and punish: The birth of the prison* (A. Sheridan, Trans.). Pantheon Books.

Frankenberg, R. (1993). *White women, race matters: The social construction of Whiteness.* University of Minnesota Press.

Frey, L. R. (1998). Communication and social justice research: Truth, justice, and the applied communication way. *Journal of Applied Communication Research, 26,* 155–164. https://doi.org/10.1080/00909889809365499

Frey, L. R., Russell, V., & German, J. (2020). Communication activism for social justice research. In H. D. O'Hair, M. J. O'Hair, E. B. Hester, & S. Geegan (Eds.), *The handbook of applied communication research* (pp. 731–746). Wiley.

Frey, L. R., & SunWolf. (2009). Across applied divides: Great debates of applied communication scholarship. In L. R. Frey & K. N. Cissna (Eds.), *Routledge handbook of applied communication research* (pp. 26–54). Routledge.

Fritz, J. H. (1997). Men's and women's organizational peer relationships: A comparison. *Journal of Business Communication, 34,* 27–46. https://doi.org/10.1177/002194369703400102

Gates, D. (2005, May). *Superior–subordinate dialogue among Caucasian, African American, and Latino/a American subordinates: Benefits of being buddies with the boss* [Paper presentation]. International Communication Association meeting, New York, NY, United States.

Gates, D. (2006, May). *Communication practices of Latino American workers: Strategizing and networking to attain organization success* [Paper presentation]. International Communication Association meeting, San Diego, CA, United States.

Gates, D. (2008, November). *Business communication: Identifying unconventional strategies to managing superior–subordinate relationships* [Paper presentation]. National Communication Association meeting, San Diego, CA, United States.

Genao-Homs, M. J., & Hull, A. (Producers & Directors). (2010). *In passing* [Film]. ATLAS Speaker Series.

Gergen, K. (1991). *The saturated self: Dilemmas of identity in contemporary life.* Basic Books.

Gibson, M. K., & Papa, M. J. (2000). The mud, the blood, and the beer guys: Organizational osmosis in blue-collar work groups. *Journal of Applied Communication Research, 28,* 68–88. https://doi.org/10.1080/00909880009365554

Giddens, A. (1984). *The constitution of society: Outline of the theory of structuration.* University of California Press.

Giles, H., & Sassoon, C. (1983). The effects of speaker's accent, social class background, and message style on British listeners' social judgments. *Language & Communication, 3,* 305–313. https://doi.org/10.1016/0271-5309(83)90006-X

Ginossar, T., & Nelson, S. (2010). La Comunidad Habla: Using Internet community-based information interventions to increase empowerment and access to health care of low-income Latino/a immigrants. *Communication Education, 59,* 328–343. https://doi.org/10.1080/03634521003628297

Givens, K. D., & McNamee, L. G. (2016). Understanding what happens on the other side of the door: Emotional labor, coworker communication, and motivation in door-to-door sales. *Journal of Ethnographic & Qualitative Research, 10*(3), 165–179.

Glaser, B. G., & Strauss, A. L. (2017). *The discovery of grounded theory: Strategies for qualitative research.* Routledge. https://doi.org/10.4324/9780203793206

Goffman, E. (1963). *Stigma: Notes on the management of spoiled identity.* Simon & Schuster.

Goffman, E. (1967). *Interaction ritual: Essays in face-to-face behavior.* Random House.

Gómez, L. E. (2018). *Manifest destinies: The making of the Mexican American race.* New York University Press.

Goodall, H. L., Jr. (2019). *Writing qualitative inquiry: Self, stories, and academic life.* Routledge.

Gordon, J., & Hartman, R. L. (2009). Affinity-seeking strategies and open communication in peer workplace relationships. *Atlantic Journal of Communication, 17,* 115–125. https://doi.org/10.1080/15456870902873184

Gordon, S., Adler, H., Day, J., & Sydnor, S. (2019). Perceived supervisor support: A study of select-service hotel employees. *Journal of Hospitality and Tourism Management, 38,* 82–90. https://doi.org/10.1016/j.jhtm.2018.12.002

Graen, G. B., & Cashman, J. (1975). A role-making model of leadership in formal organizations: A development approach. In J. G. Hunt & L. L. Larson (Eds.), *Leadership frontiers* (pp. 143–166). Kent University Press.

Graen, G. B., Dansereau, F., & Minami, T. (1972). Dysfunctional leadership styles. *Organizational Behavior and Human Performance, 7,* 216–236. https://doi.org/10.1016/0030 5073(72)90016-5

Graen, G. B., & Scandura, T. (1987). Toward a psychology of dyadic organizing. In B. M. Staw & L. L. Cummings (Eds.), *Research in organizational behavior* (Vol. 9, pp. 175–208). JAI.

Gregersen, F. (1979). Relationships between social class and language use. In J. L. Mey (Ed.), *Pragmalinguistics: Theory and practice* (pp. 171–194). Mouton.

Grosfoguel, R. (2003). *Colonial subjects: Puerto Ricans in a global perspective.* University of California Press.

Grosser, T. J., Lopez-Kidwell, V., & Labianca, G. (2010). A social network analysis of positive and negative gossip in organizational life. *Group & Organization Management, 35,* 177–212. https://doi.org/10.1177/1059601109360391

Guerra, A. (2019). *Saving public relations: Tackling the underrepresentation of Latino professionals in U.S. communications industry* [Unpublished master's thesis]. University of Southern California.

Hall, A. (2016). Exploring the workplace communication preferences of millennials. *Journal of Organizational Culture, Communications and Conflict, 20,* 35–44.

Halpern, M. (2019). Feminist standpoint theory and science communication. *Journal of Science Communication, 18*(4), C02. https://doi.org/10.22323/2.18040302

Han, E. J., & Price, P. G. (2018). Communicating across difference: Co-cultural theory, capital and multicultural families in Korea. *Journal of International and Intercultural Communication, 11*(1), 21–41. https://doi.org/10.1080/17513057.2017.1367026

Haraway, D. J. (1991). Situated knowledges: The science question in feminism and the privilege of partial perspective. In D. Haraway (Ed.), *Simians, cyborgs, and women: The reinvention of nature* (pp. 183–202). Routledge.

Harding, S. (Ed.). (1987). *Feminism and methodology: Social science issues.* Indiana University Press.

Harlos, K. P., & Pinder, C. C. (1999). Patterns of organizational injustice: A taxonomy of what employees regard as unjust. In J. Wagner (Ed.), *Advances in qualitative organizational research* (Vol. 2, pp. 97–125). JAI Press.

Hartnett, S. J. (1998). Lincoln and Douglas meet the abolitionist David Walker as prisoners debate slavery: Empowering education, applied communication, and social justice. *Journal of Applied Communication Research, 26,* 232–253. https://doi.org/10.1080/00909889809365503

Hartnett, S. J. (2018). Notes on, confessions about, and hopes for globalization. *Journal of Intercultural Communication Research, 47*(5), 434–438. https://doi.org/10.1080/17475759.2018.1480518

Hartsock, N. C. M. (1983). The feminist standpoint: Developing the ground for a specifically feminist historical materialism. In S. Harding & M. D. Hintikka (Eds.), *Discovering reality: Feminist perspectives on epistemology, metaphysics, methodology, and philosophy of science* (pp. 283–310). D. Reidel.

Hawkins, J. E. (2018). The practical utility and suitability of email interviews in qualitative research. *The Qualitative Report, 23*(2), 493–501.

Hebson, G. (2009). Renewing class analysis in studies of the workplace: A comparison of working-class and middle-class women's aspirations and identities. *Sociology, 43,* 27–44. https://doi.org/10.1177/0038038508099096

Hecht, M. L., & Choi, H. (2012). The communication theory of identity as a framework for message design. In H. Cho (Ed.), *Health communication message design* (pp. 137–152). Sage.

Hecht, M. L., Jackson, R. L., & Ribeau, S. A. (2003). *African American communication: Exploring identity and culture* (2nd ed.). Lawrence Erlbaum.

Hecht, M. L., Ribeau, S. A., & Sedano, M. V. (1990). A Mexican-American perspective on inter-ethnic communication. *International Journal of Intercultural Relations, 14,* 31–55. http://doi.org/10.1016/0147-1767(90)90046-Y

Hecht, M. L., Sedano, M. V., & Ribeau, S. A. (1993). Understanding culture, communication, and research: Applications to Chicanos and Mexican Americans. *International Journal of Intercultural Relations, 17,* 157–165. https://doi.org/10.1016/0147-1767(93)90022

Henry, P. (2001). An examination of the pathways through which social class impacts health outcomes. *Academy of Marketing Science Review, 1*(3), 165–177.

Herdman, A. O., Yang, J., & Arthur, J. B. (2017). How does leader–member exchange disparity affect teamwork behavior and effectiveness in work groups? The moderating role of leader-leader exchange. *Journal of Management, 43*(5), 1498–1523. https://doi.org/10.1177/0149206314556315

High, A. C., & Young, R. (2018). Supportive communication from bystanders of cyberbullying: Indirect effects and interactions between source and message characteristics. *Journal of Applied Communication Research, 46*(1), 28–51. https://doi.org/10.1080/00909882.2017.1412085

Hirschfeld Davis, J. (2018, May 17). Trump calls some unauthorized immigrants "animals" in rant. *The New York Times.* https://www.nytimes.com/2018/05/16/us/politics/trump-undocumented-immigrants-animals.html

Ho, S. S., Holloway, A., & Stenhouse, R. (2019). Analytic methods' considerations for the translation of sensitive qualitative data from Mandarin into English. *International Journal of Qualitative Methods, 18,* 160–174. https://doi.org/10.1177/1609406919868354

Hogg, M. A. (2018). Self-uncertainty, leadership preference, and communication of social identity. *Atlantic Journal of Communication, 26*(2), 111–121. https://doi.org/10.1080/15456870.2018.1432619

Holmer-Nadesan, M. (1996). Organizational identity and space of action. *Organization Studies, 17,* 49–81. https://doi.org/10.1177/017084069601700103

Holmes, J. (2005). Story-telling at work: A complex discursive resource for integrating personal, professional, and social identities. *Discourse Studies, 7,* 671–700. https://doi.org/10.1177/1461445605055422

Hood, J. C. (1988). From night to day: Timing and the management of janitorial work. *Journal of Contemporary Ethnography, 17,* 96–116. https://doi.org/10.1177/0891241688171004

hooks, b. (1989). *Talking back: Thinking feminist, thinking Black.* South End Press.

Hopson, M. C., & Orbe, M. P. (2007). Playing the game: Recalling dialectical tensions for Black men in oppressive organizational structures. *Howard Journal of Communications, 18,* 69–86. https://doi.org/10.1080/10646170601147481

House, J. S. (1981). *Work stress and social support.* Addison-Wesley.

Houston, M. (1997). When Black women talk with White women: Why dialogues are difficult. In A. González, M. Houston, & V. Chen (Eds.), *Our voices: Essays in culture, ethnicity, and communication* (2nd ed., pp. 187–194). Roxbury.

Houston, M., & Wood, J. T. (1996). Difficult dialogues, expanded horizons: Communicating across race and class. In J. T. Wood (Ed.), *Gendered relationships* (pp. 39–56). Mayfield.

Hsieh, Y. C. J., Sönmez, S., Apostolopoulos, Y., & Lemke, M. K. (2017). Perceived workplace mistreatment: Case of Latina hotel housekeepers. *Work, 56*(1), 55–65. https://doi.org/10.3233/WOR-162467

Huffman, T. (2018). Imagination, action, and justice: Trends and possibilities at the intersection of organizational communication and social justice. In P. J. Salem & E. Timmerman (Eds.), *Transformative practice and research in organizational communication* (pp. 292–306). IGI Global.

Hughes, E. C. (1951). Work and the self. In J. H. Rohrer & M. Sherif (Eds.), *Social psychology at the crossroads* (pp. 313–323). Harper & Brothers.

Hughes, E. C. (1962). Good people and dirty work. *Social Problems, 10,* 3–11. http://www.jstor.org/action/showPublication?journalCode=socialproblems

Hughes, E. C. (1971). *The sociological eye: Selected papers.* Aldine-Atherton.

Huspek, M. (1994). Oppositional codes and social class relations. *British Journal of Sociology, 45,* 79–102. https://doi.org/10.2307/591526

Huws, U. (2006). What will we do? The destruction of occupational identities in the "knowledge-based economy." *Monthly Review, 21,* 19–33. http://monthlyreview.org

Infante, D. A., & Gordon, W. I. (1985). Superiors' argumentativeness and verbal aggressiveness as a predictors of subordinates' satisfaction. *Human Communication Research, 12,* 117–125. https://doi.org/10.1111/j.1468-2958.1985.tb00069.x

Iwama, M. (2005). Occupation as a cross-cultural construct. In G. Whiteford & V. Wright-St. Clair (Eds.), *Occupation and practice in context* (pp. 242–253). Elsevier Health Sciences.

Jablin, F. M. (1979). Superior–subordinate communication: The state of the art. *Psychological Bulletin, 86,* 1201–1222. https://doi.org/10.1037/0033-2909.86.6.1201

Jackman, M. R. (1979). The subjective meaning of social class identification in the United States. *Public Opinion Quarterly, 1,* 444–462. https://doi.org/10.1086/268543

Jackman, M. R., & Sheuer-Senter, M. (1980). Images of social groups: Categorical or qualified? *Public Opinion Quarterly, 2,* 341–361. https://doi.org/10.1086/268601

Jackson, D., Trevisan, F., Pullen, E., & Silk, M. (2020). Towards a social justice disposition in communication and sport scholarship. *Communication & Sport, 8*(4–5), 435–451. https://doi.org/10.1177/2167479520932929

Jackson, R. L. (1999). *The negotiation of cultural identity: Perceptions of European Americans and African Americans.* Praeger.

Jacobs, T. (1971). *Leadership and exchange in formal organizations.* Human Resources Research Organization.

Ji, S., & Jan, I. U. (2020). Antecedents and consequences of frontline employee's trust-in-supervisor and trust-in-coworker. *Sustainability, 12*(2), 716–728. https://doi.org/10.3390/su12020716

Jian, G. (2012). Does culture matter? An examination of the association of immigrants' acculturation with workplace relationship quality. *Management Communication Quarterly, 26*(2), 295–321. https://doi.org/10.1177/0893318912440178

Jian, G. (2015). Leader–member exchange theory. In C. R. Berger, M. E. Roloff, S. R. Wilson, J. P. Dillard, J. Caughlin, & D. Solomon. *The international encyclopedia of interpersonal communication.* Wiley. https://doi.org/10.1002/9781118540190

Jian, G., & Dalisay, F. (2017). Conversation at work: The effects of leader–member conversational quality. *Communication Research, 44*(2), 177–197. https://doi.org/10.1177/0093650214565924

Jian, G., & Dalisay, F. (2018). Talk matters at work: The effects of leader–member conversational quality and communication frequency on work role stressors. *International Journal of Business Communication, 55*(4), 483–500. https://doi.org/10.1177/2329488415594157

Jiménez Román, M., & Flores, J. (Eds.). (2010). *The Afro-Latin@ reader: History and culture in the United States.* Duke University Press.

Jones, B. B. (2020). *Perceptions of preferential treatment at work and its effect on employee self-efficacy and job satisfaction* [Unpublished doctoral dissertation]. Trident University International.

Jones, K. P., Peddie, C. I., Gilrane, V. L., King, E. B., & Gray, A. L. (2016). Not so subtle: A meta-analytic investigation of the correlates of subtle and overt discrimination. *Journal of Management, 42*(6), 1588–1613. https://doi.org/10.1177/0149206313506466

Kahl, D. H., Jr. (2017). Addressing the challenges of critical communication pedagogy scholarship: Moving toward an applied agenda. *Journal of Applied Communication Research, 45*(1), 116–120. https://doi.org/10.1080/00909882.2016.1248468

Kamal Kumar, K., & Kumar Mishra, S. (2017). Subordinate–superior upward communication: Power, politics, and political skill. *Human Resource Management, 56*(6), 1015–1037. https://doi.org/10.1002/hrm.21814

Karreman, D., & Alvesson, M. (2001). Making newsmakers: Conversational identity at work. *Organization Studies, 22,* 59–89. https://doi.org/10.1177/017084060102200103

Kashima, Y., Kashima, E. S., Farsides, T., Kim, U., Strack, F., Werth, L., & Yuki, M. (2004). Culture and context-sensitive self: The amount and meaning of context-sensitivity of phenomenal self-differ across cultures. *Self and Identity, 3,* 125–141. https://doi.org/10.1080/13576500342000

Katz, D., & Kahn, R. L. (1966). *The social psychology of organizations.* Wiley.

Kim, K., & Baker, M. A. (2019). How the employee looks and looks at you: Building customer–employee rapport. *Journal of Hospitality & Tourism Research, 43*(1), 20–40. https://doi.org/10.1177/1096348017731130

Kim, Y. Y. (1977). Communication patterns of foreign immigrants in the process of acculturation. *Human Communication Research, 4,* 66–77. https://doi.org/10.1111/j.1468-2958.1977.tb00598.x

Kim, Y. Y. (1980). Explaining acculturation in a communication framework: An empirical test. *Communication Monographs, 47,* 156–179. https://doi.org/10.1080/03637758009376030

Kim, Y. Y. (2005). Adapting to a new culture: An integrative communication theory. In W. B. Gudykunst (Ed.), *Theorizing about intercultural communication* (pp. 375–400). Sage.

Kim, Y. Y. (2017). Cross-cultural adaptation. In J. F. Nussbaum (Ed.), *Oxford research encyclopedia of communication.* Oxford University Press. https://doi.org/10.1093/acrefore/9780190228613.013.21

Kluckhohn, F. R., & Strodbeck, F. L. (1961). *Variations in value orientations.* Greenwood Press.

Kniffin, K. M., Wansink, B., Griskevicius, V., & Wilson, D. S. (2014). Beauty is in the in-group of the beholded: Intergroup differences in the perceived attractiveness of leaders. *The Leadership Quarterly, 25*(6), 1143–1153. https://doi.org/10.1016/j.leaqua.2014.09.001

Kram, K. E., & Isabella, L. A. (1985). Mentoring alternatives: The role of peer relationships in career developments. *Academy of Management Journal, 28,* 110–132. https://doi.org/10.2307/256064

Kramarae, C. (1981). *Women and men speaking: Frameworks for analysis.* Newbury House.

Kramarae, C. (2005). Muted group theory and communication: Asking dangerous questions. *Women & Language, 28,* 55–61.

Kramer, M. W. (1995). A longitudinal study of superior–subordinate communication during job transfers. *Human Communication Research, 22,* 39–64. https://doi.org/10.1111/j.1468-2958.1995.tb00361.x

Kramer, M. W. (2017). Supervisor–subordinate communication. In C. Scott & L. K. Lewis (Eds.), *The international encyclopedia of organizational communication.* Wiley. https://doi.org/10.1002/9781118955567

Kreiner, G. E., Ashforth, B. E., & Sluss, D. M. (2006). Identity dynamics in occupational dirty work: Integrating social identity and system justification perspectives. *Organization Science, 17,* 619–636. https://doi.org/10.1287/orsc.1060.0208

Krone, K. J. (1992). A comparison of organizational, structural, and relationship effects on subordinates' upward influence choices. *Communication Quarterly, 40,* 1–15. https://doi.org/10.1080/01463379209369816

Lakoff, G., & Johnson, M. (1980). *Metaphors we live by.* University of Chicago Press.

Lakoff, R. T. (2017). The hollow man: Donald Trump, populism, and post-truth politics. *Journal of Language and Politics, 16*(4), 595–606.

Laliberte-Rudman, D., & Dennhardt, S. (2008). Shaping knowledge regarding occupation: Examining the cultural underpinnings of the evolving concept of occupational identity. *Australian Occupational Therapy Journal, 55,* 153–162. https://doi.org/10.1111/j.1440-1630.2007.00715.x

Langman, J., & Shi, X. (2020). Gender, language, identity, and intercultural communication. In J. Jackson (Ed.), *The Routledge handbook of language and intercultural communication* (2nd ed., pp. 213–231). Routledge.

Liao, S. S., Hu, D. C., Chung, Y. C., & Chen, L. W. (2017). LMX and employee satisfaction: Mediating effect of psychological capital. *Leadership & Organization Development Journal, 38*(3), 433–449. https://doi.org/10.1108/LODJ-12-2015-0275

Lindlof, T. R., & Taylor, B. C. (2017). *Qualitative communication research methods* (4th ed.). Sage.

Lloyd, K. J., Boer, D., Keller, J. W., & Voelpel, S. (2015). Is my boss really listening to me? The impact of perceived supervisor listening on emotional exhaustion, turnover intention, and organizational citizenship behavior. *Journal of Business Ethics, 130*(3), 509–524. https://doi. org/10.1007/s10551-014-2242-4

Loi, R., Chan, K. W., & Lam, L. W. (2014). Leader–member exchange, organizational identification, and job satisfaction: A social identity perspective. *Journal of Occupational and Organizational Psychology, 87*(1), 42–61. https://doi.org/10.1111/joop.12028

Lopez, G. I., Figueroa, M., Connor, S. E., & Maliski, S. L. (2008). Translation barriers in conducting qualitative research with Spanish speakers. *Qualitative Health Research, 18*, 1729–1737. https://doi.org/10.1177/1049732308325857

Love, M. S., & Dustin, S. L. (2014). An investigation of coworker relationships and psychological collectivism on employee propensity to take charge. *The International Journal of Human Resource Management, 25*(9), 1208–1226. https://doi.org/10.1080/09585192.2013.826712

Lybarger, J. E., Rancer, A. S., & Lin, Y. (2017). Superior–subordinate communication in the workplace: Verbal aggression, nonverbal immediacy, and their joint effects on perceived superior credibility. *Communication Research Reports, 34*(2), 124–133. https://doi.org/10.1080/08824096.2016.1252909

Madsen, V. T. (2016). Constructing organizational identity on internal social media: A case study of coworker communication in Jyske Bank. *International Journal of Business Communication, 53*(2), 200–223. https://doi.org/10.1177/2329488415627272

Magolda, P. M. (2016). *The lives of campus custodians: Insights into corporatization and civic disengagement in the academy.* Stylus.

Mahalingam, R., Jagannathan, S., & Selvaraj, P. (2019). Decasticization, dignity, and "dirty work" at the intersections of caste, memory, and disaster. *Business Ethics Quarterly, 29*(2), 213–239.

Maji, S., & Dixit, S. (2020). Exploring self-silencing in workplace relationships: A qualitative study of female software engineers. *The Qualitative Report, 25*(6), 1505–1525.

Major, B., & O'Brien, L. T. (2005). The social psychology of stigma. *Annual Review of Psychology, 56*, 393–421. https://doi.org/10.1146/annurev.psych.56.091103.070137

Mallison, C., & Brewster, Z. W. (2005). "Blacks and bubbas": Stereotypes, ideology, and categorization processes in restaurant servers' discourse. *Discourse & Society, 16*, 787–807. https://doi.org/10.1177/0957926505056664

Mandal, P. C. (2018). Translation in qualitative studies: Evaluation criteria and equivalence. *The Qualitative Report, 23*(10), 2529–2537.

Marra, M., & Holmes, J. (2008). Constructing ethnicity in New Zealand workplace stories. *Text and Talk, 28*, 397–419. https://doi.org/10.1515/TEXT.2008.019

Marshall, S. L., & While, A. E. (1994). Interviewing respondents who have English as a second language: Challenges encountered and suggestions for other researchers. *Journal of Advanced Nursing, 19*, 566–571. https://doi.org/10.1111/j.1365-2648.1994.tb01122.x

Martínez, D. E., & Gonzalez, K. E. (2020). "Latino" or "Hispanic"? The sociodemographic correlates of panethnic label preferences among US Latinos/Hispanics. *Sociological Perspectives,* 1–22.

Mastro, D. E., Behm-Morawitz, E., & Kopacz, M. A. (2008). Exposure to television portrayals of Latinos: The implications of aversive racism and social identity theory. *Human Communication Research, 34*, 1–27. https://doi.org/10.1111/j.1468-2958.2007.00311.x

McDonald, J. (2017). Critical methods. In J. Matthes, C. S. Davis, & R. F. Potter (Eds.), *The international encyclopedia of communication research methods.* Wiley. https://doi.org/10.1002/9781118901731

McDonald, J., & Mitra, R. (Eds.). (2019). *Movements in organizational communication research: Current issues and future directions.* Routledge.

McInnes, P., & Corlett, S. (2012). Conversational identity work in everyday interaction. *Scandinavian Journal of Management, 28*(1), 27–38. https://doi.org/10.1016/j.scaman.2011.12.004

McIntosh, P. (1998). White privilege and male privilege: A personal account of coming to see correspondences through work in women's studies. In M. Anderson & P. H. Collins (Eds.), *Race, class and gender: An anthology* (3rd ed., pp. 94–105). Wadsworth.

Meares, M. (2017). Muted group theory. In Y. Y. Kim (Ed.), *The international encyclopedia of intercultural communication.* Wiley. https://doi.org/10.1002/9781118783665

Meares, M. M., Oetzel, J. G., Torres, A., Derkacs, D., & Ginossar, T. (2004). Employee mistreatment and muted voices in the culturally diverse workplace. *Journal of Applied Communication Research, 32,* 4–27. https://doi.org/10.1080/0090988042000178121

Meisenbach, R. J. (2008). Working with tensions: Materiality, discourse, and (dis)empowerment in occupational identity negotiation among higher education fund-raisers. *Management Communication Quarterly, 22,* 258–287. https://doi.org/10.1177/0893318908323150

Meisenbach, R. J. (2017). Integrating ethics and responsibility into organizational communication research: Issues and new directions. *Management Communication Quarterly, 31*(1), 146–152. https://doi.org/10.1177/0893318916676891

Melcher, A. J., & Beller, R. (1967). Toward a theory organizational communication: Consideration in channel selection. *Academy of Management Journal, 10,* 39–52. http://www.jstor.org/action/showPublication?journalCode=acadmanaj

Meng, J., McLaughlin, M., Pariera, K., & Murphy, S. (2016). A comparison between Caucasians and African Americans in willingness to participate in cancer clinical trials: The roles of knowledge, distrust, information sources, and religiosity. *Journal of Health Communication, 21*(6), 669–677. https://doi.org/10.1080/10810730.2016.1153760

Mercer, D. L. (2019). *The colored sense of awareness: An analysis of African American perceptions of race and communication in the workplace* [Unpublished master's thesis]. Virginia Polytechnic Institute and State University.

Methot, J. R., Lepine, J. A., Podsakoff, N. P., & Christian, J. S. (2016). Are workplace friendships a mixed blessing? Exploring tradeoffs of multiplex relationships and their associations with job performance. *Personnel Psychology, 69*(2), 311–355. https://doi.org/10.1111/peps.12109

Michelson, G., van Iterson, A., & Waddington, K. (2010). Gossip in organizations: Contexts, consequences, and controversies. *Group & Organization Management, 35,* 371–390. https://doi.org/10.1177/1059601109360389

Mikkelson, A. C., Sloan, D., & Hesse, C. (2019). Relational communication messages and leadership styles in supervisor/employee relationships. *International Journal of Business Communication, 56*(4), 586–604. https://doi.org/10.1177/2329488416687267

Mikkola, L. (2020). Supportive communication in the workplace. In L. Mikkola & M. Valo (Eds.), *Workplace communication* (pp. 149–162). Routledge.

Mikkola, L., & Valo, M. (Eds.). (2020). *Workplace communication.* Routledge.

Mills, C. (1997). A view from the inside: Making sense of workplace interaction. *Australian Journal of Communication, 24,* 82–93.

Mills, C. (2002). The hidden dimensions of blue-collar sensemaking about workplace communication. *Journal of Business Communication, 39,* 288–313. https://doi.org/10.1177/002194360203900301

Mills, C. (2010). Experiencing gossip: The foundations for a theory of embedded organizational gossip. *Group & Organization Management, 35,* 213–240. https://doi:.org/10.1177/1059601109360392

Mirande, A., & Tanno, D. V. (1993). Labels, researcher perspective, and contextual validation: A commentary. *International Journal of Intercultural Relations, 17*, 149–155. https://doi.org/10.1016/0147-1767(93)90021-Y

Morton, T., Wright, R., Peters, K., Reynolds, K. J., & Haslam, S. A. (2012). Social identity and the dynamics of organizational communication. In H. Giles, C. Gallois, J. Harwood, M. Hewstone, M. Hogg, S. A. Reid, & J. C. Turner (Eds.), *Handbook of intergroup communication* (pp. 319–330). Routledge.

Mueller, B. H., & Lee, J. (2002). Leader–member exchange and organizational communication satisfaction in multiple contexts. *Journal of Business Communication, 39*, 220–244. https://doi.org/10.1177/002194360203900204

Müller, M. (2020). Escaping (into) the night . . . : Organizations and work at night. *Organization Studies, 41*(8), 1101–1122. https://doi.org/10.1177/0170840619830138

Mumby, D. K. (1993). Critical organizational communication studies: The next ten years. *Communication Monographs, 60*, 18–26. https://doi.org/10.1080/03637759309376290

Mumby, D. K. (2004). Discourse, power and ideology: Unpacking the critical approach. In D. Grant, C. Hardy, C. Oswick, & L. L. Putnam (Eds.), *Sage handbook of organizational discourse* (pp. 237–258). Sage.

Mumby, D. K. (Ed.). (2010). *Reframing difference in organizational communication studies: Research, pedagogy, and practice.* Sage.

Mumby, D. K. (2016). Organizing beyond organization: Branding, discourse, and communicative capitalism. *Organization, 23*(6), 884–907. https://doi.org/10.1177/1350508416631164

Musson, G., & Duberley, J. (2007). Change, change or be exchanged: The discourse of participation and the manufacture of identity. *Journal of Management Studies, 44*, 143–164. https://doi.org/10.1111/j.1467-6486.2006.00640.x

Muterera, J., Hemsworth, D., Baregheh, A., & Garcia-Rivera, B. R. (2018). The leader–follower dyad: The link between leader and follower perceptions of transformational leadership and its impact on job satisfaction and organizational performance. *International Public Management Journal, 21*(1), 131–162. https://doi.org/10.1080/10967494.2015.1106993

Myers, S. A. (2017). The instructor–student relationship as an alternative form of superior-subordinate relationship. *Communication Education, 66*(1), 110–112. https://doi.org/10.1080/03634523.2016.1221513

Myers, S. A., & Johnson, A. D. (2004). Perceived solidarity, self-disclosure, and trust in organizational peer relationships. *Communication Research Reports, 21*, 75–83. https://doi.org/10.1080/08824090409359969

Myers, S. A., Know, R. L., Pawlowski, D. R., & Ropog, B. L. (1999). Perceived communication openness and functional communication skills among organizational peers. *Communication Reports, 12*, 71–81. https://doi.org/10.1080/08934219909367712

Nathan, S., Newman, C., & Lancaster, K. (2019). Qualitative interviewing. In P. Liamputtong (Ed.), *Handbook of research methods in health social sciences* (pp. 391–410). Springer.

Navarro, B., Black, T., & Thomas, A. (Producers), & Nava, G. (Director). (1984). *El Norte* [Film]. Cinecom International.

Nicolas, G., & Skinner, A. L. (2017). Constructing race: How people categorize others and themselves in racial terms. In H. Cohen & C. Lefebvre (Eds.), *Handbook of categorization in cognitive science* (2nd ed., pp. 607–635). Elsevier.

Nicotera, A. M. (Ed.). (2020). *Origins and traditions of organizational communication.* Routledge. https://doi.org/10.4324/9780203703625

Nicotera, A. M., Clinkscales, M. J., Dorsey, L. K., & Niles, M. N. (2009). Race as political identity: Problematic issues for applied communication research. In L. R. Frey & K. N. Cissna (Eds.), *Routledge handbook of applied communication research* (pp. 203–232). Routledge.

Nkomo, S. M. (1992). The emperor has no clothes: Rewriting race in organizations. *Academy of Management Journal, 17,* 487–513. https://doi.org/10.2307/258720

O'Brien, R. (Producer), & Loach, K. (Director). (2000). *Bread and roses* [Film]. Lions Gate Films.

Ochs, E. (1993). Constructing social identity: A language socialization perspective. *Research on Language and Social Interaction, 26,* 287–306. https://doi.org/10.1207/s15327973rlsi2603_3

Odden, C. M., & Sias, P. M. (1997). Peer communication relationships and psychological climate. *Communication Quarterly, 45,* 153–166. https://doi.org/10.1080/01463379709370058

Olsson, C. L. K. (2017). Do leaders matter in the long run? A longitudinal study of the importance of LMX and LMX balance for followers' creative performance in research groups. In M. D. Mumford & S. Hemlin (Eds.), *Handbook of research on leadership and creativity* (pp. 228–241). Edward Elgar.

Omi, M., & Winant, H. (1986). *Racial formation in the United States: From the 1960s to the 1980s.* Routledge.

Omilion-Hodges, L. M., & Ackerman, C. D. (2018). From the technical know-how to the free flow of ideas: Exploring the effects of leader, peer, and team communication on employee creativity. *Communication Quarterly, 66*(1), 38–57. https://doi.org/10.1080/01463373.2017.1325385

Ono, K. A., & Sloop, J. M. (2002). *Shifting borders: Rhetoric, immigration, and California's proposition 187.* Temple University Press.

Orbe, M. P. (1994). "Remember, it's always Whites' ball": Descriptions of African American male communication. *Communication Quarterly, 42,* 287–300. https://doi.org/10.1080/01463379409369935

Orbe, M. P. (1996). Laying the foundation for co-cultural communication theory: An inductive approach to studying non-dominant communication strategies and the factors that influence them. *Communication Studies, 47,* 157–176. https://doi.org/10.1080/10510979609368473

Orbe, M. P. (1998a). *Constructing co-cultural theory: An explication of culture, power, and communication.* Sage.

Orbe, M. P. (1998b). An outsider within perspective to organizational communication: Explicating the communication practices of co-cultural group members. *Management Communication Quarterly, 12,* 230–279. https://doi.org/10.1177/0893318998122003

Orbe, M. P. (2000). Centralizing diverse racial/ethnic voices in scholarly research: The value of phenomenological inquiry. *International Journal of Intercultural Relations, 24,* 603–621. https://doi.org/10.1016/S0147-1767(00)00019-5

Orbe, M. P. (2017). Co-cultural theory. In Y. Y. Kim (Ed.), *The international encyclopedia of intercultural communication.* Wiley. https://doi.org/10.1002/9781118783665

Orbe, M. P., & Allen, B. J. (2008). "Race matters" in the Journal of Applied Communication Research. *Howard Journal of Communications, 19,* 201–220. https://doi.org/10.1080/10646170802218115

Orbe, M. P., Allen, B. J., & Flores, L. A. (2006). Introduction: Recognizing the diversity within and commonality between. In M. P. Orbe, B. J. Allen, & L. A. Flores (Eds.), *International and intercultural communication annual* (Vol. 29, pp. 1–3). National Communication Association.

Orbe, M. P., & Spellers, R. E. (2005). From the margins to the center: Utilizing co-cultural theory in diverse contexts. In W. B. Gudykunst (Ed.), *Theorizing about intercultural communication* (pp. 173–189). Sage.

Ore, T. E. (Ed.). (2018). *The social construction of difference and inequality: Race, class, gender, and sexuality* (7th ed.). Oxford University Press.

Ott, B. L. (2017). The age of Twitter: Donald J. Trump and the politics of debasement. *Critical Studies in Media Communication, 34*(1), 59–68. https://doi.org/10.1080/15295036.2016.1266686

Ott, B. L., & Dickinson, G. (2019). *The Twitter presidency: Donald J. Trump and the politics of White rage.* Routledge.

Parker, P. S. (2001). African American women executives' leadership communication within dominant culture organizations. *Management Communication Quarterly, 15,* 42–82. https://doi.org/10.1177/0893318901151002

Parker, P. S. (2002). Negotiating identity in raced and gendered workplace interactions: The use of strategic communication by African American women senior executives within dominant culture organizations. *Communication Quarterly, 50,* 251–268. https://doi.org/10.1080/01463370209385663

Parker, P. S., Jiang, J., McCluney, C. L., & Rabelo, V. C. (2017). Race, gender, class, and sexuality. In J. Nussbaum (Ed.). *Oxford research encyclopedia of communication.* Wiley. https://doi.org/10.1093/acrefore/9780190228613.013.204

Paustian-Underdahl, S. C., King, E. B., Rogelberg, S. G., Kulich, C., & Gentry, W. A. (2017). Perceptions of supervisor support: Resolving paradoxical patterns across gender and race. *Journal of Occupational and Organizational Psychology, 90*(3), 436–457. https://doi.org/10.1111/joop.12179

Payne, B. K., Vuletich, H. A., & Lundberg, K. B. (2017). The bias of crowds: How implicit bias bridges personal and systemic prejudice. *Psychological Inquiry, 28*(4), 233–248. https://doi.org/10.1080/1047840X.2017.1335568

Pertúz, S. B. (2017). *The chosen tokens: Exploring the work experiences and career aspirations of Latina midlevel student affairs administrators in higher education* [Unpublished doctoral dissertation]. Seton Hall University.

Phillips, A. (2017, June 16). "They're rapists": President Trump's campaign launch speech two years later, annotated. *The Washington Post.* https://www.washingtonpost.com/news/the-fix/wp/2017/06/16/theyre-rapists-presidents-trump-campaign-launch-speech-two-years-later-annotated/

Ploeger-Lyons, N. A., & Kelley, K. M. (2017). Coworker communication. In C. Scott & L. K. Lewis (Eds.), *The international encyclopedia of organizational communication.* Wiley. https://doi.org/10.1002/9781118955567

Pompper, D. (2007). The gender–ethnicity construct in public relations organizations: Using feminist standpoint theory to discover Latinas' realities. *Howard Journal of Communications, 18,* 291–311. https://doi.org/10.1080/10646170701653669

Pujiastuti, A. (2017). *Language socialization in the workplace: Immigrant workers' language practice within a multilingual workplace* [Unpublished doctoral dissertation]. The Ohio State University.

Quade, M. J., McLarty, B. D., & Bonner, J. M. (2020). The influence of supervisor bottom-line mentality and employee bottom-line mentality on leader–member exchange and subsequent employee performance. *Human Relations, 73*(8), 1157–1181. https://doi.org/10.1177/0018726719858394

Rabelo, V. C., & Mahalingam, R. (2019). "They really don't want to see us": How cleaners experience invisible "dirty" work. *Journal of Vocational Behavior, 113,* 103–114. https://doi.org/10.1016/j.jvb.2018.10.010

Ran, J. U. (2017). Communicating homosexuality online in China: Exploring the blog of a lesbian organization through the lens of co-cultural theory. *Intercultural Communication Studies, 26*(2), 79–95.

Ray, E. B. (1987). Supportive relationships and occupational stress in the workplace. In T. L. Albrecht & M. B. Adelman (Eds.), *Communicating social support* (pp. 172–191). Sage.

Ray, E. B. (1991). The relationship among communication network roles, job stress, and burnout in educational organizations. *Communication Quarterly, 39*, 91–110. https://doi.org/10.1080/01463379109369785

Ray, E. B. (Ed.). (1996). *Case studies in communication and disenfranchisement: Applications to social health issues.* Lawrence Erlbaum.

Razzante, R., & Tracy, S. J. (2019). Co-cultural theory: Performing emotional labor from a position of exclusion. In C. Liberman, A. S. Rancer, & T. A. Avtgis (Eds.), *Casing communication theory* (pp. 117–130). Kendall Hunt.

Redmond, V., Jameson, J. K., & Binder, A. R. (2016). How superior–subordinate relationship quality and conflict management styles influence an employee's use of upward dissent tactics. *Negotiation and Conflict Management Research, 9*(2), 158–176. https://doi.org/10.1111/ncmr.12072

Regmi, K., Naidoo, J., & Pilkington, P. (2010). Understanding the processes of translation and transliteration in qualitative research. *International Journal of Qualitative Methods, 9*(1), 16–26. https://doi.org/10.1177/160940691000900103

Rodriguez, G. (2007). *Mongrels, bastards, orphans, and vagabonds: Mexican immigration and the future of race in America.* Pantheon Books.

Rosnow, R. L. (1977). Gossip and marketplace psychology. *Journal of Communication, 27*, 158–163. https://doi.org/10.1111/j.1460-2466.1977.tb01811.x

Rudick, C. K., Sollitto, M., Claus, C. J., Sanford, A. A., Nainby, K., & Golsan, K. B. (2017). Comparing Hispanic-to-White co-cultural communication at four-year, public Hispanic serving and predominately White institutions. *Communication Reports, 30*(2), 104–115. https://doi.org/10.1080/08934215.2016.1268638

Sanders, M. L., & McClellan, J. G. (2015). Forum introduction: Promoting the field through organizational communication pedagogy. *Management Communication Quarterly, 29*(2), 291–294. https://doi.org/10.1177/0893318915571347

Santa Ana, O. (1999). "Like an animal I was treated": Anti-immigrant metaphor in US public discourse. *Discourse & Society, 10*, 191–224. https://doi.org/10.1177/0957926599010002004

Schatzman, L., & Strauss, A. L. (1955). Social class and modes of communication. *American Journal of Sociology, 50*, 329–338. http://www.jstor.org/action/showPublication?journalCode=amerjsoci

Schoem, D., & Hurtado, S. (Eds.). (2001). *Intergroup dialogue: Deliberative democracy in school, college, community, and workplace.* University of Michigan Press.

Segal, L. (2002). Roadblocks in reforming corrupt agencies: The case of the New York City school janitors. *Public Administrative Review, 62*, 445–460. https://doi.org/10.1111/0033-3352.00198

Shen, M. J., Peterson, E. B., Costas-Muñiz, R., Hernandez, M. H., Jewell, S. T., Matsoukas, K., & Bylund, C. L. (2018). The effects of race and racial concordance on patient–physician communication: A systematic review of the literature. *Journal of Racial and Ethnic Health Disparities, 5*(1), 117–140. https://doi.org/10.1007/s40615-017-0350-4

Shi, Y., Jimenez-Arista, L. E., Cruz, J., McTier, T. S., Jr., & Koro-Ljungberg, M. (2018). Multilayered analyses of the experiences of undocumented Latinx college students. *The Qualitative Report, 23*(11), 2603–2621.

Shuter, R., & Turner, L. H. (1997). African American and European American women in the workplace. *Management Communication Quarterly, 11*, 74–96. https://doi.org/10.1177/0893318997111004

Sias, P. M. (1996). Constructing perceptions of differential treatment: An analysis of coworker discourse. *Communication Monographs, 63,* 171–187. https://doi.org/10.1080/03637759609376385

Sias, P. M. (2005). Workplace relationship quality and employee information experiences. *Communication Studies, 56,* 375–395. https://doi.org/10.1080/10510970500319450

Sias, P. M. (2013). Workplace relationships. In L. L. Putnam & D. K. Mumby (Eds.), *The Sage handbook of organizational communication: Advances in theory, research, and methods* (3rd ed., pp. 775–801). Sage.

Sias, P. M., & Cahill, D. J. (1998). From coworkers to friends: The development of peer friendships in the workplace. *Western Journal of Communication, 62,* 273–299. https://doi.org/10.1080/10570319809374611

Sias, P. M., & Jablin, F. M. (1995). Differential superior–subordinate relations, perceptions of fairness, and coworker communication. *Human Communication Research, 22,* 5–38. https://doi.org/10.1111/j.1468-2958.1995.tb00360.x

Sias, P. M., Krone, K. K., & Jablin, F. M. (2002). An ecological systems perspective on workplace relationships. In M. L. Knapp & J. Daly (Eds.), *Handbook of interpersonal communication* (3rd ed., pp. 615–642). Sage.

Sias, P. M., & Shin, Y. (2020). Workplace relationships. In A. M. Nicotera (Ed.), *Origins and traditions of organizational communication: A comprehensive introduction to the field* (pp. 117–134). Routledge.

Simpson, R., & Simpson, A. (2018). "Embodying" dirty work: A review of the literature. *Sociology Compass, 12*(6), e12581. https://doi.org/10.1111/soc4.12581

Smith, D. E. (1987). *The everyday world as problematic: A feminist sociology.* Northeastern University Press.

Smith, S. S. (2010). A test of sincerity: How Black and Latino service workers make decisions about making referrals. *The Annals of the American Academy of Political and Social Science, 629,* 30–52. https://doi.org/10.1177/0002716210366532

Snow, D., & Anderson, L. (1987). Identity work among the homeless: The verbal construction and avowal of personal identities. *American Journal of Sociology, 92,* 1336–1371. http://www.jstor.org/action/showPublication?journalCode=amerjsoci

Sokefeld, M. (1999). Debating self, identity, and culture in anthropology. *Current Anthropology, 40,* 417–447. https://doi.org/10.1086/200042

Sollitto, M., & Myers, S. A. (2015). Peer coworker relationships: Influences on the expression of lateral dissent. *Communication Reports, 28*(1), 36–47. https://doi.org/10.1080/08934215.2014.925569

Soto Vega, K., & Chávez, K. R. (2018). Latinx rhetoric and intersectionality in racial rhetorical criticism. *Communication and Critical/Cultural Studies, 15*(4), 319–325.

Spillan, J. E., & Mino, M. (2001). Special peers' perceived use of communication openness and functional communication skills in specific organizational contexts. *Communication Research Reports, 18,* 53–66. https://doi.org/10.1080/08824090109384782

Spillan, J. E., Mino, M., & Rowles, M. S. (2002). Sharing organizational messages through effective lateral communication. *Qualitative Research Reports in Communication, 3,* 96–104.

Steele, G. A., & Plenty, D. (2015). Supervisor–subordinate communication competence and job and communication satisfaction. *International Journal of Business Communication, 52*(3), 294–318. https://doi.org/10.1177/2329488414525450

Strine, M. S. (1997). Deconstructing identity in/and difference: Voices under erasure. *Western Journal of Communication, 61,* 448–459. https://doi.org/10.1080/10570319709374589

Talbott, C. (2009, December 1). Worlds apart but on common ground. *Colorado Arts and Sciences Magazine.* https://www.colorado.edu/asmagazine/2009/12/01/worlds-apart-common-ground

Tan, N., Yam, K. C., Zhang, P., & Brown, D. J. (2020). Are you gossiping about me? The costs and benefits of high workplace gossip prevalence. *Journal of Business and Psychology,* 1–18. https://doi.org/10.1007/s10869-020-09683-7

Tanner, G., & Otto, K. (2016). Superior–subordinate communication during organizational change: Under which conditions does high-quality communication become important? *International Journal of Human Resource Management, 27,* 2183–2201. https://doi.org/10.1080/09585192.2015.1090470

Taylor, C. (2002). Modern social imaginaries. *Public Culture, 14,* 91–124. https://doi.org/10.1215/08992363-14-1-91

Teven, J. J. (2007). Effects of supervisor social influence, nonverbal immediacy, and biological sex on subordinates' perceptions of job satisfaction, liking, and supervisor credibility. *Communication Quarterly, 55,* 155–177. https://doi.org/10.1080/01463370601036036

Tracy, S. J. (2020). *Qualitative research methods: Collecting evidence, crafting analysis, communicating impact.* Wiley.

Tracy, S. J., & Geist-Martin, P. (2013). Organizing ethnography and qualitative approaches. In L. L. Putnam & D. K. Mumby (Eds.), *The Sage handbook of organizational communication: Advances in theory, research, and methods* (3rd ed., pp. 261–294). Sage.

Twinn, S. (1997). An exploratory study examining the influence of translation on the validity and reliability of qualitative data in nursing research. *Journal of Advanced Nursing, 26,* 418–423. https://doi.org/10.1046/j.1365-2648.1997.1997026418.x

Urban, E. L., & Orbe, M. P. (2007). "The syndrome of the boiled frog": Exploring international students on U.S. campuses as co-cultural group members. *Journal of Intercultural Communication Research, 36,* 117–138. https://doi.org/10.1080/17475750701478695

U.S. Bureau of Labor Statistics. (2020). *Labor force statistics from the current population survey.* https://www.bls.gov/cps/cpsaat10.htm

U.S. Census Bureau. (2020). *Data obtained from the 2018 American Community Survey* [For anonymized institution]. https://www.census.gov/quickfacts/

Uzogara, E. E. (2019). Gendered racism biases: Associations of phenotypes with discrimination and internalized oppression among Latinx American women and men. *Race and Social Problems, 11*(1), 80–92. https://doi.org/10.1007/s12552-018-9255-z

Valaei, N., & Rezaei, S. (2016). Job satisfaction and organizational commitment. *Management Research Review, 39*(12), 1663–1694. https://doi.org/10.1108/MRR-09-2015-0216

Van Laer, K., & Janssens, M. (2011). Ethnic minority professionals' experiences with subtle discrimination in the workplace. *Human Relations, 64*(9), 120–1227. https://doi.org/10.1177/0018726711409263

Villanueva, G., Gonzalez, C., Son, M., Moreno, E., Liu, W., & Ball-Rokeach, S. (2017). Bringing local voices into community revitalization: Engaged communication research in urban planning. *Journal of Applied Communication Research, 45*(5), 474–494. https://doi.org/10.1080/00909882.2017.1382711

Villegas, P. E. (2019). "I made myself small like a cat and ran away": Workplace sexual harassment, precarious immigration status and legal violence. *Journal of Gender Studies, 28*(6), 674–686. https://doi.org/10.1080/09589236.2019.1604326

Walsh, S., Shulman, S., & Maurer, O. (2008). Immigration distress, mental health status, and coping among young immigrants: A 1-year follow-up study. *International Journal of Intercultural Relations, 32,* 371–384. https://doi.org/10.1016/j.ijintrel.2008.06.007

Wang, H., Sui, Y., Luthans, F., Wang, D., & Wu, Y. (2014). Impact of authentic leadership on performance: Role of followers' positive psychological capital and relational processes. *Journal of Organizational Behavior, 35*(1), 5–21. https://doi.org/10.1002/job.1850

Wang, X., & Wang, H. (2017). How to survive mistreatment by customers: Employees' work withdrawal and their coping resources. *International Journal of Conflict Management, 28*(4), 464–482. https://doi.org/10.1108/IJCMA-11-2016-0089

Wert, S. R., & Salovey, P. (2004). A social comparison account of gossip. *Review of General Psychology, 8,* 122–137. https://doi.org/10.1037/1089-2680.8.2.122

Whiteford, G., & Wilcock, A. (2000). Cultural relativism: Occupation and independence reconsidered. *Canadian Journal of Occupational Therapy, 67,* 324–336. https://doi.org/10.1177/000841740006700505

Willems, S., De Maesschalck, S., Deveugele, M., Derese, A., & De Maeseneer, J. (2005). Socioeconomic status of the patient and doctor–patient communication: Does it make a difference? *Patient Education and Counseling, 56,* 139–146. https://doi.org/10.1016/j.pec.2004.02.011

Wilmers, N. (2019). Solidarity within and across workplaces: How cross-workplace coordination affects earnings inequality. *The Russell Sage Journal of the Social Sciences, 5*(4), 190–215. https://doi.org/10.7758/RSF.2019.5.4.07

Wilson, G. L., Hantz, A. M., & Hanna, M. S. (1995). *Interpersonal growth through communication.* WCB Brown & Benchmark.

Wodak, R. (1997). Das Ausland and anti-Semitic discourses: The discursive construction of the other. In S. H. Riggins (Ed.), *The language of politics and exclusion: Others in discourse* (pp. 65–87). Sage.

Wood, J. T. (1992). Gender and moral voice: Moving from woman's nature to standpoint epistemology. *Women's Studies in Communication, 15,* 1–24. https://doi.org/10.1080/07491409.1992.11089757

Wright, K. B. (2011). A communication competence approach to healthcare worker conflict, job stress, job burnout, and job satisfaction. *Journal for Healthcare Quality, 33*(2), 7–14. https://doi.org/10.1111/j.1945-1474.2010.00094.x

Wu, L. Z., Birtch, T. A., Chiang, F. F., & Zhang, H. (2018). Perceptions of negative workplace gossip: A self-consistency theory framework. *Journal of Management, 44*(5), 1873–1898. https://doi.org/10.1177/0149206316632057

Yang, H. C., & Cho, H. Y. (2015). Effects of individuals, leader relationships, and groups on innovative work behaviors. *The Journal of Industrial Distribution & Business, 6*(3), 19–25. https://doi.org/10.13106/ijidb/2015.vol6.no3.19

Yoder, D. (1970). *Personnel management and industrial relations* (6th ed.). Prentice Hall.

Zhuang, J., Bresnahan, M. J., Yan, X., Zhu, Y., Goldbort, J., & Bogdan-Lovis, E. (2019). Keep doing the good work: Impact of coworker and community support on continuation of breastfeeding. *Health Communication, 34*(11), 1270–1278. https://doi.org/10.1080/10410236.2018.1476802

Zirulnik, M. L., & Orbe, M. P. (2019). Black female pilot communicative experiences: Applications and extensions of co-cultural theory. *Howard Journal of Communications, 30*(1), 76–91. https://doi.org/10.1080/10646175.2018.1439422

Zlolniski, C. (2003). Labor control and resistance of Mexican immigrant janitors in Silicon Valley. *Human Organization, 62,* 39–49.

INDEX

GLOBAL LATIN/O AMERICAS

FREDERICK LUIS ALDAMA AND LOURDES TORRES, SERIES EDITORS

This series focuses on the Latino experience in its totality as set within a global dimension. The series showcases the variety and vitality of the presence and significant influence of Latinos in the shaping of the culture, history, politics and policies, and language of the Americas—and beyond. It welcomes scholarship regarding the arts, literature, philosophy, popular culture, history, politics, law, history, and language studies, among others.